THE PRACTICE
OF
LABOUR RELATIONS
AND
COLLECTIVE BARGAINING
IN
CANADA

Gerald E. Phillips
B. Comm., M. A.

Butterworth and Co. (Canada) Ltd.
Toronto

CANADA:
BUTTERWORTH & CO. (CANADA) LTD.
TORONTO: 2265 MIDLAND AVENUE, SCARBOROUGH, M1P 4S1

UNITED KINGDOM:
BUTTERWORTH & CO. (PUBLISHERS) LTD.
LONDON: 88 KINGSWAY, W2C B 6AB

AUSTRALIA:
BUTTERWORTH PTY. LTD.
SYDNEY: 586 PACIFIC HIGHWAY, CHATSWOOD, NSW 2067
MELBOURNE: 343 LITTLE COLLINS STREET, 3000
BRISBANE: 240 QUEEN STREET, 4000

NEW ZEALAND:
BUTTERWORTHS OF NEW ZEALAND LTD.
WELLINGTON: 26/28 WARING TAYLOR STREET, 1

SOUTH AFRICA:
BUTTERWORTH & CO. (SOUTH AFRICA) (PTY.) LTD.
DURBAN: 152/154 GALES STREET

Phillips, Gerald E., 1943
The Practice of Labour Relations
and Collective Bargaining in Canada

Includes index.
ISBN 0-409-859001

I. Title. II. Series.

346'.71'034   C77-001005-9

1 2 3 4 5   80 79 78 77 76

TO

ELAINE,

CINDI,

SOPHIA

Preface

In recent years there has been a rapid expansion in the quantity and quality of studies, reports and academic publications on industrial relations in Canada. Unfortunately, there is still a scarcity of introductory Canadian teaching materials designed to upgrade students' knowledge of industrial relations to a level such that these studies are meaningful.

Because the field of "industrial relations" covers a very broad territory, any effort to produce a comprehensive textbook on Canadian industrial relations would be an extremely demanding task for any single person. Any textbook which attempts to integrate the contributions of economists, lawyers, psychologists, historians, sociologists, corporate managers and countless others interested in industrial relations could take on the aspects of a nightmare for both the author and the student. An alternative to this integrated approach involves developing teaching materials on a gradual basis for the various sub-disciplines of industrial relations.

This introductory book has been written with the modest objective of introducing the reader to the practice of labour relations and collective bargaining in Canada. To fulfil this objective, digressions into other disciplines, abstract theoretical discussions and terse legalistic phrases have been minimized. However, a listing of advanced readings is provided at the end of each chapter. After completing the book, the reader will be knowledgeable about the practical aspects of labour relations in Canada's private employment sector. In addition to this, he will also have an awareness of current developments and practices in collective bargaining by public employees, professional employees and special interest groups.

It should be noted that the book rarely expresses opinions on what are obviously controversial topics. Until the reader has completed the book and the suggestions for advanced reading provided at the end of each chapter, he may find the evaluation of diverse opinions more confusing than enlightening.

Many individuals have provided assistance and inspiration over the three-year period in which this book was "in progress". I wish to express my sincere appreciation to Lakehead University for the small but timely stipends from the Chancellor's Fund which kept this project alive in 1975 and 1976; to my friends and colleagues, especially Professors Tony Seuret and Walter Crowe for their support and encouragement in this project; to Professor Frances Bairstow of McGill University for her helpful advice and suggestions on an earlier draft; to my former students, especially Ms. Beryl Kirk, for many constructive comments on the organization and content of the manuscript; to Mr. David Godden of Butterworth and Company (Canada) Ltd. for his confidence in this project; to Mrs. Susan Joseph and Ms. Arlene Smith for their efforts in typing the manuscript; and of course, to my wife and daughters for their understanding, encouragement and assistance in completing this book.

Gerald E. Phillips

General Introduction

During the past thirty years, the practice of labour relations and its consequences have become major facts of life for an increasing number of Canadians.

Each year the number of Canadians who are aware of and are involved in this process continues to grow for a variety of reasons. Rising education levels and improvements in Canada's news media have stimulated an awareness of the issues and consequences in a variety of employee-employer disputes. Also, the right to use collective bargaining has been fought for and won by an expanding group of public and professional employees. Further, there has been a growing tendency for special-interest groups to use collective bargaining techniques to deal with pressing economic and social problems. For many individuals, the process of collective bargaining represents a healthy alternative to the radical political philosophies advocated during the 1960's.

Regardless of the reasons for this upsurge of Canadian interest in labour relations, it is unlikely that there will be any decrease in this trend in the forseeable future. Consequently, the need for a thorough understanding of the institutions and procedures of labour relations is extremely important.

The six interrelated parts of this book have been written to introduce the reader to the most relevant aspects of labour relations in Canada.

As a starting point, it must be recognized that the practice of labour relations in Canada involves two primary participants, the employee organization and the employer, and a multitude of external institutions and procedures. Part A examines each of these aspects of labour relations and their inter-relationships in the collective bargaining process.

The negotiation process is a vital part of labour relations and there are certain fundamentals that should be considered in all contract negotiations. Consequently, Part B is devoted to the critical traits of effective negotiation practices.

Labour relations in Canada is most formalized with respect to employee-employer relationships in the private sector. Part C considers specific institutions and practices which influence the practice of labour relations in the private sector.

Recent tendencies by government employees and self-governing professionals to opt for free collective bargaining have generated increasing concern about labour relations outside the private sector. Part D deals with the nature of labour relations when public employees and professional associations are required to negotiate with powerful agencies and institutions.

There are interaction processes other than collective bargaining which have a profound influence on the conduct of labour relations. Part E summarizes some of the most relevant aspects of personnel administration, labour market analysis, and labour standards legislation.

Included in the final part of this book is a series of assignments designed to provide students with an "experiential" approach to understanding labour relations.

Contents

Contents

Contents

Contents

Part A: The Canadian Setting For Labour Relations

It is essential that anyone concerned with labour relations in Canada should have some basic knowledge and understanding of the nature of the collective bargaining process, the parties involved in this process, and the external institutions and procedures which influence the actions of these parties. The purpose of the next four chapters is to provide the reader with a basic understanding of these subjects in a Canadian context.

The meanings that should be attached to such terms as "industrial relations", "labour relations", "personnel management", "labour economics", and "collective bargaining" are explored in Chapter 1.

An entity that is a part of each concept discussed in Chapter 1 is the employee organization. Because of its crucial importance to the collective bargaining process, it would be impossible to understand the practice of labour relations without sufficient knowledge of the various aspects of employee organizations. Chapter 2 provides a perspective on the history, objectives and structure of employee organizations in Canada.

But the employee organization is only one component of the bargaining process. The employer represents the focal point for the activities of the employee organization. Chapter 3 analyzes the attitude of employers to employee organizations and then goes on to describe employer associations.

Finally, the actions of both the employee organization and the employer are heavily influenced by a variety of external institutions and procedures. Chapter 4 presents an overview of Canadian public policy, labour relations boards, and the conciliation and arbitration processes. In addition, alternatives to existing institutions and procedures are outlined.

Chapter 1

Introduction:
Labour Relations
and the
Collective Bargaining
Process

I   ESTABLISHING A VIEWPOINT

Collective bargaining is a highly complex inter-disciplinary field of study. In many textbooks and studies, collective bargaining is examined as a subfield of one of four broader subject areas: industrial relations, labour relations, personnel management, or labour economics. Although some authorities on collective bargaining still tend to regard these three terms as synonyms, it should be pointed out that each area of study approaches collective bargaining in a somewhat distinctive way.

1.   Industrial Relations

There have been many attempts to design a general system or structure that facilitates the study of the parties and variables which are a part of the area of study referred to as "industrial relations". The model provided by one expert, John Dunlop, is still regarded by most authorities as a "classic" that should be familiar to all students of labour issues (1.1).

Dunlop's model involves four basic elements:

a) The actors: Dunlop emphasizes the role of three groups, which he refers to as "actors". These actors consist of employees and their organizations and spokesmen; management and their organizations and spokesmen; and government agencies and specialized private agencies concerned with employee relationships.

b) The contexts or environment in which the actors interact: According to Dunlop, interactions among the actors are conditioned by such things as the technological characteristics of the workplace, market constraints, and the relative prestige or power of the actors in society.

c) The nature of the ideology held by the actors: The working of the industrial relations system is strongly influenced by the extent to which the actors share a common view or ideology of how the economy does work and should work, and the role that each actor does play and should play. There must be a compatibility of ideologies among the actors and between each actor and the general public if any kind of stability is to prevail within the industrial relations system.

d)   The web of rules: The fourth element of Dunlop's model is the body of rules and regulations that governs the actors in the economy and the work-place. This system of rules and procedures is strongly influenced by the contexts and ideologies which prevail among the actors.

According to Professor Montague:

"The Dunlop model permits a succinct description of the Canadian Industrial Relations System. The actors include managements that bargain largely on a plant-by-plant basis; a labour force with about one-third of its members belonging to a well organized labour movement; and governments that have played active roles in the shaping of the labour market. The working of the "contexts" emerging from the Canadian economy to shape the actors and the role they play is evident. Certainly the commitment of the actors to the pursuit of a mixed free-enterprise economy reflects the binding force of a common ideology, and the partial coverage of the bargaining process in the economy means a significant role for government in the conduct of the labour market." (1.2)

A more recent conceptual model that is now regarded as a "classic" on the Canadian scene was prepared by Professor Alton Craig and adapted for use by the Woods Task Force in 1967 (1.3). In this report, the industrial relations system was described as "the complex of market and institutional arrangements, private and public, which society permits, encourages or establishes to handle superior-subordinate relationships growing out of employment and related activities." (1.4) The diagram presented in Figure 1.1 categorizes the environmental factors, parties of interest, interaction processes and the results, which together form the Canadian Industrial Relations System. In this context, collective bargaining is but one of many interrelated components of the industrial system.

Figure 1.1

A Schematic Presentation of the Canadian Industrial Relations System

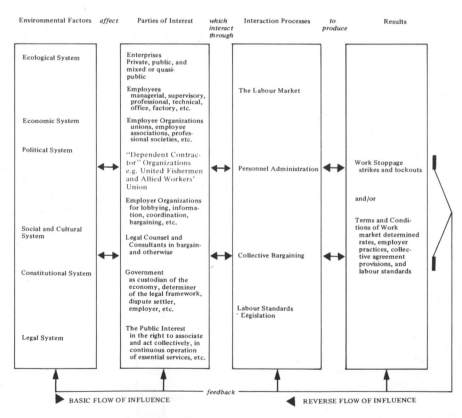

Source: Canadian Industrial Relations. The Report of the Task Force On Labour Relations, Ottawa: Queen's Printer, 1969, p. 10.

Figure 1.2

A Schematic Presentation of The Labour Relations Subsystem

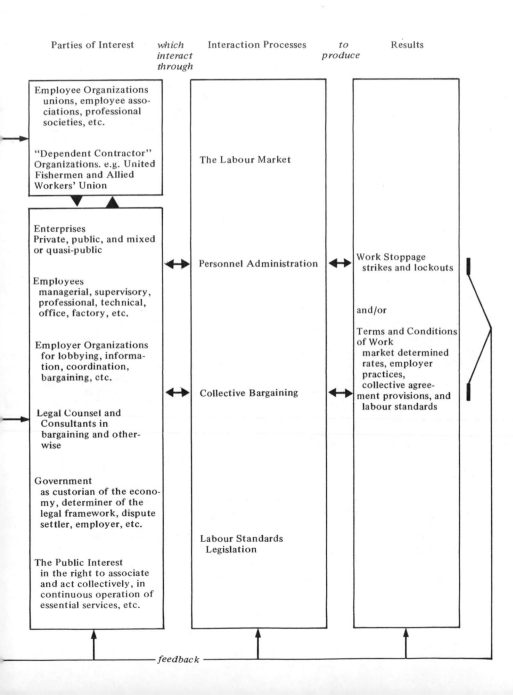

2.   Labour Relations

An important party of interest in the industrial relations system is the employee organization. The field of study that concentrates on interactions between employee organizations and other parties of interest in the industrial relations system is generally referred to as "labour relations". Figure 1.2 illustrates the fact that labour relations is a subsystem of the industrial relations system which categorizes collective bargaining as one of four interaction processes.

It should be stressed that labour relations and environmental factors are examined as two separate subsystems only for academic convenience. Such an approach can be compared to the practice of initially separating basic athletic skills from overall game strategies when the fundamentals of any sport are being introduced. However, if one wishes to become proficient in the sport, it is necessary to learn the strategic aspects of the game and modify some of the basic skills to suit various game conditions. The same approach is necessary in the practice of labour relations. To successfuly apply the basic concepts of labour relations in the real world, the practitioner must become thoroughly acquainted with the intricate linkages that exist between the labour relations and environmental subsystems.

3.   Personnel Management

It can be seen in Figure 1.1 and Figure 1.2 that personnel management is but one of four interaction processes in the industrial relations system and labour relations subsystems. Although personnel management does include the study of problems relevant to understanding industrial and labour relations, it does so almost exclusively from the viewpoint of the employer.

According to Megginson, the term "personnel management" refers to those activities of a particular firm associated with the interpersonal relationships between subordinates and superiors (1.5). Interacting with employee organizations is but one of many "personnel" activities for an organization.

Departments which are involved in these types of activities have been given a variety of names, the most common of which include "industrial relations departments", "labour relations departments", and "personnel departments". The upshot of this differing terminology has been an increasing tendency for some individuals to conclude that the study of the personnel practices of a particular firm is the complete body of knowledge referred to under the heading of industrial relations or labour relations. This is, of course, incorrect and misleading.

4.   Labour Economics

The study of labour economics involves the study of the supply and demand of labour. Supply analysis involves an exploration of the variables that affect labour force participation, the investment in human capital, hours of work and so on. Demand analysis concentrates on the productivity of workers, the value of workers' production to the firm and a multitude of related topics. Supply and demand analysis is combined to concentrate on the theoretical study of such topics as unemployment and wage trends.

A succinct description of the relationship between labour economics and industrial relations has been provided by Professor Rees:

"It is of course impossible to draw a sharp boundary, and in one sense all of labour economics is part of the interdisciplinary field of industrial relations. However, for many purposes it is useful to draw some distinctions. Industrial relations has as its principal focus the relation between the employer and his workers within a particular establishment or firm, while labour economics is concerned with larger aggregates. It is because of this focus of industrial relations on smaller units that sociology and psychology can make an important contribution to it. For much the same reasons, training in industrial relations is primarily the training of practitioners while training in labour economics is largely the training of teachers and researchers. In a sense, industrial relations is related to basic social science disciplines, including economics, as engineering is to the physical sciences or medicine to the biological sciences." (1.6)

This book is written for individuals who wish to gain an appreciation of the practical aspects of labour relations in Canada. Because labour relations is such a complex area of study, much of the emphasis will be placed upon the interaction of the parties of interest through the collective bargaining process. This is not intended to imply that interactions which involve the Canadian labour market, personnel administration or labour standards legislation are unimportant. Rather, one has to begin somewhere to build knowledge and understanding. It is the writer's opinion that an examination of the Canadian collective bargaining process is a good place to start.

Individuals who have no understanding of personnel administration, labour market analysis or Canadian labour standards legislation will find a concise summary of related subtopics in Part E.

II   THE NATURE OF COLLECTIVE BARGAINING

As members of a democratic Canadian society, individuals and groups of individuals must constantly resolve their differences and seek workable solutions to a broad spectrum of disputes. Some of these disputes may be settled by the dictates of government. Others may be resolved by a person-to-person relationship with little or no formality in the procedures leading to or the contents of the final agreement. Still others may be unilaterally decided by the actions of one predominating party. None of these situations represent a true collective bargaining relationship.

The fact that "collective bargaining" is by no means easy to define is reinforced by one expert who stated:

"I am a great believer in collective bargaining: the only trouble is that after thirty years of watching it at close range in dozens of industries, large and small, I am not sure I know what it is." (1.7)

Because different individuals attach varying interpretations to the term, it is desirable at this point to clarify some existing ambiguities about collective bargaining.

Collective bargaining is a multi-dimensioned concept. The following are the five most significant dimensions of this concept:

1. Collective Action. To begin with, it is useful to distinguish between the terms "collective action" and "collective bargaining". Collective action is a single-dimensioned concept which implies only the existence of a formalized organization of individuals who have a common purpose. A special type of collective action, "trade unionism", refers to organizations of workers acting collectively to protect and improve their conditions of employment. Although collective action does constitute one very important facet of the collective bargaining process, there are other dimensions of equal significance.

2. Recognition. A second dimension of equal significance is the requirement that collective action be supplemented by recognition from some other individual, group, or organization. Such recognition must be real rather than token and permit meaningful dialogue between the relevant parties. Historically, sanctions frequently had to be invoked to secure recognition for employee organizations that were not under employer influence.

3. *Written Agreement.* Collective bargaining implies the formulation of a formal written contract or collective agreement. Such an agreement sets the wages, hours, and working conditions which will apply to a defined group of employees for a specified time period. Bargaining that results only in verbal and implicit understandings between the parties is considered often as being tantamount to an absence of a formal collective bargaining relationship.

4. *Adherence.* Collective bargaining implies that both parties will adhere to an agreement for a negotiated time period. Obviously, the entire process will break down if there is a lack of certainty that one or both parties will live up to the provisions of an agreement.

5. *Deadline Procedures.* To be effective, a collective bargaining relationship must, at a specified point in time, allow the parties to invoke some types of actions designed to encourage the opposition to seek a meaningful settlement. Otherwise, it could be in the interest of one party (often the employer) to continue the negotiations for an indefinite time period.

It should be stressed that labour unions are by no means the only group in our present society to employ a collective bargaining strategy to resolve conflicts with relatively powerful adversaries. Since the latter part of the 1960's, a divergent variety of groups has attempted to adapt the labour union model as a vehicle for resolving economic and social conflicts. However, each successful simulation of labour's methods can usually be analyzed in terms of the five dimensions just outlined (1.8).

These five dimensions provide a useful framework for assessing those factors working against a viable collective bargaining process. Organizing a formal group of individuals with a common purpose can be a difficult and complex process. Gaining recognition by another party is by no means an easy exercise. The process of arriving at a mutually acceptable written agreement is filled with uncertainties. Interpreting and administering the conditions of a mutually acceptable contract is a demanding task. And the question of what constitutes acceptable sanctions when the parties reach a defined deadline is still a contentious issue.

As a result of long years of experience with these difficulties in the labour setting, specific agencies and policies have gradually evolved to better accommodate labour relations in Canada. Such agencies and policies will be examined in Chapter 4. Before doing so, however, it is useful to know more about the two primary participants in the collective bargaining process, the employee and his organization and the employer and his organization.

Summary

1.   Collective bargaining is closely associated with the study of industrial relations, labour relations, personnel management, and labour economics.
2.   Industrial relations is the broadest of these fields of study, including both labour relations and personnel management.
3.   Labour relations is a study of interactions associated with various types of employee organizations. As such it includes both personnel management and collective bargaining as subfields.
4.   Personnel management deals with interpersonal relationships between

superiors and subordinates within a particular firm. Relationships which involve employee organizations are analyzed primarily from the point of view of the employer.

5. Labour economics is concerned with the study of the supply and demand of labour and focuses primarily upon the "macro" or larger aggregates of the economy, such as labour force participation and unemployment.

6. The most important aspects of a collective bargaining relationship were described as collective action, recognition, a written agreement, adherence to that agreement, and the ability of the parties to invoke meaningful sanctions once a specified deadline has passed.

References

1.1   Dunlop, J.T. *Industrial Relations Systems.* New York, Rinehart and Winston, 1958.

1.2   Montague, J.T. *Labour Markets in Canada.* Toronto, Prentice-Hall, 1970, p. 167.

1.3   Craig, A.W. "A Model for the Analysis of Industrial Relations Systems." *In Canadian Labour and Industrial Relations* by H. C. Jain. Toronto, McGraw-Hill, 1975.

1.4   Canadian Industrial Relations. *The Report of the Task Force on Labour Relations.* Ottawa, Queen's Printer, 1969, p. 9.

1.5   Megginson, L.C. *Personnel: A Behavioural Approach to Administration,* Homewood, Illinois, Irwin, 1967, p. 51.

1.6   Rees, A. *The Current Status of Labour Economics.* Kingston, Ontario, Industrial Relations Centre, Queen's University, 1971, p. 1.

1.7   Raskin, A.H. and John T. Dunlop. "Two Views of Collective Bargaining", in Ulman, ed. *Challenges to Collective Bargaining.* Englewood Cliffs, N.J., Prentice-Hall, 1967, p. 155.

1.8   Barber, Christie, Kuyek and Whyte. "The Collective Labour Relations Model Applied to Social Welfare Programs". *U.T.L.J.,* Vol. 22, 1972.

Suggested Readings for Further Study

Barbash, Jack. "The Elements of Industrial Relations". *British Journal of Industrial Relations,* Vol. 4, October, 1964.

Blain and Gennard. "Industrial Relations Theory — A Critical Review". *British Journal of Industrial Relations,* Vol. 8, No. 3, 1970.

Canadian Industrial Relations. "Report of the Task Force on Labour Relations". Ottawa, Queen's Printer, 1968.

Craig, Alton W. J. "A Model for the Analysis of Industrial Relations Systems", in *Canadian Labour and Industrial Relations* edited by H. C. Jain. Toronto, McGraw-Hill Ryerson, 1975.

Dunlop, John T. *Industrial Relations Systems.* New York, Holt, Rinehart and Winston, 1958.

Goodman, *et.al.,* "Rules in Industrial Relations Theory: A Discussion". *Industrial Relations Journal,* Spring, Vol. 6, No. 1, 1975.

Hameed, S.M.A. "A Theory of Collective Bargaining". *Industrial Relations,* Vol. 25, No. 3, August, 1970.

Hameed, S.M.A. "Theory and Research in the Field of Industrial Relations". *British Journal of Industrial Relations,* Vol. V, No. 2, July, 1967.

Heneman, Herbert, G. "Toward a General Conceptual System of Industrial

Relations: How Do We Get There?", in *Essays in Industrial Relations Theory*, edited by G. G. Somers. Ames, Iowa State University Press, 1969.

Kerr C. et al. *Industrialism and Industrial Man*. Cambridge, Harvard University Press, 1960.

Laffer, K. "Is Industrial Relations an Academic Discipline?" *Journal of Industrial Relations*, March, 1974.

Pentland, H.C. A Study of the Changing Social, Economic and Political Background of the Canadian System of Industrial Relations. A study for the Task Force on Labour Relations, Ottawa, 1968.

Shister, Joseph. "Collective Bargaining", in *A Decade of Industrial Relations Research*, 1946-1956. New York, Harper and Bros., 1958.

Tripp, L. Reed. "Collective Bargaining Theory", in *Labour, Management and Social Policy*, edited by G. G. Somers. Madison, University of Wisconsin Press, 1963.

Tripp, L. Reed. "The Industrial Relations Discipline In American Universities". *ILRR*, July 1964.

Experiential Assignment

List some of the specific interest groups (other than traditional unions) in your province that are now making use of collective bargaining techniques. Describe the "dimensions" of collective bargaining that are being stressed by these groups.

Chapter 2

The Participants In The Collective Bargaining Process: The Employee And His Organization

I   INTRODUCTION

Up to this point our discussion has been about some of the primary concepts associated with labour relations. Each of these is important, but there are some other basic elements still to be considered: the employee and his organization, the employer, and external institutions and procedures. In this chapter we will consider some important aspects of the employee and his organization

II   AN HISTORICAL PERSPECTIVE
ON EMPLOYEE ORGANIZATIONS IN CANADA

In order to fully understand the present legal status of employee organizations in Canada, it is necessary to review briefly the evolution of collective bargaining since the early 1800's.

1.   Pre-Confederation Labour Laws

The English labour laws which applied in Canada during the early part of the nineteenth century emphasized economic freedom and free competition in the marketplace. The British Combines Acts of 1799, 1800 and 1825, for example, outlawed trade unions as criminal conspiracies and decreed that workers could be prosecuted for attempting to associate for the purpose of altering wages or working conditions. The repressive nature of these English laws severely inhibited the development of employee organizations in Canada.

2.   Legalization of Employee Organizations in Canada

The British Parliament's new Criminal Law Amendment Act and Trade Union Act of 1871 came at a time when Canada was experiencing a series of troublesome labour confrontations. In 1872, some Toronto printers decided to go on strike to support their demands for a 54-hour week. The publishers' group laid criminal charges and had a number of union members arrested. The ensuing mass demonstration to protest these arrests put pressure on the government of Sir John A. Macdonald to sponsor legislation similar to that of Britain. The Canadian Government acceded to the pressure and passed the Canadian Trade Unions Act and the Canadian Criminal Law Amendment Act of 1872. The latter statute brought an end to the prosecution of the striking printers and legalized the existence of employee organizations registered under the provisions of the Canadian Trade Unions Act. Thus, members of employee organizations which were registered under the Act were no longer liable to prosecution for criminal conspiracy, and labour-management agreements were no longer invalid due to restraint of trade restrictions.

This legal right of Canadian workers to join employee organizations was not readily accepted by many employers. It was not uncommon for disgruntled employers to counter the legislation by requiring employees to sign "yellow-dog" contracts as a condition of employment. Such contracts guaranteed that the employee would not join an employee organization. It was also not uncommon for unions to abstain from registering under the Act, thereby denying themselves access to its protective provisions.

3.   Legalization of the Use of Sanctions by Employee Organizations

The Criminal Law Amendment Act, also passed in 1872, legalized all strikes except those that were intended to coerce the employer or eliminate his ability to carry on business. This latter exception was extremely important in that any combination (union) which performed a legal act (using sanctions) by illegal means (eliminating an employer's ability to carry on business) was a criminal conspiracy. In 1875 and 1876, further amendments were enacted so that an individual was no longer liable to prosecution for criminal conspiracy for any legal acts directly or indirectly connected with a "trade combination". In addition, provision was made to permit peaceful picketing "at or near a house or place of business to obtain or communicate information".

4. Limiting the Effectiveness of Employee Sanctions

Between 1890 and 1935, the labour surplus generated by economic depressions combined with increasing public concern over the effects of strikes, resulted in a series of setbacks for the labour movement. In 1892, the Criminal Law of Canada was codified. All trade unions, registered or unregistered, were permitted to pursue lawful objectives without fear of criminal prosecution. However, the Criminal Code of 1892 concomitantly declared that it was illegal to "beset or watch" and made no mention of any exceptions for "peacefully obtaining or communicating information". Until 1934, when such "exceptions" were reintroduced many employees received harsh reprimands from Canadian courts for actions related to picketing.

5. Involvement of the Federal Government In Dispute Settlement

A series of disruptive strikes in Canada at the turn of the century provided the impetus for new legislation designed to promote the settlement of labour-management disputes. The Conciliation Act of 1900 established the Federal Department of Labour and provided for voluntary conciliation to assist the disputing parties in arriving at an agreement. A strike by trackmen in 1902 led to the enactment of the Railway Labour Disputes Act of 1903, which established compulsory conciliation for Canadian railways. Another strike in the Lethbridge coal fields led to the passage of the Industrial Disputes and Investigation Act of 1907, which required compulsory investigation by a conciliation board and the postponement of the right to strike until a conciliation report had been issued. On balance, these "new approaches" did little to help or hinder the function of labour-management relations in Canada.

6. Limiting the Employer's Ability to Exploit the Vulnerability of Employee Organizations

In 1935, an American statute entitled the National Labour Relations Act (or Wagner Act) was passed. This Act, which had a profound influence on the shape of Canadian labour legislation during the next decade, recognized that much of the labour strife of previous years centered on the ability of employers to prevent employee organizations from establishing a collective bargaining relationship. Even though employee organizations were legal, employers had the ability to fire union members, to refuse to negotiate, or to replace strikers. In many cases, employees retaliated with violent and coercive tactics in order to inflict retributive costs on their employers. In return, employers adopted equally violent retaliation techniques and "preventative" measures.

The Wagner Act established the principle that employees had the right to join the union of their choice and to be represented by that union in the collective bargaining process. The Act provided for an administrative tribunal to ensure that employees were represented by the union of their choice (if they desired to be represented by one), that neither party should engage in "unfair labour practices", and that both parties "bargained in good faith".

These concepts were gradually incorporated into Canadian jurisdictions over the following decade. In 1944, the War Measures Act gave the Federal Government authority for labour relations in Canada. Under this Act the Federal Government was able to by-pass normal parliamentary procedure and pass "Orders-in Council" which dealt with emergency legislation. The Government used this opportunity to introduce Wagner – style labour relations provisions for the entire country. Some of the most significant principles that were incorporated into the 1944 Wartime Labour Relations Regulations (P.C. 1003) included:

a) the right of employees to form and join unions;

b) protection against unfair labour practices which, if allowed to continue, would result in discouraging the exercise of the right to form and join unions;

c) a system for defining bargaining units and certifying bargaining representatives;

d) compulsory collective bargaining;

e) compulsory postponement of strikes and lockouts coupled with compulsory two-stage conciliation;

f) the right to resort to strikes and lockouts after compulsory conciliation procedures were completed;

g) compulsory negotiation and arbitration, if necessary, of disputes arising during the life of an agreement (2.1).

When the federal wartime regulations were abolished in 1948, virtually all provincial jurisdictions (as well as the Federal Government) enacted statutes that contained provisions similar to those introduced in 1944. However, since that time the level of uniformity across the country has gradually been eroded as a result of the changing economic, political, and social pressures facing each jurisdiction.

7.   Postwar Developments in Canadian Labour Relations

A number of significant changes in Canadian labour relations legislation have occurred between 1948 and the present time. Most Canadian jurisdictions have studied or enacted various statutes which:

a) increase the protection of the parties against "unfair labour practices" and the formation of "company unions";

b) extend collective bargaining rights to "employees" who were not previously covered under the legislation;

c) widen the jurisdiction and specify the composition of labour relations boards;

d) invest the Minister of Labour with a wider choice of options in dispute settlement procedures;

e) safeguard employees from the effects of rapid technological change.

8.   The Woods Task Force

Many of these changes or proposals for change have come during the past decade and can be traced directly or indirectly to the work of the Woods Task Force on Labour Relations.

In the mid-1960's a serious rash of strikes resulted in public pressure on the government to take some corrective action. The Federal Government was convinced that research should precede any legislative action and, in 1966, commissioned a task force to conduct an intensive study of Canadian industrial relations problems. This Task Force under the direction of Professor H. D. Woods of McGill University, undertook one of the most comprehensive series of studies ever conducted in Canada in any single research area. On the basis of these studies, the Task Force arrived at a wide range of recommendations that covered the structure and operation of collective bargaining, union and management rights and responsibilities, potential emergency disputes, picketing and boycotting and enforcement of the law, adaptation of collective bargaining to industrial conversion, the role and powers of labour relations boards, and constitutional obstacles to the reformation of national labour policy. In July, 1971, the Federal Government incorporated many of these recommendations into a new Canada Labour Code which replaced the Industrial Disputes and

Investigation Act of 1948. Since 1971, most provincial jurisdictions have also made significant legislative revisions which reflect the spirit of the Task Force recommendations. However, there has been a pronounced variation in the timing and interpretation of these revisions in each jurisdiction.

III REASONS FOR THE COLLECTIVE NATURE OF EMPLOYEE BARGAINING

Collective bargaining is a process that usually involves dealings between representatives of the employee and employer, rather than individual relationships between the principals. The reasons why an individual employee finds it necessary to join an employee organization are extremely complex and are linked to the immediate environment of the individual involved. However, two broad hypotheses provide some useful perspectives on individual motivations. The first will be referred to as the "union-pull" explanation and the second as the "union-push" explanation.

1. The "Union-Pull" Explanation. This hypothesis theorizes that employees are "pulled" into unions or employee associations by the benefits they feel union membership will bring. Even though employees are not overly dissatisfied with their present conditions of employment, they feel that by joining an employee organization, they can obtain "more" benefits. The types of benefits desired may be economic (more wages, less hours, more fringe benefits), physiological (improved safety standards, better clean-up facilities), psychological (having a shop steward to whom to complain), or sociological (the sense of belonging to a social group). There are a number of research studies which show that the "union-pull" hypothesis does have validity in certain instances (2.2).

2. The "Union-Push" Explanation. A second hypothesis proposes that employees join employee organizations because they are forced or "pushed" into doing so. In other words, the disadvantages of non-membership exceed the disadvantages of membership (2.3). Three distinct factors can initiate this "push" phenomenon: the employee organization, the employer, or government decree.

a) An existing employee organization may create disadvantages of non-membership that are economic (loss of a job without membership), physiological (threats of physical harm to non-members – which are now, hopefully, relics of a turbulent past), psychological (arbitrary and unfair actions undertaken by union representatives to "hound" and harass non-members), or sociological (making social outcasts of non-members).

b) Employers may push reluctant employees into employee organizations in a variety of ways. In the past, many employers failed to furnish employees with any type of job security and few employees were able to negotiate job security individually. Therefore, the only alternative was to form or join an employee organization. Also, in the absence of an employee organization, certain employers acted irrationally and discriminatorily towards their employees. Once again, this encouraged employees to seek redress through collective action. In this context, a five-year survey conducted by Professor Goodfellow of the University Research Center at Chicago, showed that "what motivates most employees against their employer is the feeling that their company doesn't treat them fairly, decently and honestly" (2.4).

c) Some experts on the subject choose to add federal and provincial laws to the "push" factors already cited. It is argued that cases do exist where employees do not have the legal right to refrain from collective bargaining.

However, it is difficult to find examples of Canadian jurisdictions where government legislation explicitly requires union membership as a condition of employment. Generally, it is a clause in a collective agreement negotiated by employee representatives and management, not a legislative decree, which governs the right of employees to join or not to join a union.

It would be unrealistic to attempt to choose which of the two explanations is the most relevant. In some settings the first might provide the best explanation, while in other settings the second hypothesis might be more valid. But in the majority of cases, both hypotheses must be considered in order to understand the complex forces that condition employees to join a particular employee organization at a particular time.

After the employee has joined an employee organization, there is no guarantee that he will show a strong allegiance to it. In a study carried out by Tagliacozzo and Seidman, the authors distinguished seven ranges of allegiance that may be demonstrated by rank and file members (2.5):

1.   The Ideological Unionist
This type of individual, who is extremely enthusiastic and loyal, regards management as an oppressor and the union as a vehicle for class struggle.

2.   The Good Union Man   *Person* *Rick ...*
The good union man is also extremely enthusiastic and loyal. However, he does not regard management as a class enemy, but rather as an adversary at the bargaining table.

3.   The Loyal, But Critical, Member
This type of individual differs from the two types already discussed in terms of his attitude towards his local. While remaining a staunch supporter of unionism in general, he will not be reluctant to express his displeasure with the leaders or members of his local.

4.   The Crisis Activist
The crisis activist tends to be a passive supporter of the union who generally permits other commitments to come before union activities. However, this type of individual will participate in meetings and other activities when a crisis develops in negotiations or within the union.

5.   The Dually Oriented Member
Some union members tend to hold the union in high regard and support its policies, but at the same time adopt a managerial point of view towards production and efficiency.

6.   The Indifferent Member   *(Percentage high?)*
Workers of this type do not have any strong feelings either for or against unionism. They usually join the union because "everyone else does" and have no interest in their obligations as union members.

7.   The Unwilling Unionist
Unwilling unionists are generally individuals who have been forced to join the organization against their will by legal or social pressures. If given the opportunity, such individuals would readily revoke their union status.

IV   THE OBJECTIVES OF EMPLOYEE ORGANIZATIONS

Collective bargaining is a representative process. Representatives of employees and employers are responsible for most of the decision-making and administrative tasks associated with their respective organizations. It is generally assumed that most of these decisions and tasks are consistent with the beliefs of the membership of that particular organization. Therefore, it should not be surprising to find that the objectives of employee organizations are easily traceable to the reasons why employees join employee organizations. The theoretical objectives of employee organizations have been defined as:

1. Maintenance of the organization. Opposition to employee organizations continues to be a fact of life even after a significant majority of the population has come to regard them as a permanent feature of our industrial system. The Task Force on Labour Relations pointed out that they:

"... do not believe that most employers have a very positive orientation toward trade unions and collective bargaining. Although employers in general are prepared to accept the fact that these institutions are indispensable instruments in a modern industrial liberal democratic state, the majority would be more than pleased if they were to restrict their activities or confine them to enterprises other than their own. To the individual employer, activities of unions are seen as one more force, along with some of the activities of suppliers, customers, government officials and politicians, making business more complicated. It is, therefore, not surprising that at the enterprise level employers' reaction toward unions and collective bargaining should range from positive approval, through reluctant acceptance and grudging toleration, to outright rejection." (2.6)

In addition to hostile employers, employee organizations must deal also with a growing apathy among union members and an increasingly less tolerant attitude towards unions by the general public. Thus, employee organizations must constantly seek to improve their capacity for long range survival.

2. Rationing of scarce job opportunities. Without an employee organization, the employer is free to hire and fire, or to promote and demote anyone at any time. Most employees do not wish to live under the constant threat of job displacement, either because of the inconvenience associated with being forced to switch jobs, or the uncertainty of being able to find another suitable job. Therefore, an important objective of the employee organization is to maintain or increase the total number of jobs in an industry, ensure that its members get first chance at these jobs, and to see that the different jobs are distributed among employees in a fair and reasonable manner.

3. Improvement of wages and working conditions. Members of employee organizations feel that the profits of an enterprise should be shared with the employees through better wages and working conditions. Their logic is that because employees have contributed to earning these profits, employees should be entitled to share in such profits. In this respect, the objectives of employee organizations have been condensed to read "more!", or "more now!"

4. Ensuring that negotiated rules are equitably applied and that the rights of employees are fully protected. A collective agreement sets out the basic rules and rights which govern union members and management in their dealings with each other. However, as the representatives of management initiate decisions in the areas covered by the collective agreement, there is always the possibility that managerial actions will run contrary to the provisions of the agreement. Employee organizations have demonstrated a firm commitment to developing rules, procedures and competent individuals capable of handling such matters.

5. Lobbying on behalf of unorganized segments of Canadian society.
While certain segments of Canadian society are represented by powerful employee organizations, there still exist large groups of individuals who lack any form of organized representation. For a variety of reasons, ranging from pure self-interest to a genuine concern for humanity, existing employee organizations have sought to lobby for conditions and legislation that would benefit the unorganized.

Over the years employee organizations have attached varying degrees of significance to these five objectives and have engaged in a complex assortment of programmes and procedures to accomplish them. In most cases the public has been willing to accept these objectives, but has frequently reacted against the programmes and procedures used to accomplish them.

V   THE STRUCTURE OF EMPLOYEE ORGANIZATIONS

To understand the operation of employee organizations it is necessary to examine the various categories of institutional structures associated with such organizations. Three of the most common categories of structures will be described in this section.

1.   The market for members

Any survey of the types of employees eligible for membership in employee organizations must deal with five distinctive categories of organizations which exist in Canada:

a) Craft employee organizations – "one skill, one union": The historical pattern of employee organizations in Canada was dominated by craft unionism from the early beginnings of Canadian trade unions to the late 1930's. Craft organizations were founded on the belief that employees should bargain together if they share common skills. These skills could be practiced in a single industry or across many industries. Thus, craft organizations include such unions as the United Brotherhood of Carpenters and Joiners of America, the Amalgamated Meat Cutters and Butcher Workmen of North America, and the Painters and Decorators of America.

The objectives of craft organizations are quite simple. They seek to protect the interests of their members by controlling the allotment of jobs. This is accomplished by regulating the qualifying process for each job and by requiring employers to hire only union members at a rate negotiated by the union.

Since the 1930's, the movement towards mass production technologies in an increasingly industrialized economy has severely limited the growth of craft unions. Today, the largest proportion of craft unions are found in the construction industry.

b) Industrial employee organizations – "one shop, one union": The growth of mass production industries led to the increasing popularity of industrial employee organizations that were founded on a set of postulates quite different from those applying to craft unions. Industrial employee organizations include in their membership all employees of a given industry or group of related industries, irrespective of the type or presence of skills. Thus, such organizations may encompass in their ranks varying combinations of skilled, semi-skilled and unskilled employees. Included in the category of "industrial" employee organizations would be such unions as the Canadian Food and Allied Workers, the United Steelworkers of America, and the United Automobile, Aerospace and Agricultural Implement Workers.

c) Public employee associations: The "employer" in the public sector is usually some type of federal, provincial, or municipal government agency which has a monopoly over certain goods and services. Historically, governmental agencies have been reluctant to grant their employees full collective bargaining rights for a variety of reasons which range from genuine concern for the welfare of Canadian society to purely political considerations. As a result, public employee organizations were required to depend upon lobbying tactics and "collective begging" to obtain improvements in pay and working conditions.

These organizations, which frequently resemble the "industrial" union model previously described, have rapidly increased their memberships in recent years and are now demanding and achieving improved collective bargaining rights. The reasons for these developments are discussed in Chapter 13 of this book.

d) Professional associations: A professional association is theoretically a self-disciplining organization concerned with the imposition and maintenance of high standards and a code of ethics to govern its members (2.7). During the past decade there has been a dramatic shift in emphasis from standards and ethics to protection of the economic well-being of members. A number of analysts have commented that the behaviour of professional employee organizations is surprisingly similar to the behavior of early Canadian craft unions. Such organizations will be discussed more fully in Chapter 14.

e) Dependent contractor organizations: The distinctive feature of these organizations is their inclusion of members whose economic status is dependent upon such variables as a percentage share of a total catch in the case of fishermen, a price paid per load in the case of truckers, and gross revenues per day in the case of lunch-wagon operators. Individuals such as these have found it profitable to maintain a united stand against those buying their services or products. Although dependent contractor organizations perform a variety of functions, many of their activities are clearly related to the terms and conditions under which their services and products will be provided to defined individuals or enterprises.

In the absence of specific statutory provisions dealing with dependent contractors, the following interrelated issues remain unresolved in some Canadian jurisdictions (2.8):
— are dependent contractors bona fide employees?
— are dependent contractors a source of unfair competition for organized workers?
— can dependent contractors join an existing union?
— should employers have the right to convert employees into dependent or independent contractors?

In actual situations, it is difficult to find "pure" examples of many of these categories. Even so, it is often possible to discern a significant, though not perfect, fulfillment of the requirements of a particular classification. More will be said about this in the discussion of appropriate bargaining units which appears in Chapter 10.

2. The decision-making capacity of employee organizations.
A second method of classifying the structure of employee organizations is based upon where the decision-making capabilities of that organization are concentrated.

a) The independent local employee organization: The independent local union is controlled by the majority vote of its members and seeks to represent its members in relation to their employer. In other words, it is independent both of the employer and the rest of the union movement. Independent local unions do not form an important part of total union membership in Canada, representing fewer than two percent of Canadian union members in 1975.

b) National employee organizations: Because their memberships are relatively small, independent local unions are often incapable of influencing powerful decision makers in industry and government. As a result, many locals have found it advantageous to become a part of a much larger superstructure of employee organizations. National employee organizations include locals from the various regions of Canada. Such locals may be composed of from ten to a few thousand members, depending upon which arrangement provides the best combination of administrative convenience and bargaining strength. Over the years the head offices of such organizations have been accumulating a great deal of decision-making power, taking an increasing share of the responsibility for negotiations and using their right to veto decisions made by locals. In 1975 about 46 percent of unionized Canadian employees belonged to purely Canadian employee organizations.

   c) International employee organizations: International employee organizations charter locals in other countries as well as Canada, and most of them have their head offices located outside Canada (primarily in the United States). As is the case with national organizations, power and authority reside primarily in the head offices. In 1975 it was estimated that about fifty-one percent of Canadians who belong to an employee organization are members of an international organization. This is a sharp drop when compared to the seventy-two percent figure that prevailed in 1962.

   The presence of international unions in Canada gives rise to some important issues. Much of the concern about this structural arrangement can be traced to the degree of freedom possessed by Canadian locals of international unions. In examining the question of the potential domination of Canadian locals by their international headquarters in the United States, Professor Jamieson has noted that if one employs a legalistic interpretation:

   "... most Canadian unions, as local branches and subsidiary bodies of
   international unions are not distinct entities in themselves and have no
   character that distinguishes them in any significant way from their
   American counterparts. If the central executives of all internationals at all
   times exerted to the full the powers and prerogatives allowed them under
   most union constitutions, most of them could, legally, have complete
   control over their Canadian branches and American domination would be
   a fact... Attempts by the officials of Canadian locals to break away from
   Internationals have been defeated on a number of occasions, even when
   they were supported by the majority of local members. Courts have
   usually ruled that the locals' assets and bargaining rights, under existing
   agreements, were the property of parent bodies." (2.9)

But not all breakaway attempts have been defeated. The formation of a separate Canadian union (The Canadian Paperworkers Union) by former members of the United Paperworkers International Union in 1974 caused a number of internationals to reshape their policies for Canadian locals. Recently, the 25,000 Canadian members of the Brotherhood of Railway, Airline and Steamship Clerks were permitted to establish their own division within this 250,000-member international union. According to the first president of the Canadian division, the Canadian members were not setting up

   "a separate and independent national entity by breaking away from the
   international as some have done and as some others have misinterpreted
   the intention of this event.
   Nor are we here to indulge in a mock ritual to change the image but not
   the substance of our Brotherhood in Canada. We are here to establish a
   fully functioning Canadian division of a truly international union, a
   division with its own constitution, its own policies and its own financial

and administrative officers who will be accountable to a convention of Canadian members." (2.10)

It has been reported that the Teamsters Union is also in the process of building a new Canadian structure with three regional divisions and five trade divisions.

The subject of international unionism is too complex and controversial to be covered effectively in this book. Those interested in pursuing this topic would be well advised to start with John Crispo's *International Unionism,* published by McGraw-Hill.

3. Federations of employee organizations.

A third aspect of the structure of employee organizations involves the affiliation of such organizations with a municipal, provincial, federal, or international federation. There are many such groups in Canada designed to correspond to the three levels of government. The primary purposes of these federations are to coordinate the relations between the labour movement and the various levels of government and to act as an arbitrator of disputes among member unions.

A brief historical perspective on the formation of labour federations in Canada appears in Figures 2.1 and 2.2 Some of the highlights worthy of careful attention include:

a) The Pre-Confederation Era: The few trade unions that existed in the early nineteenth century were composed primarily of journeymen and craftsmen, carpenters, printers and shoemakers. At first the union movement grew slowly, both in terms of the number of unions and the size of their membership, because of the agrarian nature of the Canadian economy, the individualistic outlook of so many Canadian pioneers, depressions that generated labour surpluses, and the lack of cooperation between French and English-speaking workers. The influx of both English and American workers who had been members of unions in their fatherland gave some momentum to the Canadian labour movement prior to Confederation.

b) The Dominance of Craft Unionism − The TLC: In the years following Confederation, attempts were made to link the various trade union locals and to form district labour councils. The objectives of these councils were to lobby for laws beneficial to the labour movement, to increase union membership and to provide financial assistance to striking unions. This movement led to the establishment of the Trades and Labour Congress in 1887, which was intended to be a national organization speaking for all Canadian unions. Unfortunately, this aim was never realized.

c) Schisms in the Canadian Labour Movement: With the realization of Canada's potential as an industrial nation, more and more disputes developed within the Canadian labour movement. Controversies over the place of semi-skilled and unskilled workers in the labour movement, the need for national as opposed to international unionism, and the degree of political involvement that would best serve the labour movement led to the formation of a variety of labour organizations with few common goals.

d) Polarization of the Labour Movement − The CCL: a gradual polarization of the various labour organizations was climaxed in 1940 with the formation of the Canadian Congress of Labour. The membership of this organization was composed chiefly of industrial unions which represented workers in the mining, manufacturing, automobile, and clothing industries. The Canadian Congress of Labour achieved considerable success in competing with the craft-dominated TLC until the two organizations merged in 1956 to form the Canadian Labour Congress.

e) The Present Situation: There are presently two national federations of union organizations in Canada: The Canadian Labour Congress and the

Figure 2.1

Summary of Attempts to Bring Canadian Trade Unions Within One National Body

Year	Name of the Organization	Geographic Scope	Philosophy/Policy	Outcome
1873	Canadian Labour Union	Ontario	Unite all unions in Canada	Failed due to depression
1881	Knights of Labour	Canada	Organize workers into trades and district assemblies	
1883	Canadian Labour Congree	Canada	Unite independent union within K of L	Not successful
1887	Trades and Labour Congress (TLC) of Canada	Canada	Canadian wing to the American Federation of Labor-craft unionism	Continued until merger with CCL to form CLC in 1956
1908	Canadian Federation of Labour (CFL)	Canada	Nationalism and industrial unionism —opposed to TLC	Could not continue
1919	One Big Union (OBU)	Western Canada	Revolutionary industrial unionism—opposed to TLC-type craft unionism	Could not survive due to internal dissensions, opposition from government and TLC
1920	Canadian Federation of Labour (Revived again)	Canada	Opposed to craft as well as revolutionary radical unionism— against TLC and OBU	Suffered due to general decline of union movement
1927	All Canadian Congress of Labour	Canada	Complete independence of Canadian labour movement	Could not succeed due to depression and inadequate nationalism
1930-1934	Workers' Unity League	Canada	Revolutionary ideology—Communist sponsored	Disbanded by the Communist party
1936	Canadian Federation of Labour (a new body)	Canada	Reaction to internal conflicts within the ALC, Canadian Congress of Labour	Lost workers' support
1940	Canadian Congress of Labour (CCL)	Canada	Industrial unionism— rival to TLC formed by CIO affiliates expelled by TLC and remaining units of ACCL	Merged with TLC to form CLC in 1956
1956	Canadian Labour Congress (CLC)	Canada	International business/economic unionism	Continuing

Source: Thakur, C. P. "The Structure of the Labour Movement" In *Canadian Industrial Relations* by S.M.A. Hameed. Toronto, Butterworths, 1975, pp. 126-7.

Figure 2.2

The History and Development of the Canadian Labour Movement

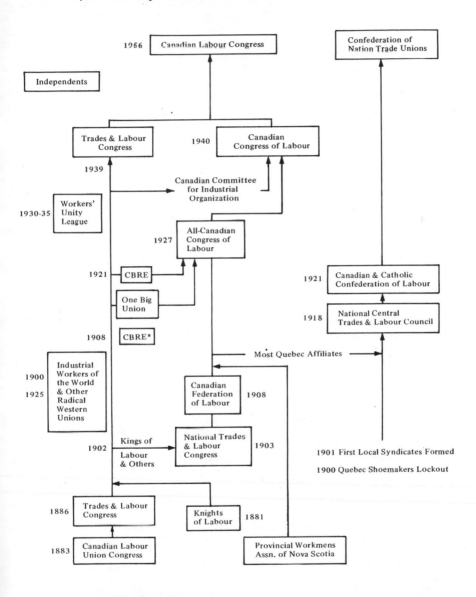

1873-1877 Canadian Labour Union
    1871 Local Trade Assemblies Begin to Emerge
    1867 Knights of St. Crispin
1825-1860 Numerous Weak & Isolated Locals
1800-1825 Scattered Friendly Societies & Labour Circles
*Canadian Brotherhood of Railway Employees
Source: M. Lazurus. *Years of Hard Labour.* Don Mills, Ontario Federation of Labour,
       1974, p. 70.

Confederation of National Trade Unions. The structure of the CLC segment of the Canadian labour movement is shown in Figure 2.3. This segment includes more than three-quarters of Canadian union members, ten provincial federations, and more than one hundred municipal labour councils. It is interesting to note that the majority of the CLC membership is affiliated with international unions, which are in turn affiliated with the AFL-CIO (the national labour federation in the United States). This dual loyalty has been the cause of growing skepticism concerning the autonomy of the CLC. The CLC is also affiliated with the 50 million member International Confederation of Free Trade Unions.

The other national federation, the Confederation of National Trade Unions, accounts for about 10 percent of the total membership in Canadian Unions. Although most of its present members reside in Quebec, an attempt is being made to expand this membership base into other provinces. The CNTU is presently made up of 12 federations which consist of more than 800 locals. These federations are involved directly in labour relations matters involving their members. Political lobbying activities are normally left to a system of regional councils.

The structure of Canadian employee organizations is by no means a neat, well coordinated structure. The structure has evolved over a long period of time, surviving many serious political and economic struggles. Most experts agree that this evolutionary process is far from complete. Searching questions are being raised as to where newly organized employees of the public, professional and service sectors of the Canadian economy fit into the labour movement. Opinion is divided on the usefulness of the formal affiliation of unions with the New Democratic Party. Increasing pressure is being generated to reconsider the value of our ties with the United States labour movement. Consequently, it is not surprising to find that recent forecasts predicting more schisms in the Canadian labour movement far outnumber the forecasts of polarization.

VI   THE MEMBERSHIP IN CANADIAN EMPLOYEE ORGANIZATIONS (2.11)

The statistical tables which appear in this chapter present some interesting data on the structure of employee organizations in Canada.

Union membership as a percentage of the non-agricultural Canadian labour force has been remarkably stable since the mid-1950's. The membership figures for selected years which appear in Figure 2.4 show that about one-third of the non-agricultural labour force has been consistently unionized. In addition, it must be remembered that employee organizations involved in collective bargaining in Canada include certain groups other than the traditional craft and industrial trade unions. The membership of public employee associations, professional associations, and dependent contractor associations must be calculated if a true picture of the proportion of Canada's labour force covered by collective bargaining is to be obtained. Additional estimates are also necessary to determine the magnitude of those affected where collective agreements apply to non-members of employee organizations as well as to members of a particular organization.

Although estimates of traditional trade union membership are available, the other relevant data is difficult to obtain. But, according to the Task Force on Labour Relations 1968:

"even if all these groups were totalled, it is unlikely they would surpass forty-five or fifty percent of the non-agricultural work force." (2.12)

Figure 2.4 shows that although the long-run growth trend of union membership appears to have stabilized at about one-third of the non-agricultural labour force, the level of unionization in Canada has risen from thirty to thirty-six percent.

Figure 2.3

The Structure of the CLC Segment of the Canadian Labour Movement

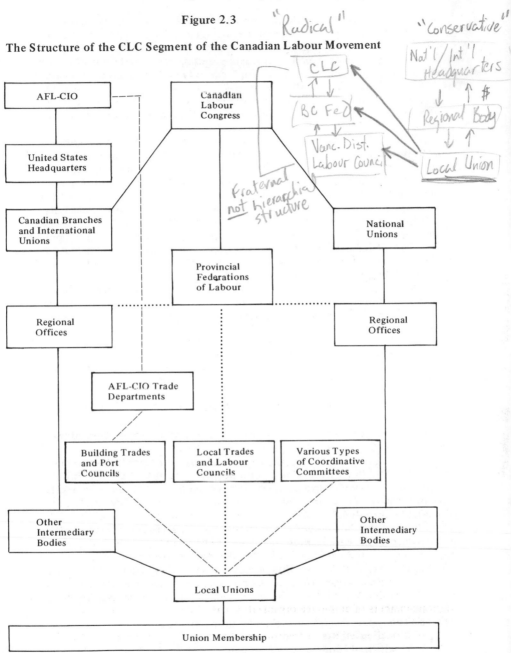

——— Obligatory links   ······· Voluntary links   ———— More specialized
links

Source: Thakur, C.P. *op. cit.,* p. 134. Adapted from John Crispo, *International Unionism:*
A Study of Canadian-American Relations. Toronto, McGraw-Hill, 1967, p. 167.

between 1962 and 1973. In addition, there has been considerable variation in terms of industrial, geographical, and occupational categories.

An examination of Figure 2.5 reveals negligible increases in unionization in such industrial sectors as commerce, finance, and insurance between 1962 and 1973, but very significant increases in the service (which includes education and health) and public administration sectors.

Seventy percent of all unionized workers in Canada are concentrated in Quebec and Ontario. In Figure 2.6 it is apparent that, while unionism has increased in all geographical regions between 1967 and 1973, the percentage increases have been very substantial in both the Atlantic and Prairie regions. It must be noted, however, that the 1973 figures overestimate the real growth of unionism in comparison with other years since, from that point of time, professional associations representing groups such as teachers and nurses have been considered as "unions".

Data on the occupational distribution of unionized workers is relatively sparse. However, in view of the fact that an estimated 90 percent of white collar workers are employed in the public sector, the growth of unionism in the public sector gives some indication of the occupational trend among white collar workers. Figure 2.7 provides some relevant information on the extent of unionism among office and non-office employees.

The turn of events since 1970 would also seem to indicate that an increasing proportion of individuals are becoming members of non-traditional types of employee organizations and this trend should continue for some time to come. More will be said about this in Part D of this book.

Summary

1.   The history of employee organizations in Canada deals with the struggle waged by employees to gain the right to associate, organize, bargain, and use sanctions.

2.   There are two basic categories of reasons why employees desire to bargain collectively. The first category deals with positive factors that tend to "pull" members into employee organizations. The second category deals with negative aspects of a particular employment situation that "push" employees into a collective relationship.

3.   Some of the most important objectives of employee organizations include: maintenance of the organization, the rationing of scarce job opportunities, improving wages and working conditions, developing a judicial system for deciding disputes concerning rights of individual employees, and lobbying on behalf of certain unorganized segments of Canadian society.

4.   The structure of employee organizations in Canada can be described in the following manner:

    a) The types of employees eligible for membership.
        −craft employee organizations
        −industrial employee organizations
        −public employee associations
        −professional associations
        −dependent contractor organizations
    b) The decision-making capacity of employee organizations.
        −independent local employee organizations
        −national employee organizations

Figure 2.4

Union Membership 1911-1975 with Estimates of Total Paid Workers in Non-Agricultural Industries in Canada (1921-1975) and Union Membership as Percentage of the Civilian Labour Force and the Total Non-Agricultural Paid Workers, 1921-1975.

Year	Union Membership (Thousands)	Total Non-Agricultural Paid Workers' (Thousands)	Union Membership as Percentage of civilian labour force	Union Membership as Percentage of non-agricultural paid workers
1911	133			
1912	160			
1913	176			
1914	166			
1915	143			
1916	160			
1917	205			
1918	249			
1919	378			
1920	374			
1921	313	1,956	9.4	16.0
1922	277	2,038	8.2	13.6
1923	278	2,110	8.1	13.2
1924	261	2,138	7.5	12.2
1925	271	2,203	7.6	12.3
1926	275	2,299	7.5	12.0
1927	290	2,406	7.7	12.1
1928	301	2,491	7.8	12.1
1929	319	2,541	8.0	12.6
1930	322	2,451	7.9	13.1
1931	311	2,028	7.5	15.3
1932	283	1,848	6.7	15.3
1933	286	1,717	6.7	16.7
1934	281	1,931	6.5	14.6
1935	281	1,941	6.4	14.5
1936	323	1,994	7.2	16.2
1937	333	2,108	8.5	18.2
1938	332	2,075	8.3	18.4
1939	359	2,079	7.7	17.3
1940	362	2,197	7.9	16.3
1941	462	2,566	10.3	18.0
1942	578	2,801	12.7	20.6
1943	665	2,934	14.6	22.7
1944	724	2,976	15.6	24.3

Figure 2.4 (Continued)

Year	Union Membership (Thousands)	Total Non-Agricultural Paid Workers' (Thousands)	Union Membership as Percentage of civilian labour force	Union Membership as Percentage of non-agricultural paid workers
1945	711	2,937	15.7	24.2
1946	832	2,986	17.1	27.9
1947	912	3,139	18.4	29.1
1948	978	3,225	19.4	30.3
1949	1,006(a)	3,326	19.3	29.5
1950	– (b)	–	–	–
1951	1,029	3,625(a)	19.7	28.4
1952	1,146	3,795(c)	21.4	30.2
1953	1,220	3,694	23.4	33.0
1954	1,268	3,754	24.2	33.8
1955	1,268	3,767	23.6	33.7
1956	1,352	4,058	24.5	33.3
1957	1,386	4,282	24.3	32.4
1958	1,454	4,250	24.7	34.2
1959	1,459	4,375	24.0	33.3
1960	1,459	4,522	23.5	32.3
1961	1,447	4,578	22.6	31.6
1962	1,423	4,705	22.2	30.2
1963	1,449	4,867	22.3	29.8
1964	1,493	5,074	22.3	29.4
1965	1,589	5,343	23.2	29.7
1966	1,736	5,658	24.5	30.7
1967	1,921	5,953	26.1	32.3
1968	2,010	6,068	26.6	33.1
1969	2,075	6,380	26.3	32.5
1970	2,173	6,465	27.2	33.6
1971(d)	2,231	6,637	26.8	33.6
1972	2,371	6,893	27.6	34.4
1973	2,610	7,181	29.4	36.3
1974	2,726	7,637	29.4	35.7
1975	2,875	7,817	29.7	36.8

(a)   Includes Newfoundland for the first time.

(b)   Data on union membership for all years up to and including 1949 are as of December 31. In 1950 the reference date was moved ahead by one day to January 1, 1951. Thus, while no figure is shown for 1950, the series is, in effect, continued without interruption. The data on union membership for subsequent years are also as of January.

(c)   Figures for all years up to and including 1952 are as of the first day in June. Data for subsequent years are as of January.

(d)   Revised.

*   The figures shown in this column from 1921 to 1930 inclusively represent Total Non-Agricultural Workers.

Source: Labour Organizations in Canada, 1974-75 Organisations de travailleurs au Canada. Labour Canada/Travail Canada, Ottawa, 1975.

Figure 2.5

Percentage of unionized employees in relation to:

Industrial sectors	Total number of unionized employees			Total number of workers in the industry		
	1962	1967	1973	1962	1967	1973
Manufacturing	40.8	39.5	30.6	42.5	45.3	44.7
Transportation, communication and public utilities	23.1	18.8	15.4	73.6	68.1	56.9
Construction	10.1	10.9	10.1	60.2	57.4	74.5
Socio-cultural, commercial and personal services	7.1	8.8	20.8	9.5	11.7	26.5
Forestry and fishing	2.6	2.5	1.2	45.6	58.5	54.0
Mines, quarries and oil wells	3.5	3.0	2.8	62.5	53.6	66.2
Commerce	2.9	4.1	4.1	5.2	8.0	8.5
Agriculture	*	*	*	*	*	1.8
Public administration	5.4	10.8	14.8	22.1	50.2	69.1
Finance, insurance and real estate	*	*	*	*	*	*
Others	4.5	1.6	*	*	*	*

* Negligible percentage

Sources: *Union Growth in Canada, 1921-1967,* Economics and Research Branch, Canada Department of Labour, Ottawa 1970 (by Ashagrie, K. and Eaton, J.K.).

The Labour Force, Statistics Canada, January 1973.

Figure 2.6

Union membership according to region, expressed as a percentage of the total unionized work force in Canada and as a percentage of the wage-earners in the region (in brackets).

Region	1927	1947	1967	1973
Atlantic	10 (*)	8 (23.3)	6 (25.7)	7.7 (38.8)
Quebec	26 (*)	27 (22.6)	31 (33.0)	28.7 (38.7)
Ontario	32 (*)	37 (22.2)	39 (31.0)	38.2 (34.2)
Prairies	20 (*)	13 (22.6)	11 (21.8)	12.1 (30.2)
British Columbia	12 (*)	15 (35.0)	13 (40.6)	12.6 (41.6)
Canada	100 (*)	100 (28.0)	100 (31.9)	100.0 (36.0)

* Not available

Sources: See the preceding table.

Figure 2.7

Percentage of employees covered by a collective agreement*

	1967	1968	1969	1971	1972	1973	1974
Office employees	14	15	19	28	32	31	33
Non-office employees and others	58	59	62	63	63	65	67

Percentage of employees covered by a collective agreement by industry (1974)*

	Office Employees	Non-office Employees
Meat packing	21	78
Mines	7	81
Manufacturing	9	74
Transportation, communications and other public utilities	42	87
Commerce, finance	3	37
Services	21	40
Civil Service	93	98
All industries	33	70

*The number of employees covered by a collective agreement overestimates the number of union members.

Source: *Working Conditions in Canadian industry, 1974,* Report No. 18, Economics and Research Branch, Labour Canada.

–international employee organizations

c) Federations of employee organizations which are designed to correspond to various levels of government in Canada.

References

2.1 Woods, H.D. *Labour Policy in Canada.* Toronto, Macmillan of Canada, 1973, p. 93.

2.2 Sherman, V.C. "Unionism and the Non-Union Company." *Personnel Journal,* June 1969, pp. 413-22.

2.3 Beal, E.F. et. al. *The Practice of Collective Bargaining.* Homewood Ill., Richard D. Irwin, Inc., p. 8.

2.4 Wood, W.D. *The Current Industrial Scene in Canada 1974.* Kingston, Industrial Relations Centre Queen's University, 1974, p. SU-22.

2.5 Tagliacozzo, D.L. and Joel Seidman. "Rank and File Union Members", in *Unions, Management and the Public,* by E.W. Bakke, et al. New York, Harcourt, Brace & World, 1967, pp. 162-167.

2.6 *Canadian Industrial Relations: The Report of the Task Force on Labour Relations.* Ottawa, Queen's Printer, 1969, p. 92.

2.7 Carrothers, A.W. "Collective Bargaining and the Professional Employee," in *Collective Bargaining and the Professional Employee,* by J. Crispo. Toronto, Centre for Industrial Relations, University of Toronto, 1966, p. 7.

2.8 Arthurs, H.W. "The Dependent Contractor: A Study of Legal Problems of Countervailing Power". *U.T.L.J.* Vol. 16, 1965.

2.9 Jamieson, S. *Industrial Relations In Canada.* Toronto, Macmillan, 1973, pp. 53-54.

2.10 *Labour Gazette.* May, 1976, p. 239.

2.11 Beaucage, A. *An Outline of the Canadian Labour Relations System.* Ottawa, Canada Department of Labour, 1976.

2.12 Task Force on Labour Relations. *op. cit.,* p. 35.

Suggested Readings for Further Study

Abella, Irving. *The Struggle For Industrial Unionism in Canada.* Toronto, University of Toronto Press, 1972.

Carrothers, A.W. *Collective Bargaining Law in Canada.* Toronto, Butterworths, 1965, pp. 3-71.

Confederation of National Trade Unions. *Quebec Labour – The Confederation of National Trade Unions Yesterday and Today.* Montreal, Black Rose Books, 1972.

Crispo, John. *International Unionism. A Study in Canadian-American Relations.* Toronto, McGraw-Hill, 1967.

Goldenberg, S.B. and Frances Bairstow, eds., *Domination or Independence? The Problem of Canadian Autonomy in Labour Management Relations.* Montreal: Labour Relations Centre, McGill University, 1965.

Jamieson, Stuart M. *Industrial Relations In Canada.* Toronto, Macmillan, 1973.

Kruger, A.M. "The Direction of Unionism in Canada". *In Canadian Labour in Transition,* edited by R.U. Miller and A.F. Isbester. Toronto, Prentice-Hall, 1971.

Miller, Richard U. "Organized Labour and Politics in Canada". In *Canadian Labour in Transition,* edited by R.U. Miller and A.F. Isbester. Toronto, Prentice-Hall, 1971.

Perlman, Mark. *Labour Union Theories In America.* Illinois, Row, Peterson and Co., 1961.

Rees, A. *The Economics of Trade Unions.* Chicago, University of Chicago Press, 1969.

Woods, H.D. *Labour Policy in Canada,* Toronto, Macmillan, 1973. Chapter III.

Experiential Assignment

Survey the membership of a particular union in your community and attempt to determine the relative significance of the "push" and "pull" factors discussed in this chapter that contributed to their decision to join the union.

STATISTICAL APPENDIX TO CHAPTER 2

Figure A.2.1

Labour organizations in Canada

At the beginning of 1975, union membership in Canada totalled 2,875,464 compared with 2,726,144 in 1974, an increase of 5.5 per cent, according to *Labour Organizations in Canada*, an annual Labour Canada publication.

In the past 10 years union membership has increased by 65.6 per cent compared with the 25.3 per cent increase in the previous decade, 1957 to 1966.

In 1975, union membership in Canada represented 29.7 per cent of the labour force and 36.8 per cent of non-agricultural paid workers, compared with the marginally lower 1974 figures of 29.4 per cent and 35.7 per cent, respectively.

Seventy-one per cent of all union members in Canada, representing a membership of 2,043,484, belonged to Canadian Labour Congress – affiliated unions. Members in unaffiliated national unions have increased their share of total membership in Canada from 4.8 per cent in 1966, to 16.4 per cent in 1975.

The extension of collective bargaining rights to government employees, teachers, nurses and some groups of professionals has been the main contributing factor in the increased number of members in national unions.

There are now 37 unions with more than 20,000 members, representing 70 per cent of the membership of national and international unions. In 1966, 21 unions represented 55 per cent of the membership.

A comparison of 1966 and 1975 figures shows the number of small unions remains relatively high. In 1966 there were 116 national and international unions with less than 10,000 members comprising 20 per cent of the membership, compared with 120 unions in 1975, representing 14 per cent of the membership.

Only two national unions in 1966 were represented in the 10 largest unions: the Canadian Union of Public Employees (CLC) and the Canadian Brotherhood of Railway, Transport and General Workers (CLC). In 1975 there were four: Canadian Union of Public Employees (CLC), Public Service Alliance of Canada (CLC), Centrale de l'enseignement du Québec (Ind.), and Fédération des affaires sociales (CNTU). In 1975 the Canadian Union of Public Employees replaced the United Steelworkers of America as the largest union in Canada (see accompanying list of unions with 50,000 or more members).

More information is available in the recently-published edition of *Labour Organizations in Canada 1974-1975.*

Union Membership by Congress Affiliation, 1975

Congress Affiliation	Membership Number	Per Cent
Canadian Labour Congress	2,043,484	71.1
AFL-CIO/CLC	1,239,971	43.1
CLC only	803,513	28.0
CNTU	173,610	6.0
CSD	40,275	1.4
CCU	20,358	0.7
AFL-CIO only	626	*
Unaffiliated International Unions	84,963	3.0
Unaffiliated National Unions	471,909	16.4
Independent Local Organizations	40,239	1.4
TOTAL	2,875,464	100.0

*Less than 0.1 per cent.

Unions with 50,000 or more members, 1975

	1975 Membership	Relative Position in 1974
1. Canadian Union of Public Employees (CLC)	198,872	(2)
2. United Steelworkers of America (AFL-CIO/CLC)	186,996	(1)
3. Public Service Alliance of Canada (CLC)	135,998	(3)
4. International Union, United Automobile Aerospace and Agricultural Implement Workers of America (CLC)	117,486	(4)
5. United Brotherhood of Carpenters and Joiners of America (AFL-CIO/CLC)	89,010	(6)
6. Québec Teachers' Corporation (Ind.)	84,905	(5)
7. International Brotherhood of Teamsters, Chauffeurs, Warehousemen and Helpers of America (Ind.)	75,638	(7)
8. International Brotherhood of Electrical Workers (AFL-CIO/CLC)	63,463	(8)
9. Social Affairs Federation (CNTU)	61,130	(11)
10. International Association of Machinists and Aerospace Workers (AFL-CIO/CLC)	57,209	(13)
11. International Woodworkers of America (AFL-CIO/CLC)	56,741	(10)
12. Canadian Paperworkers Union (CLC)	56,000	(**)
13. Civil Service Association of Ontario, The	55,448	(*)
14. Canadian Food and Allied Workers, District 15 Council (AFL-CIO/CLC)	50,000	(14)

*Fewer than 50,000 members in 1974.
**Separate Canadian union formed in 1974, membership formerly in United Paperworkers International Union (AFL-CIO/CLC).

Source: *The Labour Gazette.* January, 1976, p. 34.

Figure A.2.2

Locals, Collective Agreements, Membership, and Female Membership of Labour Organizations in Canada, 1972

Name of Labour Organization	Locals	Collective Agreements	Membership 1962	Membership 1972	Change (%) 1962-1972	Women Members 1962	Women Members 1972	Net Change 1962-1972
INTERNATIONAL UNIONS (Data relate to locals, collective agreements, and membership in Canada)								
Actors' Equity Assoc. (AFL-CIO/CLC)	1	55	1,500	4,009	+ 167.3	861	1,394	+ 533
Artists, American Guild of Variety (AFL-CIO/CLC)	2	8	651	331	− 49.2	381	234	− 147
Asbestos Workers, International Assoc. of Heat & Frost Insulators & (AFL-CIO/CLC)	9	15	1,397	2,459	+ 76.0	--	--	--
Automobile, Aerospace & Agricultural Implement Workers of America, International Union, United (CLC)	110	434	61,284	107,266	+ 75.0	5,975	13,426	+ 7,451
Bakery and Confectionery Workers' International Union of America (AFL-CIO/CLC)	28	149	8,621	11,316	+ 31.3	2,804	2,784	− 20
Barbers, Hairdressers, Cosmetologists & Proprietors' International Union of America, Journeymen (AFL-CIO/CLC)	6	--	1,988	898	− 54.8	41	47	+ 6
Boilermakers, Iron Shipbuilders, Blacksmiths, Forgers & Helpers, International Brotherhood of (AFL-CIO/CLC)	31	89	5,482	9,427	+ 72.0	--	--	--
Brewery, Flour, Cereal, Soft Drink and Distillery Workers of America, International Union of United (AFL-CIO/CLC)	84	235	7,330	11,963	+ 63.2	222	361	+ 139
Bricklayers, Masons and Plasterers' International Union of America (AFL-CIO/CLC)	48	182	7,608	10,541	+ 38.6	--	--	--
Broadcast Employees and Technicians, National Assoc. of (AFL-CIO/CLC)	43	32	2,246	3,648	+ 62.4	101	133	+ 32
Carpenters & Joiners of America, United Brotherhood of (AFL-CIO/CLC)	212	1,210	59,794	74,547	+ 24.7	415	1,650	+ 1,235

Union								
Cement, Lime and Gypsum Workers' International Union, United (AFL-CIO/CLC)	50	73	4,076	4,943	+ 21.3	—	—	—
Chemical Workers' Union, International (AFL-CIO/CLC)	93	147	12,724	15,097	+ 18.6	1,209	2,035	+ 826
Clothing Workers of America, Amalgamated (AFL-CIO/CLC)	49	40	12,457	16,444	+ 32.0	8,183	11,350	+ 3,167
Communications Workers of America (AFL-CIO/CLC)	6	7	2,672	2,774	+ 3.8	1,248	1,576	+ 328
Distillery, Rectifying, Wine and Allied Workers' International Union of America (AFL-CIO/CLC)	20	24	3,377	3,285	− 2.7	953	831	− 122
Dolls, Toys, Playthings, Novelties and Allied Products of the United States and Canada, International Union of (AFL-CIO/CLC)	1	9	—	800	—	—	670	+ 670
Electrical, Radio and Machine Workers, International Union of (AFL-CIO/CLC)	65	65	8,920	12,370	+ 38.7	3,309	5,804	+ 2,495
Electrical, Radio & Machine Workers of America, United (Ind.)	47	93	18,841	20,100	+ 6.7	3,260	4,774	+ 1,514
Electrical Workers, International Brotherhood of (AFL-CIO/CLC)	122	322	33,131	59,700	+ 80.2	3,988	6,460	+ 2,472
Elevator Constructors, International Union of (AFL-CIO/CLC)	10	1	1,277	2,209	+ 73.0	—	—	—
Engineers, International Union of Operating (AFL-CIO/CLC)	20	199	12,955	26,355	+ 103.3	—	—	—
Engineers, American Federation of Technical (AFL-CIO/CLC)	2	30	815	1,042	+ 27.9	25	28	+ 3
Fire Fighters, International Assoc. of (AFL-CIO/CLC)	166	166	13,315	16,187	+ 21.6	—	—	—
Firemen and Oilers, International Brotherhood of (AFL-CIO/CLC)	45	22	2,363	2,085	− 11.8	69	73	+ 4
Flint Class Workers Union of North America, America (AFL-CIO)	2	2	—	189	—	—	60	+ 60
Garment Workers' Union, International Ladies (AFL-CIO/CLC)	30	117	16,787	23,402	+ 39.4	13,193	19,400	+ 6,207
Garment Workers of America, United (AFL-CIO/CLC)	11	21	1,882	2,272	+ 20.7	1,463	1,920	+ 457

Continued . . .

Figure A.2.2 (Continued)

Locals, Collective Agreements, Membership, and Female Membership of Labour Organizations in Canada, 1972 (continued)

Name of Labour Organization	Locals	Collective Agreements	Membership 1962	Membership 1972	Change (%) 1962-1972	Women Members 1962	Women Members 1972	Net Change 1962-1972
Glass and Ceramic Workers of North America, United (AFL-CIO/CLC)	48	48	5,695	8,772	+ 54.0	939	2,068	+ 1,129
Grain Millers, American Federation of (AFL-CIO/CLC)	7	11	1,586	1,950	+ 23.0	692	692	—
Graphics Arts International Union (AFL-CIO/CLC)	31	333	3,402	10,236	+ 200.9	1,928	1,753	− 175
Guard Workers of America, International Union, United Plant (Ind.)	3	19	174	553	+ 217.8	—	—	—
Hatters, Cap and Millinery Workers' International Union, United (AFL-CIO/CLC)	9	59	2,389	1,343	− 43.8	1,453	678	− 775
Hotel & Restaurant Employees' and Bartenders' International Union, (AFL-CIO/CLC)	34	339	12,728	23,444	+ 84.2	3,984	10,082	+ 6,098
Iron Workers, International Assoc., of Bridge, Structural and Ornamental (AFL-CIO/CLC)	24	143	7,495	15,333	+ 104.6	—	—	—
Jewelry Workers' Union, International (AFL-CIO/CLC)	3	13	297	523	+ 76.1	29	91	+ 62
Labourers' International Union of North America (AFL-CIO/CLC)	40	1,540	21,296	48,618	+ 128.3	—	—	—
Lathers' International Union, Wood, Wire and Metal (AFL-CIO/CLC)	16	60	919	1,353	+ 47.2	—	—	—
Laundry, Dry Cleaning and Dye House Workers' International Union (CLC)	4	15	1,827	2,433	+ 33.2	1,554	2,006	+ 452
Leather Goods, Plastic and Novelty Workers' Union, International (AFL-CIO/CLC)	2	34	1,167	1,442	+ 23.6	818	968	+ 150
Locomotive Engineers, Grand International Brotherhood of (Ind.)	98	6	8,938	7,334	− 17.9	—	—	—
Longshoremen's Association, International (AFL-CIO/CLC)	36	60	8,372	7,013	− 16.2	—	—	—
Longshoremen's and Warehousemen's Union, International (CLC)	11	5	2,391	3,433	+ 43.6	—	40	+ 40
Machinists & Aerospace Workers, International Assoc. of (AFL-CIO/CLC)	171	521	38,968	49,511	+ 27.1	2,113	3,427	+ 1,314
Maintenance of Way Employees, Brotherhood of (AFL-CIO/CLC)	175	10	23,982	17,464	− 27.2	—	—	—

Union								
Marble, Slate & Stone Polishers, Rubber & Sawyers, Tile Helpers & Finishers, Marble Setters' Helpers, Marble Mosaic & Terrazzo Workers' Helpers, International Assoc. of (AFL-CIO)	3	23	408	286	– 29.9	—	—	—
Meat Cutters and Butcher Workmen of North America, Amalgamated (AFL-CIO/CLC)	146	432	8,835	50,790	—	3,508	15,481	+ 11,973
Mine Workers of America, United (IND.)	23	16	9,192	6,371	– 30.7	1	—	+ 1
Molders' and Allied Workers' Union, International (AFL-CIO/CLC)	30	86	5,756	5,844	+ 1.5	57	704	+ 647
Musicians, American Federation of (AFL-CIO/CLC)	37	—	15,080	28,800	+ 91.0	1,500	2,847	+ 1,347
Newspaper Guild, The (AFL-CIO/CLC)	6	19	3,220	3,051	– 5.2	1,288	969	– 319
Office & Professional Employees' International Union (AFL-CIO/CLC)	63	426	5,728	13,011	+ 127.1	2,433	6,439	+ 4,006
Oil, Chemical & Atomic Workers' International Union (AFL-CIO/CLC)	90	163	12,115	14,868	+ 22.7	800	1,236	+ 436
Painters and Allied Trades, International Brotherhood of (AFL-CIO/CLC)	59	395	6,657	12,686	+ 90.6	—	—	—
Papermakers and Paperworkers, United (AFL-CIO/CLC)	69	70	9,832	11,151	+ 13.4	—	—	—
Pattern Makers' League of North America (AFL-CIO/CLC)	4	22	349	280	– 19.8	244	162	– 82
Plasterers' and Cement Masons' International Assoc. of the United States & Canada, Operative (AFL-CIO/CLC)	31	93	3,468	4,400	+ 26.9	—	—	—
Plumbing and Pipe Fitting Industry of the United States & Canada, United Assoc. of Journeymen & Apprentices of the (AFL-CIO/CLC)	69	194	18,656	36,967	+ 98.2	—	—	—
Porters, Train, Chair Car, Coach Porters and Attendants, Brotherhood of Sleeping Car (AFL-CIO/CLC)	4	1	449	219	– 51.2	—	7	+ 7
Pottery and Allied Workers, International Brotherhood of (AFL-CIO/CLC)	18	17	524	1,783	+ 240.3	31	683	+ 652
Printing Pressmen and Assistants' Union of North America, International (AFL-CIO/CLC)	57	283	8,150	10,023	+ 23.0	952	1,697	+ 745

Continued . . .

Figure A.2.2 (Continued)

Locals, Collective Agreements, Membership, and Female Membership of Labour Organizations in Canada, 1972 (continued)

Name of Labour Organization	Locals	Collective Agreements	Membership 1962	1972	Change (%) 1962-1972	Women Members 1962	1972	Net Change 1962-1972
Pulp, Sulphite and Paper Mill Workers, International Brotherhood of (AFL-CIO/CLC)	141	196	37,196	40,193	+ 8.1	1,724	1,509	– 215
Railroad Signalmen, Brotherhood of (AFL-CIO/CLC)	21	3	1,473	1,147	– 22.1	—	—	—
Railway Carmen of the United States and Canada, Brotherhood of (AFL-CIO/CLC)	81	6	19,485	12,858	– 34.0	7	9	+ 2
Railway, Airline & Steamship Clerks, Freight handlers, Express & Station Employees, Brotherhood of (AFL-CIO/CLC)	146	42	19,029	22,683	+ 19.2	1,168	1,955	+ 787
Retail Clerks' International Assoc. (AFL-CIO/CLC)	8	186	9,733	32,805	+ 237.0	4,328	14,244	+ 9,916
Retail, Wholesale and Department Store Union (AFL-CIO/CLC)	40	366	16,272	21,689	+ 33.3	4,242	7,106	+ 2,864
Rubber, Cork, Linoleum & Plastic Workers of America, United (AFL-CIO/CLC)	78	82	11,591	16,777	+ 44.7	2,381	3,359	+ 978
Seafarers' International Union of North America (AFL-CIO/CLC)	2	2	15,009	5,700	– 62.0	390	200	– 190
Service Employees' International Union (AFL-CIO/CLC)	22	264	14,061	41,503	+ 195.2	8,447	28,989	+ 20,542
Sheet Metal Workers' International Assoc. (AFL-CIO/CLC)	43	288	7,795	15,199	+ 95.00	38	—	—
Shoe Workers of America, United (AFL-CIO/CLC)	5	5	148	929	+ 527.7	60	466	+ 406
Shoe Workers' Union, Boot and (AFL-CIO/CLC)	11	11	1,025	1,393	+ 35.9	541	844	+ 303
Stage Employees and Moving Picture Machine Operators of the United States and Canada, International Alliance of Theatrical (AFL-CIO/CLC)	50	199	2,981	2,527	– 15.2	449	308	– 141
Steelworkers of America, United (AFL-CIO/CLC)	867	1,146	102,962	174,347	+ 69.3	5,906	10,536	+ 4,630
Stereotypers' and Electrotypers' Union of North America, International (AFL-CIO/CLC)	11	37	773	473	– 38.8	—	—	—

INTERNATIONAL

	locals	Coll.agree	Membership 62	Membership 72	Δ	Women members 62	Women members 72	Δ
Teamsters, Chauffeurs, Warehousemen and Helpers of America, International Brotherhood of (Ind.)	34	1,474	42,161	61,102	+ 44.9	1,610	3,420	+ 1,810
Telegraph Workers, United (AFL-CIO/CLC)	14	3	5,030	3,348	− 33.4	1,204	918	+ 286
Textile Workers' Union of America (AFL-CIO/CLC)	103	107	11,013	16,073	+ 45.9	5,221	7,140	+ 1,919
Textile Workers of America, United (AFL-CIO/CLC)	52	53	8,479	10,156	+ 19.8	3,012	4,041	+ 1,029
Tobacco Workers' International Union (AFL-CIO/CLC)	21	21	5,743	6,050	+ 5.3	3,333	2,920	− 413
Transit Union, Amalgamated (AFL-CIO/CLC)	30	51	13,858	15,631	+ 12.8	81	262	+ 181
Transportation Union, United (AFL-CIO/CLC)	155	29	—	24,041	—	—	—	—
Typographical Union of North America, International (AFL-CIO/CLC)	52	164	8,040	6,963	− 13.4	140	252	+ 112
Upholsterers' International Union of North America (AFL-CIO/CLC)	14	89	3,587	7,561	+ 110.8	459	1,030	+ 571
Woodworkers of America, International (AFL-CIO/CLC)	61	480	35,408	54,618	+ 54.3	1,017	2,769	+ 1,752
Previously reporting unions not reporting in 1972	—	—	65,278	—	—	4,688	—	− 4,688
TOTAL	4,804	14,507	1,011,676	1,442,710	+ 42.6	122,471	219,317	+ 96,846

NATIONAL UNIONS

	locals	Coll.agree	Membership 62	Membership 72	Δ	Women members 62	Women members 72	Δ
Air Line Dispatchers' Assoc., Canadian (CLC)	4	4	—	113	—	—	—	—
Air Line Flight Attendants' Assoc., Canadian (CLC)	12	5	1,165	3,317	+ 184.7	978	2,698	+ 1,720
Air Line Pilots' Assoc., Canadian (Ind.)	11	5	823	1,954	+ 137.4	—	—	—
Air Line Employees' Assoc., Canadian (CLC)	38	2	1,515	2,669	+ 76.2	666	1,579	+ 913
Artists, Assoc. of Canadian Television and Radio (CLC)	10	21	—	3,871	—	—	1,837	+ 1,837
Barbers and Hairdressers, Federation of the Province of Quebec Inc. (Ind.)	16	—	1,073	1,066	− 0.7	375	809	+ 434
Building and Woodworkers' Union, Inc., National Federation of (CNTU)	61	28	9,708	16,869	+ 73.8	—	—	—
Canadian Labour, National Council of (Ind.)	61	54	5,867	9,177	+ 56.4	1,640	1,827	+ 187

Continued . . .

Figure A.2.2 (Continued)

Locals, Collective Agreements, Membership, and Female Membership of Labour Organizations in Canada, 1972 (continued)

Name of Labour Organization	Locals	Collective Agreements	Membership 1962	Membership 1972	Change (%) 1962-1972	Women Members 1962	Women Members 1972	Net Change 1962-1972
Canadian Labour Congress (Ind.)	130	134	18,594	15,492	− 16.7	2,146	4,568	+ 2,422
Communications Workers, Canadian Union of (Ind.)	4	2	7,809	6,037	− 22.7	2,822	2,478	− 344
Christian Labour Association of Canada (Ind.)	58	34	961	2,676	+ 178.5	--	198	+ 198
Christian Trade Unions of Canada (Ind.)	3	11	206	390	+ 89.3	22	130	+ 108
Clothing Workers Inc., National Federation of (CSD)	41	88	4,560	7,597	+ 66.6	3,878	4,897	+ 1,019
Commerce, Federation, Inc. (CNTU)	112	111	--	13,650	--	--	4,080	+ 4,080
Engineers, Canadian Union of Operating (Ind.)	7	116	1,134	1,368	+ 20.6	--	--	--
Engineers, Federation of Quebec (CNTU)	25	17	--	4,890	--	--	4	+ 4
Fishermen and Allied Workers' Union, United (Ind.)	32	33	7,793	5,426	− 30.4	1,304	1,120	− 184
Forestry Workers, Quebec Federation of (Ind.)	8	29	4,551	4,521	− 0.7	--	1	+ 1
Hospital Employees' Union (Ind.)	76	76	--	10,595	--	--	8,846	+ 8,846
Institutional Employees' Union (Ind.)	3	6	811	1,041	+ 28.4	576	762	+ 186
Industrial, Mechanical and Allied Workers, Canadian Assoc. of (Ind.)	7	33	--	2,889	--	--	231	+ 231
(Marconi), Salaried Employees' Association (Ind.)	4	4	--	667	--	--	136	+ 136
Marine Workers' Federation (CLC)	10	21	--	2,461	--	--	11	+ 11
Merchant Service Guild Inc., Canadian (CLC)	3	63	2,133	3,602	+ 68.9	--	2	+ 2
Metals, Mines and Chemical Workers, Federation of (CSD)	39	49	--	7,207	--	--	327	+ 327
Miramichi Trades and Labour Union (Ind.)	3	7	430	243	− 43.5	--	--	--
Municipal and School Employees Inc., Federation of (Ind.)	109	130	2,829	6,513	+ 130.2	263	1,811	+ 1,548
National Trade Unions, Confederation of (Ind.)	22	22	13,330	2,440	− 81.7	2,000	205	− 1,795

Northern Electric Office Employee Association (Ind.)	1	1	—	2,064	—	—	820	+ 820
Nurses, Alberta Assoc. of Registered (Ind.)	62	62	—	13,207	—	—	13,207	+ 13,207
Nurses' Association of British Columbia, Registered (Ind.)	94	94	+ 309.9	14,474	3,531	3,529	14,329	+ 10,800
Peace Officers, B.C. Federation of (Ind.)	11	11	+ 34.2	1,212	903	22	22	—
Public Employees, Canadian Union of (CLC)	911	1,294	—	171,038	—	—	59,009	+ 59,009
Public Service Employees Inc., Federation of (CNTU)	283	324	—	26,674	—	—	9,021	+ 9,021
Paper and Forestry Workers, Federation of (CNTU)	74	77	+ 69.6	12,196	7,190	405	556	+ 151
Pulp and Paper Workers of Canada (Ind.)	10	27	—	5,223	—	—	209	+ 209
Quebec Teachers' Corporation (Ind.)	57	57	—	87,546	—	—	58,767	+ 58,767
Railways Police Association, Canadian National (Ind.)	12	1	— 2.7	359	369	—	—	—
Railway, Transport and General Workers, Canadian Brotherhood of (CLC)	193	272	+ 11.5	38,296	34,342	3,529	4,234	+ 705
R.C.A. Victor Employees' Assoc. (Ind.)	4	4	+ 44.2	937	650	203	242	+ 39
Retail Employees, Union of Canadian (CLC)	9	4	+ 84.7	5,634	3,050	897	2,477	+ 1,580
Seafood Workers' Union, Canadian (CLC)	18	18	+ 53.2	3,002	1,960	598	1,217	+ 619
Services, National Federation of, Inc. (CNTU)	266	271	+ 282.3	58,379	15,272	12,214	39,175	+ 26,961
Shipyard General Workers' Federation (CLC)	3	34	+ 9.9	2,198	2,000	6	1	— 5
Telephone Employee's Association, Canadian (Ind.)	65	8	+ 16.5	18,572	15,943	6,706	9,067	+ 2,361
Telephone Workers of British Columbia (Clerical Division) Federation of (CLC)	8	3	+ 102.5	2,238	1,105	859	1,907	+ 1,048
Telephone Workers of British Columbia (Plant Division), Federation of (CLC)	16	1	+ 105.3	4,305	2,097	5	98	+ 93
Telephone Workers of British Columbia (Traffic Division), Federation of (CLC)	8	1	+ 80.0	1,703	946	942	1,703	+ 761
Textile and Chemical Union, Canadian (Ind.)	6	4	+ 91.5	1,620	846	380	1,160	+ 780
Textile Workers, Canadian Federation of, Inc. (CSD)	42	43	+ 3.0	8,872	9,144	3,660	2,766	— 894

Continued

Figure A.2.2 (Continued)

Locals, Collective Agreements, Membership, and Female Membership of Labour Organizations in Canada, 1972 (continued)

Name of Labour Organization	Locals	Collective Agreements	Membership 1962	Membership 1972	Change (%) 1962-1972	Women Members 1962	Women Members 1972	Net Change 1962-1972
Traffic Employees' Assoc. (Ind.)	27	2	6,665	6,602	− 0.9	6,665	6,602	− 63
Transportation Employees' Canadian Union (Ind.)	18	——	——	653	——	——	——	——
Wheat Pool Employees' Association, Saskatchewan (CLC)	21	5	1,618	2,100	+ 37.2	171	239	+ 68
Previously reporting organizations not reporting in 1972	——	——	131,127	——	——	26,093	——	−26,093
TOTAL	3,128	3,723	324,050	627,845	+ 93.7	83,554	265,385	+181,831
GOVERNMENT EMPLOYEES[1]								
Agricultural Union (CLC)	66	——	1,134	6,428	+ 466.8	102	693	+ 591
Air Traffic Control Assoc. Inc., Canadian (CLC)	27	1	——	1,870	——	——	17	+ 17
Civil Service Association of Ontario, (Ind.)	453	5	31,897	41,433	+ 29.9	9,174	16,940	+ 7,766
Civil Service Association of Alberta (Ind.)	62	10	10,194	22,334	+ 119.1	4,055	9,698	+ 5,643
Customs Excise Union (CLC)	23	——	6,576	7,061	+ 7.4	564	892	+ 328
Economic Security Employees' National Assoc. (CLC)	303	——	7,143	10,932	+ 53.0	3,284	5,300	+ 2,016
Environment Component (CLC)	52	——	——	5,076	——	——	709	+ 709
Government Employees' Assoc., Nova Scotia (Ind.)	13	1	——	6,478	——	——	3,463	+ 3,463
Government Employees' Assoc., Manitoba (Ind.)	48	8	——	11,046	——	——	4,120	+ 4,120
Government Employees' Assoc., Saskatchewan (Ind.)	18	6	6,539	8,975	+ 41.1	2,364	3,262	+ 898
Government Employees' Union, B.C. (CLC)	63	——	8,568	17,700	+ 106.6	2,515	3,503	+ 988
Health and Welfare Union, National (CLC)	31	——	797	5,130	+ 543.7	402	2,911	+ 2,509

Letter Carriers' Union of Canada (CLC)	254	1	7,005	13,880	+ 98.1	—	34	+ 34
Manpower and Immigration Union (CLC)	9	—	1,358	2,106	+ 55.1	136	271	+ 135
National Component of the Public Service Alliance of Canada (CLC)	173	—	—	16,456	—	—	4,493	+ 4,493
National Defence Employees, Union of (CLC)	118	—	18,257	28,712	+ 57.3	3,414	6,616	+ 3,302
Public Employees' Assoc. Inc., New Brunswick (Ind.)	14	—	—	2,520	—	—	1,125	+ 1,125
Northwest Territories Component (CLC)	6	—	—	1,295	—	—	351	+ 351
Postal Officials of Canada, Assoc. of (Ind.)	27	1	—	2,896	—	—	28	+ 28
Postal Workers, Canadian Union of (CLC)	312	1	10,537	19,143	+ 81.7	516	4,573	+ 4,057
Postal-Communications Component (CLC)	17	—	601	3,096	+ 415.1	—	959	+ 959
Postmasters' Assoc., Canadian (Ind.)	8	1	—	8,012	—	—	4,674	+ 4,674
The Professional Institute of the Public Service of Canada (Ind.)	50	9	9,570	15,055	+ 57.3	1,315	3,348	+ 2,033
Public Works Component (CLC)	52	—	2,035	6,042	+ 196.9	223	583	+ 360
Public Service Alliance of Canada (CLC)	16	13	—	(118,913)²	—	—	(31,929)²	—
Research Council Employees' Assoc. (Ind.)	3	4	1,818	1,984	+ 9.1	452	390	− 62
Solicitor General Component (CLC)	72	—	—	6,784	—	—	1,463	+ 1,463
Supply and Services Union (CLC)	22	—	2,796	6,295	+ 125.1	1,438	2,025	+ 587
Taxation Component (CLC)	30	—	5,145	9,665	+ 87.9	2,174	4,267	+ 2,093
Union of Canadian Transport Employees (CLC)	82	—	—	10,810	—	—	933	+ 933
Veterans' Affairs Component, Department of (CLC)	27	—	7,873	7,431	− 5.6	3,016	3,241	+ 225
Previously reporting organizations not reporting in 1972	—	—	39,516	—	—	7,715	—	+ 7,715
TOTAL	2,451	61	179,179	306,646	+ 71.1	42,859	90,882	+ 48,023

1 Organizations of federal and provincial employees whose bargaining rights are established by special legislation.
2 Not included in total.

Source: Statistics Canada

Chapter 3

The Participants In The
Collective Bargaining Process:
The Employer And His Organization

I   INTRODUCTION
The preceding chapter outlined some prominent features of Canadian employee organizations. Now we turn our attention to the other key participant in the collective bargaining process – the employer.

Although the following topics focus on aspects of employer practices which are directly related to collective bargaining, it must be remembered that the activities of employers extend far beyond the collective bargaining process. "Management" is a term that is used to describe anyone who is a representative of the employer and whose principal tasks are oriented to a particular set of functions. These functions are traditionally categorized as planning, organizing, staffing, directing and controlling. Through the collective bargaining process, employee organizations attempt to influence the actions of management in many of these areas. But the interests and aspirations of employees represent only one aspect of the environment with which management must deal. Some of the most significant environmental forces which have a direct and significant influence on employer decisions are shown in Figure 3.1.

II   REASONS WHY EMPLOYERS OPPOSE EMPLOYEE ORGANIZATIONS
When an employee organization is introduced into an enterprise, the employer will frequently resent the intrusion of this "outsider" into his affairs. Such individuals realize that if they recognize an employee organization, their future activities will be affected in a variety of ways.

1.   Inconvenience. Many employers dislike employee organizations simply because they necessitate greater amounts of detail, and promote frustration and uncertainty. The existence of an employee organization often means that where employees are concerned, rigid rules and procedures cannot be easily short-circuited, those that disagree with the employer or his representatives cannot always be dismissed, and attempts to obtain the agreement of employees can involve a long and costly process.

2.   Loss of authority without a concomitant lessening of responsibility. It has already been mentioned that employers and their representatives must make decisions in a complex setting which includes a multitude of groups other than employees. It is the employer whom these groups ultimately hold responsible for the success or failure of the enterprise. Therefore, if the employer feels that an employee organization will upset the existing balance between authority and responsibility in a detrimental way, one can expect a hostile reaction towards employee organizations.

3.   Modifications of employees' attitudes to an employer. Once employees have joined an employee organization, they may adopt a hostile attitude towards the employer and his enterprise. Many employers fear that employee organizations will attempt to fabricate problems to justify their continued existence. In addition, anything the employer grants to his employees is treated as something the employee organization has won for its employees and not as a benevolent act on the part of the employer.

4.   The perceived failure of employee organizations to act in the best interest of their members. Employers who have conscientiously adopted progressive personnel programs are frequently distressed when they discover their employees may be represented by what they perceive to be an "irresponsible" employee organization. A primary concern of employers is that the representatives speaking for a particular employee organization may simultaneously represent employees of competitive companies. Under these circumstances, the survival of a particular enterprise and the jobs of its employees may not be foremost in the minds of the employee representatives.

Figure 3.1

Claimant to the business firm	General nature of the claim
Stockholders	Participate in distribution of profits, additional stock offerings, assets on liquidation; vote of stock, inspection of company books, transfer of stock, election of board of directors, and such additional rights as established in the contract with corporation.
Creditors	Participate in legal proportion of interest payments due and return of principal from the investment. Security of pledged assets; relative priority in event of liquidation. Participate in certain management and owner prerogatives if certain conditions exist within the company (such as default of interest payments).
Employees	Economic, social, and psychological satisfaction in the place of employment. Freedom from arbitrary and capricious behavior on the part of company officials. Share in fringe benefits, freedom to join union and participate in collective bargaining, individual freedom in offering up their services through an employment contract. Adequate working conditions.
Customers	Service provided the product; technical data to use the product; suitable warranties; spare parts to support the product during customer use; R & D leading to product improvement; facilitation of consumer credit.
Supplier	Continuing source of business; timely consummation of trade credit obligations; professional relationship in contracting for, purchasing, and receiving goods and services.
Governments	Taxes (income, property, etc.), fair competition, and adherence to the letter and intent of public policy dealing with the requirements of "fair and free" competition. Legal obligation for businessmen (and business organizations) to obey anti-trust laws.
Union	Recognition as the negotiating agent for the employees. Opportunity to perpetuate the union as a participant in the business organization.
Competitors	Norms established by society and the industry for competitive conduct. Business statesmanship on the part of contemporaries.
Local communities	Place of productive and healthful employment in the local community. Participation of the company officials in community affairs, regular employment, fair play, local purchase of reasonable portion of the products of the local community, interest in and support of local government, support of cultural and charity projects.
The general public	Participation in and contribution to the governmental process of society as a whole; creative communications between governmental and business units designed for reciprocal understanding; bear fair proportion of the burden of government and society. Fair price for products and advancement of the state-of-the-art in the technology which the product line offers.

Source: *Cleland, D.I., and W.R. King. Management: A   Systems Approach,* New York, McGraw-Hill, 1972, p. 104.

5.   Influence on the efficiency of an enterprise. Employee organizations can prevent employers from adopting labour-saving techniques and thereby endanger the survival of an enterprise in either national or international markets. In some cases these labour-saving techniques could take the form of more efficient men taking the place of less efficient men. In other cases, such techniques involve machines taking the place of men.

6.   Misinterpretations and misunderstandings of the other party's attitudes and behavior. A project conducted by Blake, Mouton and Sloma in 1965 delved into the contradictory assumptions and attitudes which prevailed among the ranks of management and a union of a particular company. The lists which appear in Figure 3.2 demonstrate the behavioural foundation for hostility that is prevalent in many union – management relationships

III   THE RELATIONSHIP BETWEEN THE EMPLOYER AND THE EMPLOYEE ORGANIZATION

As we have seen, there are a variety of reasons why employers may choose to resist the establishment and operation of employee organizations. Let us now turn our attention to the more "positive" side of union-management relations. A report prepared for the Task Force on Labour Relations found four factors or conditions to be associated significantly with the existence of a cooperative relationship between management and unions (3.1).

1.   The maturity of the relationships. Unions and management having less than five years dealings with one another also had developed significantly more cooperative relations.

2.   The independence of the local organization from outside control and influence. Organizations which were not subsidiaries, were not members of employer associations, were independent from central office control, were final authorities during negotiations and which sought no outside help regarding industrial relations problems also tended to manifest more cooperative relations than did their opposites.

3.   The expansion of the organization. Those organizations which were expanding rather than contracting or in a static state, tended to have significantly more cooperative relations with their unions.

4.   Organizations whose management held positive attitudes towards the union tended to be cooperative. This was reflected in management's views of the union as being reasonable, non-interfering and a useful channel of communications. In addition, the union-management relationship was generally viewed positively by members of companies who had a cooperative relation with their union.

As a result of these and other factors, a broad range of attitudinal postures between employers and employee organizations is possible. The "classic" categorization of these postures is that provided by the late Professor Selekman. According to Selekman (3.2), there are eight possible categories, some of which may overlap in particular instances:

1.   Ideology. The employee organization is dedicated primarily to some ideology, such as "socialism" or "class equality", which the employer opposes. Ultimately, each party seeks to destroy the other.

2.   Conflict. Such cases can be likened to a "hot" war. The employer seeks to eliminate the employee organization while the employee organization fights for

Figure 3.2

"Self" and "Other" Images Developed by Management and the International Union During Phase 2 of the Union-Management Laboratory

Management's Image

Of Itself	*By the Union*
1. Concerned with running the business effectively	1. .... (an issue not considered)
2. We show equal concern for production and people	2. Management is concerned only with production
3. Autonomous, decentralized decision-making body	3. They follow all of headquarters' policies and dictates
4. Want to learn to work better with international	4. Opposed to all organized labor
5. Prefer to deal with independent unions	5. Prefer to deal with independent unions
6. Strive continually to upgrade supervision	6. ....
7. Goal is to establish problem-solving relationship with the international	7. Their goal is to drive us out of the plant
8. Maintain flexibility in areas concerning our "rights to manage"	8. Management wants power and control over every aspect of a worker's life — they are "fatherly dictators"
9. We are inconsistent in how we treat independents and the international	9. They treat the independents one way and us another
10. Honest and aboveboard in our dealings	10. They are underhanded and they lie

The Union's Image

By Management	*Of Itself*
1. Little concern shown for the profit picture of the company	1. Concerned primarily with people
2. They are skillful and have intense pride	2. Proud of our craft and skills
3. Controlled by a scheming professional leader and a minority clique	3. We are governed by the will of the total membership
4. Legalistic and rigid in interpreting contract	4. Approach problems and contract with open mind
5. The union pushes every grievance to the point of arbitration. When they want to establish a precedent they want to arbitrate	5. Do not want to have to arbitrate every grievance. We want to work them out with management
6. They want to prove they can "win" — they don't care what, just so it is something	6. We want good relations and to solve our problems with management
7. They want to co-manage. They want a say in every decision we make	7. We want a voice in those areas that directly concern us
8. The union wants the training of their people back under their control	8. We want joint control of the training and apprenticeship program
9. The union does not communicate internally. Their people don't know what is going on	9. Our people always know what is going on and what important union business is coming up
10. Union is concerned only with seniority and job security. They are not concerned with our problems.	10. We want greater consideration for our skills and what we can contribute to the plant

Source: Blake, R. R. *et al*, "The Union-Management Intergroup Laboratory: Strategy for Resolving Intergroup Conflict", in *Canadian Labour and Industrial Relations,* Edited by H. C. Jain. McGraw-Hill, 1975, pp. 229-230.

survival and improved security arrangements.

3.   Containment-aggression. The employer seeks to contain the employee organization within limited bounds while the employee organization presses for extending its scope of activities.

4.   Power Bargaining. Here, both the employer and the employee organization accept the existence of the other party. Emphasis is placed on tough bargaining tactics to get all that is possible from the opposing side.

5.   Accommodation. This is characterized by serious bargaining within established boundaries and a willingness to compromise whenever necessary. Familiar routines are followed and both parties maintain a "live and let-live" policy.

6.   Cooperation. Both the employer and the employee organization accept problems of the other party as being problems of their own. Even though the parties will have their differences on traditional collective bargaining issues, each carefully regards the other as a responsible party.

7.   Deal bargaining. This refers to secret "deals" between employers and representatives of the employee organization. Each side gives up something, but employees not a party to the negotiations are never told the true extent of or reasons for the compromise. In some cases, the end result may be detrimental to the membership.

8.   Collusion. This implies that employers and employee representatives make illegal agreements that adversely affect the interests of other employers, other employees and the consuming public.

Over a period of time, the two parties may move back and forth between Selekman's postures as the factors influencing the degree of resistance among the parties are modified. When the employer decides the employee organization is no longer a serious threat to his enterprise, there will be less reason to seek to destroy the other party. An unfavourable shift in economic conditions which endangers the survival of the enterprise could encourage both parties to seek cooperative solutions to this mutual problem. A drastic shakeup in the leadership of the employee organization may lead to a breakdown in familiar routines developed in the past and set the stage for a "hot war" atmosphere. On the other hand, as an employer gains more experience in dealing with a particular employee organization, more accomodation between the parties may become possible.

IV   EMPLOYER ORGANIZATIONS

Some employers have found that it makes sense to form their own associations to deal with powerful employee organizations. At present in Canada, employer association bargaining is an established practice in certain provinces and appears to be growing more prevalent each year. For example, recent amendments to the Canada Labour Code now empower the Canada Labour Relations Board to force certain enterprises into employer associations in some circumstances.

The reasons why employers have formed associations for the purposes of collective bargaining all have one common denominator: the desire to avoid or eliminate power deficiencies by presenting a united position against employee organizations.

More specifically, employers increasingly prefer to introduce employer organizations into the collective bargaining process for the following reasons:

1.   To reduce competition among companies based on wage differences. When powerful employee organizations bargain with many small competitive companies, unequal wage levels and fringe benefits can result providing some companies with a competitive advantage over others. When an employer association becomes involved, uniform standards can be negotiated. This effectively eliminates labour costs as a competitive item.

2.   To discourage "whipsawing" practices. A common strategy used by employee organizations is to settle first with the employer that has the weakest bargaining position and then extend these terms to other employers. The existence of an employer organization makes it difficult to implement such a strategy.

3.   Ruinous industrial disputes are less likely. Where a single employer is involved, the public may be unaware of or unconcerned about a particular dispute. One by one, these disputes do irreparable harm to the firms and ultimately to the industry. Where a dispute involves a group of employers simultaneously, the potential adverse effects become much easier to recognize.

4.   Convenience. Chaos could prevail if each small employer had to negotiate agreements with the different types of employees required at the various stages of a construction project. An employer association can negotiate master agreements with the employee organizations representing each group of workers, providing employers with the security of an established agreement whenever they need a particular type of employee.

5.   Specialized negotiators. An employer organization can often employ full-time negotiators of a much higher calibre than could any individual firm.
    To achieve these benefits, the more than 300 official employers' associations in Canada carry out their activities in a variety of ways (3.3):
1. *The lobbying association.* The activities of such organizations as the Canadian Manufacturers' Association and the Chamber of Commerce are concerned with lobbying and speaking on behalf of employers in the general field of labour relations.
2. *The educational association.* Le Centre des dirigeants d'enterprise in Quebec is a typical example of an educational association. This type of organization concentrates on the education of members in all facets of industrial relations. Other organizations that concentrate primarily on training and informing their members include the Canadian Construction Association and the Canadian Pulp and Paper Association.
3. *The consultative association.* In this type of organization, individual employers still bargain for themselves. Prior to any negotiations, they consult with each other in an attempt to develop a strategy for dealing with a particular employee organization. Information sharing, constant communication and coordination are key objectives of such associations as the Railway Association of Canada.
4. *The negotiatory association.* This type of organization concentrates its efforts on negotiating a master contract for its members. However, acceptance of the master contract is not always mandatory and members may be allowed to include modifications that suit their particular circumstances. Such organizations are most common in the printing, clothing, construction and trucking industries where there are large numbers of relatively small firms confronted by a common union or group of unions. According to Labour Canada, about twenty percent of employers with more than 500 employees negotiated in groups or associations between 1953 and 1968. These negotiatory associations were responsible for negotiating with about thirty percent of the unionized workers employed by companies with more than 500 employees.

5. The administrative association. Certain employer organizations may assume
the responsibility for a variety of activities other than contract negotiations.
Questions of interpretation, grievance processing and grievance arbitration are
examples of the administrative details which some organizations look after.
6. The mutual aid association. Some employers have also developed mutual aid
pacts whereby the members agree to share losses arising out of strikes that
interrupt their operation.

No matter which of these approaches a particular employer organization
decides to use, certain problems are difficult to avoid. Three prevalent
difficulties include the following:

1. Employers are reluctant to give up their rights to make individual decisions.
As a result most employer organizations permit individual members to "opt out"
of certain agreements and few conditions of membership are binding in any legal
sense.
*2. Individual members may attempt to obtain some degree of control over their
weaker competitors.* Where significant inequities in power exist among members,
the general procedure to eliminate this problem involves hiring a "neutral"
professional expert to conduct the business of the employer organization.
*3. It is difficult to guarantee adherence to the "constitution" of the employer
organization.* Most employer associations adopt a "code of ethics" for
members and provide punitive measures such as fines and expulsion for
breaches of these ethics. For the most part, however, the voluntary nature
of the organization makes such measures extremely ineffective.

The widespread opinions expressed about employer associations have been
somewhat mixed in recent years. There are those who fear that employer
organizations formed for collective bargaining purposes may be used for
regulating other aspects of the members' operations. Others argue that employer
associations lead to greater stability in labour relations and should be extended
to the point where a few employer associations bargain with a few associations
of unions (3.4).
    On balance, it would appear that public opinion at present tends to favor
the latter group and more legislation which is supportive of employer
associations can be expected in the future. Such legislation, referred to as
"accreditation" legislation, gives an employers' organization exclusive bargaining
rights for a unit of employers. At present, the most sophisticated examples of
accreditation legislation pertain to the construction industry (3.5).
    In the construction industry there are two alternative ways accreditation
legislation can be granted. These include:
1. A Trade Basis. Trade accreditation (which applies in Alberta, Ontario, and
New Brunswick) specifies that accreditation decisions of the labour relations
board depend on existing bargaining rights between an employee organization
and an employers' organization.
2. A Sector Basis. The term "sector" refers to a division of the construction
industry such as the commercial sector, the residential sector or the institutional
sector. Where sector accreditation applies (in Nova Scotia and Prince Edward
Island for instance), an employers' organization can apply for accreditation in
any sector and geographic area for which it claims support, regardless of existing
bargaining rights.
    Accreditation legislation may include any one of a number of definitions
of "majority" support. Some of the alternative definitions available are:
1 A simple majority test.

2. *A double majority test.* This refers to the support of a majority of the unionized employers in the unit who, in turn, employ a majority of the employees in the designated unit.
3. *A "compromise" test.* An employers' organization must either have the e support of the majority of the unionized employers in the unit *or* the employers' organization must represent not less than, say, 35 percent of the employers who employ a majority of the employees in the designated geographic area and sector.

Most accreditation legislation is analogous to that which governs union certification (discussed in Chapter 10) with respect to the existence of a properly constituted organization and the non-existence of union interference in the formation of the employers' organization.

Summary:

1.   It should be kept in mind that employee organizations are not the only groups, nor always the most important groups with which employers must be concerned.
2.   Some of the main reasons why employers may resent employee organizations include inconvenience, the fear of lost authority, the tendency of such organizations to modify employee attitudes, the suspicion that employee organizations will not act in the best interests of their members, and the adverse effects such organizations may have on the efficiency of an enterprise.
3.   The degree of resistance which individual employers offer against employee organizations depends upon such things as ideology, economic conditions, the leadership of the employee organization, and the bargaining experience of the employer. All of these factors could influence which of Professor Selekman's eight attitudinal postures would prevail in a particular relationship. Selekman's categories include containment, aggression, ideology, conflict, power bargaining, deal bargaining, collusion, accommodation and cooperation.
4.   The composition, problems and future prospects for employer organizations are becoming increasingly important aspects of the bargaining relationship.

References

3.1   Mikalachki, A., G. Forsyth, and J. Wettlaufer. "Management's Views of Union-Management Relations at the Local Level". A Study for the Task Force On Labour Relations. Ottawa, Queen's Printer, 1970, pp. 33-34.
3.2   Selekman, B. "Varieties of Labour Relations". *Harvard Business Review*, Vol. 27, March 1949, pp. 177-85.
3.3   Canadian Industrial Relations. *The Report of the Task Force On Labour Relations.* Ottawa, Queen's Printer, 1968, pp. 30-31.
3.4   Craig, A.W. and H.J. Waisglass. "Collective Bargaining Perspectives". *Relations Industrielles*, Vol. 23, No. 4, 1968, p. 582.
3.5   Arthurs, H.W. and John Crispo. "Countervailing Employer Power: Accreditation of Contractor Association", in *Construction Labour Relations*, edited by H.C. Goldenberg and John Crispo. Ottawa, Canadian Construction Association, 1968.

Suggested Readings for Further Study

Bakke, E.W. *Unions, Management and the Public.* New York, Harcourt, Brace & World, 1967, pp. 187-239.

Belanger, L. "Management Attitudes Toward Management Associations, Unions, and Strikes". A Study for the Task Force On Labour Relations, Ottawa, 1968.

Blake, David H. "Multinational Corporation, International Union and International Collective Bargaining", in *Transnational Industrial Relations,* edited by Hans Gunter. International Institute for Labour Studies, 1972.

Crysler, A.C. *Handbook of Employer-Employee Relations in Canada.* Don Mills, Ontario, CCH Canadian Limited, 1969.

Malles, P. *Industrial Relations In The Construction Industry.* Ottawa, Economic Council of Canada, 1976.

McFarland, D.E. "The Labour Relations Consultant as Contract Negotiator". *Personnel,* Vol. XXXIV, May-June 1958, pp. 44-51.

Mikalachki, A. *et.al.* "Managment's Views of Union-Mangement Relations at the Local Level". A Study for the Task Force On Labour Relations, Ottawa, Queen's Printer, 1970.

Simmons, C. Gordon. "Coordinated Bargaining by Unions and Employers". A Study for the Task Force on Labour Relations. Ottawa, 1970.

Wood, W. Donald. *The Current Status of Labour Management Cooperation In Canada.* National Conference on Labour Management Relations, Ottawa, 1964.

Experiential Assignment

Survey at least five managerial personnel in your community to determine the relative importance of "the reasons why employers oppose employee organizations" that were discussed in this Chapter.

Chapter 4

Participants In The Collective Bargaining Process: External Institutions And Procedures

I   INTRODUCTION

Up to this point, we have examined the evolution of the legal foundation for collective bargaining, the employee and his organization, and the employer and his organization. In this chapter we will be looking at certain institutions and procedures which influence these three elements.

II   THE CONSTITUTIONAL JURISDICTION OVER LABOUR RELATIONS IN CANADA

The federal and provincial governments derive their authority from the British North America Act. Under this Act, legislative authority with regard to certain classes of subjects is assigned exclusively to the federal jurisdiction, while various other subjects are exclusively within the legislative jurisdiction of the provinces. However, the failure of the B.N.A. Act to designate either level of government as having authority over labour relations causes confusion in this area.

1.   Federal Jurisdiction In Labour Relations.

Over the years, court decisions have established a general rule that a labour relations law was valid if it was *primarily* connected with an enumerated power of the federal or provincial level of government that passed it (even though such a law might be connected in a "minor" way with a subject assigned to the other level of government). Consequently, the federal government has claim to jurisdiction in a number of significant areas:

1.   Employees engaged in work that falls within the federal jurisdiction. Where the federal government has specific power over a particular agency (the Post Office, for example), the Courts have ruled that the federal government also has the authority for labour relations matters pertaining to the employees of that agency.

2.   Employees engaged in work that does not fall within the legislative jurisdiction of any province.

3.   Employees engaged in work that connects provinces or extends beyond the limits of a province. i.e., connects Canada to another country.

4.   Employees engaged in work that the federal government declares to be for the "general advantage of Canada". To date the federal government has declared such diverse undertakings as railways, canals, grain elevators and Ontario's Chalk River atomic energy plant to be for the general advantage of Canada.

5.   All Canadian employees in the event of a "national emergency". This power is derived from the federal right to enact laws necessary for "peace, order, and good government".

2.   Provincial Jurisdiction In Labour Relations.

The constitutional jurisdiction over labour relations in Canada has been assigned for the most part to provincial governments. It has been estimated that over ninety percent of the Canadian labour force comes under provincial jurisdiction.

The provinces' claim to jurisdiction in labour relations matters is based primarily on their powers under the B.N.A. Act to make laws in relation to "property and civil rights". According to the Canada Year Book:

> "Because it imposes conditions on the rights of the employer and employee to enter into a contract of employment, labour legislation is, generally speaking, law in relation to civil rights and provincial legislatures are authorized to make laws in relation to both local works and to property and civil rights. Power to enact labour legislation has become, therefore, largely a provincial prerogative, under which a large body of legislation has been enacted affecting the employment relationship in such fields as working hours, minimum wages, the physical conditions of

workplaces, apprenticeship and training, wage payment and wage collection, labour-management relations and workmen's compensation." (4.1)

Provinces also derive a certain amount of jurisdiction from their right under the B.N.A. Act to make laws which pertain to "generally all matters of a merely local or private nature in the province".

In spite of the fact that the Canadian policy framework influencing employee-employer relations is really a compendium of eleven independent jursidictions (all of which have experimented freely), it is possible to distinguish some common threads in all Canadian jurisdictions:

1. All jurisdictions have substituted administrative tribunals for courts of law to determine who has the right to associate for collective bargaining and what agencies should be permitted to represent those who are organized.
2. All jurisdictions have some guidelines for delaying or preventing work stoppages.
3. All jurisdictions require that certain clauses appear in all collective agreements and that no clauses violate existing Canadian laws.
4. All jurisdictions describe and prohibit certain "unfair practices" by the parties involved in collective bargaining. (4.2)

III   LABOUR RELATIONS BOARDS   *see Labour Code*

As previously noted, all eleven Canadian jurisdictions make use of administrative tribunals in dealing with employee-employer relationships. These tribunals or agencies are commonly referred to as labour relations boards. Their composition is normally determined by the government in office and is subject to change at the government's will. The purpose of these agencies is to provide a superior institutional alternative to traditional courts of law for matters pertaining to employee-employer relations. However, each jurisdiction differs in the specific functions assigned to its labour relations board. In some provinces, British Columbia and Alberta for example, the board may be involved substantially in social policy matters which range far beyond traditional collective bargaining issues. In other provinces, such as Ontario, the board's primary function is to resolve narrow collective bargaining issues concerning representation rights and unfair labour practices. Specific examples of issues considered by the Ontario Labour Relations Board include (4.3):

1.   applications for certification;
2.   applications for termination of bargaining rights;
3.   applications for successor rights declarations;
4.   applications for early termination of collective agreements;
5.   applications for exemption from union security provisions;
6.   applications for access rights;
7.   applications for accreditation;
8.   applications for declarations respecting unlawful strikes;
9.   applications for consent to prosecute;
10.   applications respecting status as employee or guard;
11.   applications to supply provisions relating to recognition and to modify provisions relating to arbitration;
12.   applications for reconsideration;
13.   applications to extend trusteeship;
14.   complaints respecting financial statements;
15.   complaints respecting unfair labour practices;
16.   complaints respecting jurisdictional disputes;
17.   references relating to the authority of the Minister of Labour to

appoint a conciliation officer or arbitrator.

Labour relations boards must carry out a variety of interdependent administrative, procedural and judicial functions to fulfil their responsibilities. Administrative functions are usually handled by a support staff of examiners, field officers and clerical personnel.

Procedural matters primarily involve providing answers to such questions as:

- the right of an individual to a hearing
- the kind of evidence which a board may receive (frequently evidence that would not be admissable in a court of law)
- the powers to enter and inspect both premises and records
- the conducting of votes on matters upon which boards wish to ascertain the views of the employees
- the confidentiality of information obtained by boards and their staff
- the obligation of boards to keep records of proceedings.

The legislation which creates labour relations boards often gives such boards wide powers of discretion in carrying out their judicial responsibilities. In contrast to traditional courts of law, labour relations boards substitute relevant expertise for rigid precedents, compromise for the adversary system, and "flexible solutions" for predetermined remedies. Thus, the proponents of the "tribunal" concept claim that in matters involving employee-employer relationships such boards theoretically have more potential than traditional courts of law for operating in an optimal manner.

In order not to erode any of these positive characteristics, provisions exist to keep the matters under the jurisdictions of the boards out of the courts. As a rule, the courts will only become substantially involved in assertions which pertain to boards operating outside their statutory jurisdiction, boards failing to exercise their powers when a party has submitted a legitimate claim, and boards acting in a manner which is procedurally or judicially unfair. Even in cases where the decision of the board is not complied with, resort to the courts is usually unnecessary. Generally, boards are empowered to investigate, report and issue orders to ensure that their rulings are complied with.

IV   CONCILIATION, MEDIATION AND FACT-FINDING
It has already been mentioned that all eleven jurisdictions have some guidelines for delaying or preventing work stoppages which result from a breakdown in the collective bargaining process. Three common methods employed to delay work stoppages include conciliation, mediation and fact-finding.

1.   Conciliation vs. Mediation
In the United States conciliation is traditionally defined as an "attempt by a third party to help in the settlement of disputes between employers and employees through interpretation, suggestion, and advice". In practice the term conciliation is synonymous with mediation. The ultimate goal of conciliation or mediation, then, is to help disputants to arrive at their own agreement and the conciliator or mediator is in no way vested with the power to force a settlement.

In Canada, however, the labour laws of many jurisdictions specify both a technical and legalistic distinction between the terms. From a technical standpoint, "conciliation" is used to imply a passive role of merely bringing the disputing parties together and keeping them talking. "Mediation" connotes a more affirmative role. The mediator may be expected to contribute suggestions and recommendations which could lead to possible areas for agreement.

On the legalistic side, nearly all jurisdictions require that if the negotiating parties reach an impasse, they must go through conciliation before they can legally engage in a work stoppage.

A conciliation officer is normally appointed by the Minister of Labour and charged with three functions. These include:

i) conferring with the parties to assist them to conclude a collective agreement;

ii) making recommendations respecting matters upon which the parties cannot agree;

iii) making a recommendation as to the advisability of appointing a conciliation board.

Once the conciliation officer (and, if necessary, the conciliation board) reports to the Minister of Labour, the Minister will send a letter to the parties acknowledging receipt of the report. After a specified number of days (referred to as a "cooling off" period), a work stoppage becomes legal.

The Minister of Labour may also offer the services of a mediator at any time during the negotiations. The mediator does not make a formal report to the Minister and has nothing to do with determining the legality of a work stoppage.

2. Fact-Finding

Fact-finding involves the submission of a dispute to a group of neutrals who are requested to conduct hearings, collect and analyze all relevant statistics and contentions, and issue a report. In some cases the group may be requested to issue a report that lets the facts "speak for themselves." In other instances the group may be requested to specify recommendations for a settlement that the parties might adopt. However, no fact-finding board has the inherent right to make recommendations for the settlement of a dispute.

Fact-finding can be either voluntary or compulsory. Voluntary fact-finding occurs when the procedure is requested by the parties to the dispute. A common form of voluntary fact-finding involves an agreement by the parties at the time of negotiations to refer certain issues to a committee for further study during the forthcoming contract term. Such a device, if used judiciously, has the potential to permit a thorough and objective study of the problem and its long term ramifications. Compulsory fact-finding, as the name implies, is forced upon the disputing parties by some external agency.

The terms "conciliation", "mediation" and "fact-finding" can reflect somewhat different shades of meaning, but all imply intervention in the collective bargaining process by an impartial individual or panel which lacks both the authority and responsibility for deciding one or more of the unresolved issues: the disputing parties always have the right to say "no" to any proposals that result from such processes.

V ARBITRATION

The most common substitute for the use of sanctions in the collective bargaining process is arbitration. The fundamental difference between the tactics previously described and arbitration is the responsibility and authority which the arbitrator has to determine the outcome of a dispute. Once an arbitrator has given his decision, it becomes binding on the parties involved. The arbitrator cannot, even for obvious errors, make a second award or amend his original award and, in Canada, even the courts cannot interfere with an arbitrator's award unless there is an error in law, the arbitrator has exceeded his authority, or there is a breach of natural justice, proven corruption, or fraud. A more detailed description of the arbitration process appears in Chapters 8 and 11.

VI   GOVERNMENT GUIDELINES

In October, 1975 the Federal Government enacted the Anti-Inflation Act which was designed to restrain profits, prices, dividends and compensation in designated sections of the economy. The provisions of such a statute which relate to compensation can be of strategic importance to those involved in the collective bargaining process.

1.   Definitions

In order to understand the guidelines on compensation, there are four basic terms that must be understood:

1.   The Base Date. This refers to the last day of the last compensation plan being replaced. It is assessed individually for each group of employees, and different groups of employees of one employer may have different Base Dates.

2.   The Programme Year. The Anti-Inflation Act was originally set up to run for a period of three years from October 14, 1975 to October 13, 1978. The periods from October 14 to the following October 13 are described as the first, second, or third Programme Years.

3.   The Guideline Year. This refers to the one year period immediately following the Base Date or an anniversary of the Base Date. Each group subject to the programme has its own Guideline Years and will have as many Guideline Years as are needed for the last one to extend beyond the end of the programme. If a group's first Guideline Years starts in the first Programme Year, it will be subject to the programme for three Guideline Years; if its first Guideline Year is retroactive to a date prior to the first Programme Year, it will have four Guideline Years.

4.   Compensation. If all forms of compensation were not subject to the guidelines there could be a process of substitution of improved benefits and incentives for increases in salaries and wages. The guidelines would then be neither effective nor equitable.

The methods set out in the Federal Anti-Inflation Regulations attempt to measure changes in pay and benefits of groups of employees. They also take into account the kinds of payments which are called direct incentives – such as piece work and sales commissions. If employees receive part of their compensation in the form of shares of profits, bonuses, or options to buy stock in a firm, changes in these indirect incentives are also measured and included in the total compensation of each group of employees.

The complex details of how all the components of total compensation are calculated and brought together are beyond the scope of this book. However, the reader should be aware of a number of expenditures which are "excluded" from the compensation subject to the guidelines. For example: expenditures in the form of special payments to maintain pension plans, changes in pay or benefit plans to eliminate sex discrimination, to improve the health or safety of employees in the working environment, to offset the effects of technological changes and to offset measures to eliminate restrictive work practices.

These concepts provide the framework for the compensation guidelines.

2.   Arithmetic Guidelines

A maximum allowable rate of increase in compensation from the Base Date to the last day of the Guideline Year is calculated for each group of employees. This limit is determined by four factors:

1.   The Basic Protection Factor. The first of these, the "Basic Protection

Factor", is meant to protect employees against the anticipated rise in the cost of living. Increases of 8%, 6% and 4% in the Consumer Price Index are anticipated for the three Programme Years. This factor is the same for all groups.

If the rate of increase in the Consumer Price Index should prove to be higher than the Basic Protection Factor in any Programme Year, the Basic Protection Factor will be increased for the following Programme Year by the excess percentage rise in the Consumer Price Index. There is no reduction in wages if the cost-of-living increase is less than the Basic Protection Factor in any Programme Year.

2. The National Productivity Factor. In addition to the Basic Protection Factor, each group of workers is entitled to an additional 2% for each Guideline Year to account for increases in national productivity.

3. The Experience Adjustment Factor. The third factor, the "Experience Adjustment Factor", is calculated separately for each group of employees. Its purpose is to ensure that those groups of employees whose compensation has fallen behind the general level may receive higher increases in order to "catch up", while those groups whose increases have forged ahead of the general level will be subject to a tighter restraint. No group is constrained by more than 2% in any Guideline Year to ensure that the maximum permissible increase is at least equal to the anticipated increase in the Consumer Price Index.

4. Lower and Upper Limits. At the extremes of compensation, the three arithmetic factors just described can be overridden so that some employees will be able to get greater increases while others may get less. At the low end of the spectrum, there is the provision that an individual may receive an increase of up to $600 (or 3.50 per hour) in Guideline Year without being subject to the Guidelines. On the high side of the spectrum, a group's average compensation increase may not exceed $2400 per year.

Adding up these first three "arithmetic" factors gives the maximum permissible limits for compensation increases of from 8% to 12% in the first Programme Year, 6% to 10% in the second Programme Year, and 4% to 8% in the third Programme Year. These permissible limits may then be modified by the lower and upper limits previously described.

It should be noted that these are limits, not guaranteed rates of increase for any group of employees. How much a group actually will receive is determined in collective bargaining or unilaterally by the employer. The market forces which affect pay determination can and do result in increases at rates lower than the guidelines permit.

3. Discretionary Elements

There are "particular circumstances" under which increases in excess of the arithmetic guidelines can be approved by the Anti-Inflation Board.

The most frequently used pertain to "historical relationships". This concept is defined quite precisely in the guidelines as being a situation in which:

a) there is a demonstrable relationship between the groups being compared in "the level, timing and rates of increase in compensation" obtained in the last two years; and in which

b) the groups have a common employer, or are in the same industry or the same labour market and in which the jobs relate to the same product, process or service.

The Anti-Inflation Board may also approve an increase in excess of the arithmetic guidelines if a group has been working under a previous agreement which was entered into prior to January 1, 1974, which has not been revised sufficiently during the subsequent period in response to the accelerating increases in the cost-of-living, and during which the "slippage" in compensation has been so great that it cannot be recovered during the programme by the application of the Experience Adjustment Factor for the group involved.

In these situations a group may be given "Special Consideration", and the Anti-Inflation Board may authorize a maximum permissible increase greater than the arithmetic guidelines by an amount which is consistent with the objectives of the programme. This gives the Anti-Inflation Board discretion (in that there are no amounts specified in the Regulations), because the increases obtained by the "target groups" before October 14 varied so much in amount that it is impossible to quantify once and for all the necessary variation needed to prevent the opening of an "unreasonable" gap.

4.   Institutions For Enforcing The Guidelines
The Anti-Inflation Act specifies a number of agencies to promote compliance with its provisions.

a) The Anti-Inflation Board (AIB)
The Anti-Inflation Board is charged with monitoring the operation and effectiveness of the guidelines and recommending modifications of them. The Board is also empowered to (a) identify changes which contravene or would, if implemented, contravene the guidelines either in fact or in spirit; (b) identify changes that would have a significant impact on the economy and endeavour through consultations and negotiations to modify these changes to accord with the spirit and limits of the guidelines; (c) refer the matter to the Administrator (see below) where the above consultation and negotiation have failed; (d) promote public understanding of the government's policies; and (e) conduct an inquiry upon the direction of the Cabinet and to advise the Cabinet whether to make certain private sector employers and their employees subject to the guidelines.

b) The Administrator
The Administrator is an appointed official. He is responsible for hearing appeals from parties who are dissatisfied with the decision of the Anti-Inflation Board and for investigating alleged violations of the guidelines upon receiving advice from the Cabinet or Anti-Inflation Board that there are reasonable grounds for believing that a contravention of the guidelines is imminent, occurring, or has occurred.

The Administrator is also responsible for issuing binding orders that will stand up to legal appeals to the Anti-Inflation Tribunal and/or the courts. This fact, together with the broader powers possessed by the Administrator to seize documents and subpoena information, can cause the Administrator to modify opinions of the Anti-Inflation Board. The Act provides that those who contravene its provisions can be fined from $200. to $10,000. and/or face imprisonment for a term of from two to five years. A person who fails to comply with an order of the Administrator is subject to a fine of up to $5,000 and/or imprisonment for a term of one year. The Administrator can make any order he deems appropriate to prohibit contravention of the guidelines and can also order persons violating them to pay the excess revenues and compensation thus acquired to the government. The Administrator can require any trade union to submit relevant information or produce relevant books, statements, documents and records. The Administrator may also impose a penalty of 25% of the excess compensation accepted by persons violating the guidelines and can request the Attorney-General to apply to a superior court for an injunction to prevent the contravention of an order.

c) The Anti-Inflation Appeal Tribunal

Any person against whom an order has been made by the Administrator may take his case to an Appeal Tribunal within 60 days provided there has been compliance with the order. The Appeal Tribunal, which is not bound by the strict rules of evidence, can then dispose of the appeal by

a) dismissing it; or

b) allowing it an

    i)   vacating the order appealed against,

    ii)   varying the order appealed against, or

    iii)   referring the matter back to the Administrator for reconsideration and variation of the order.

d) The Federal Court of Appeal

Any decision of the Tribunal is subject to review by the Federal Court of Appeal when the Tribunal has:

    a)   failed to observe a principle of natural justice or otherwise acted beyond or refused to exercise its discretion;

    b) erred in law in making its decision or order;

    c) based its decision on erroneous findings of fact that it made in a perverse or capricious manner, or without regard for the material before it.

e) The Federal Cabinet

The Act allows the Federal Cabinet to review the decisions of the Administrator and to rescind or vary any order of the Administrator. Thus, the Cabinet has the ultimate authority in any ruling made under the Anti-Inflation Act.

5.   Impact on Collective Bargaining

The Anti-Inflation Act of 1975 was supposedly designed to rationalize inflationary expectations without disrupting the existing collective bargaining system. In an attempt to achieve these objectives, the Anti-Inflation Board employed three basic tactics.

a) Recognition of historical relationships

The AIB has feared that rigid enforcement of the maximum allowable wage limits could cause the negotiating parties to misinterpret these limits as "reasonable settlements". Therefore, the AIB has chosen to be flexible on the question and make allowances for special circumstances in various occupations and regions.

b) Refusing to rule on settlements until the two parties have reached agreement

This is supposed to encourage the parties to use the arithmetic limits as guides while conducting "negotiations as usual".

c) Using an all-inclusive definition of compensation

Those who designed the guidelines attempted to avoid loopholes which substituted redistribution (among categories of wages, benefits and incentives) for restraint. Thus the guidelines were expressed in terms of total compensation.

Many critics of the Anti-Inflation Act feel that the guidelines can disrupt normal collective bargaining results. It has been suggested that unions will be more likely to:

1. propose a one-year agreement with heavy emphasis on wage increases at the expense of fringe benefits improvements;

2. propose that increases clearly above the maximum permissible percentage

increase be "taken to the Board" on the fuzzy basis that the Board might rule such increases to be appropriate;

3. seek new ways to justify their existence, such as emphasis on work rules, working conditions and the processing of grievances.

It has also been suggested that management may be:

1. caught between the legal requirements of the AIB, the desire to avoid a strike and the need to attract and retain qualified manpower during the restraint period;

2. tempted to hide behind the guidelines and make such guidelines the villains in any bargaining situation.

As a result, the guidelines may provide incompetent negotiators on both sides of the bargaining table with an excuse for suboptimal performance.

VII   LABOUR COURTS

The concept of a labour court is by no means something new to Canada. In 1943, the province of Ontario set up the Ontario Labour Court as a division of the High Court of Justice to enforce its newly adopted collective bargaining statutes. However, the Labour Court proved to be a short-lived institution, being pre-empted by the Federal Government's War Measures Act of 1944. The Labour Court was later replaced by the establishment of the Ontario Labour Relations Board, following the repeal of the federal regulation in 1948.

A labour court would have exclusive jurisdiction over all disputes pertaining to collective bargaining issues. Over the years, a body of labour law would become established and provide a rational basis for the formulation of statute law.

There are individuals in Canada who advocate the establishment of such an institution. However, each proposal contains certain refinements and variations of the Ontario Labour Court with respect to:

a) the issues within its jurisdiction;

b) the degree of compulsion that would be generated upon the parties to make use of the institution;

c) the remedies available for non-compliance with a labour court judgement.

It has been argued that establishing a system of labour courts could destroy Canada's collective bargaining system. The claim is made that replacing strikes with labour courts could dissuade one or both of the negotiating parties from bona fide bargaining. One refinement of the "labour court concept" that has been suggested to encourage serious bargaining includes the following procedures (4.4):

1. Compulsory arbitration should replace the strike.

2. Specialist "courts of arbitration" should be established to encourage "uniform" decisions.

3. These courts of arbitration would be financed through an assessment of only those union and management negotiating teams that find it necessary to use these courts.

4. The assessment would be related to the amount of difference between either the union's or management's final negotiating position and the arbitrator's ruling. For example, suppose an impasse was reached when the union's position was $8.00 per hour and management's position was $ 7.00 per hour. If the arbitration court ruled that a "reasonable settlement" was $7.80 per hour, the union would be assessed 20 ¢ per hour and the company 80 ¢ per hour for a definite period of time.

This idea of a "non-stoppage strike" (where employees remain on the job, but some wages and profits are lost by the disputing parties), is by no means new, but its use in conjunction with a "labour court" is extremely creative.

It is interesting to note that a substantial number of "labour court attributes" were built into the objectives and functions of the Anti-Inflation Board which was established in October, 1975.

VIII THE FUTURE FOR FREE COLLECTIVE BARGAINING IN CANADA

The Canadian system of labour relations has thus far been modified by gradual evolution, rather than by any dramatic revolution. But the possiblity that some viable alternative system will ultimately supplant the present one can never be overlooked.

Dunlop has noted that there are three basic tasks that must be performed in every economy, either by the collective bargaining process or by some acceptable alternative (4.5):

1. Rule-making at the workplace.

2. Determining the compensation of employees and the distribution of the economic pie.

3. Settling disputes during the life of an agreement and on the expiration of the agreement.

Canadian society has at least three broad alternatives available for accomplishing these tasks.

1. Do Nothing

One of the easiest options available is to leave things as they are. Let the two adversary organizations continue to attempt to reach a voluntary agreement on their own; require them to make use of conciliation services before using sanctions of any kind; accept the consequences of these sanctions until they become intolerable; and pass emergency legislation when such sanctions result in unacceptable public hardship. The latter part of this process, emergency legislation, presents a number of problems (4.6):

a) There is some unfairness in having the government change the rules in the middle of the dispute.

b) The weaker party often finds it attractive to bring in the government rather than capitulate.

c) Both parties may enjoy having the government take the responsibility for unpopular decisions.

2. Prohibit the use of Sanctions

A second option that is often advocated involves the prohibition of strikes and lockouts. The advocates of such a proposal rarely provide any detailed analysis of how this would work. Some suggest that bargaining should continue as before. However, with the employees being deprived of their ultimate source of power it is difficult to envision "bargaining in good faith" on the part of the employer. In many cases he has nothing to lose by extending the negotiations for an indefinite period of time.

Others propose that a settlement could be arrived at by binding arbitration if the parties cannot reach an agreement by an established deadline. This presumes the existence of a school of skilled arbitrators who will make wiser decisions than the two adversaries. Recent examples of questionable arbitration awards, one of which granted a salary below existing provincial minimum wages, raise serious doubts about the benefits to be derived by replacing sanctions with compulsory arbitration.

It has also been proposed that strikes could be eliminated by allowing one of the parties of interest to make a binding unilateral decision. Those with a fascist philosophy favour the employer, those with a democratic socialist philosophy prefer the employee, and those with a communistic outlook favour the government. Then there are others who favour some form of public referendum whereby major disputes would be submitted to a public ballot.

Obviously, unilateral action in any of these forms results in some group being required to accept terms that they consider inadequate or unfair. Sooner or later discontent will build up to a point where rebellion and violence become inevitable. Consequently, the end result could be a choice between establishing a police state or re-establishing many elements of our existing collective bargaining system.

Finally, there are advocates of a technocratic type of system whereby compensation is determined by some pattern or mathematical formula. A current example of such a system involves an agreement covering 11½ years and prohibiting strikes and lockouts which has been signed between Manitoba Hydro and the Allied Hydro Council of Manitoba (which represents workers at two big construction projects that are part of the hydroelectric development on the Nelson River). This agreement provides for settlement of grievances and jurisdictional disputes by arbitration, while wages and benefits are escalated with reference to agreements that are negotiated in the Winnipeg area.

In the United States, the Minneapolis Star and Tribune and the International Typographical Union recently signed a 10-year collective agreement. It guarantees lifetime jobs to the dailies' present 389 printers, but gives management the absolute right to automate the composing room and to assign work as it sees fit.

The contract provides that manpower cuts may be made only through attrition, and it ties wage increases to those won by other blue collar unions at the newspaper.

Since 1934, Quebec has had a "Collective Agreement Decrees Act". This Act provides for the extension of the provisions of a collective agreement to all employees (union and non-union) and employers in a particular regional industry at the request of one of the parties to the original agreement. A number of highly competitive industries such as hairdressing, service stations and printing have made use of the provisions of this Act.

This "technocratic" approach is not without its problems. Those individuals who belong to the group required to negotiate the "reference agreement" do not normally display a very positive orientation towards outsiders "riding on their coattails". Also, outside interference in "reference" negotiations can seriously distort wages and working conditions in a particular plant or industry.

3. Move Away From An Adversary System.

A third option is to modify our entire industrial relations system in such a way that cooperation replaces confrontation. Strikes and lockouts are avoided by making them unnecessary, rather than illegal. The systems of cooperation or "industrial democracy" which have been advocated involve different degrees of worker participation in management. At one end of the spectrum there is joint consultation which implies an obligation on the part of management to consult with its workers or their representatives before making decisions in a broad range of areas (many of which are normally regarded as management prerogatives). At the other end of the spectrum is worker control which involves the transformation of an enterprise from a privately-owned to a communal type of operation. In the middle of the spectrum is co-management or co-determination, which requires co-decision-making over a broad range of activities.

These proposals have been met with a certain amount of skepticism in Canada. It has been argued that such systems require the existence of a cooperative attitude which is not found presently in Canada. Such an attitude developed over many decades in the Scandinavian countries in a social climate that is quite different from that which exists in Canada. Also, the point has been made that under present conditions, rank and file union members would be extremely suspicious of "cooperative" union leaders. Many union members fear that cooperation can degenerate into conspiracy either against the public or against the rank and file members themselves.

One thing is certain in the future: we can expect a continuing series of changes in our present labour relations system. It is hoped that those responsible for instigating and implementing such changes will heed the following warning issued by the Task Force on Labour Relations:

"Any tampering with the system must be based on an appreciation of the implications of such adjustments, not merely at the point of impact but everywhere in the system." (4.7)

Summary

1.   Collective bargaining in the private sector of Canada is primarily under provincial jurisdiction. However, a small percentage of employees and employers do come under federal jurisdiction.
2.   Labour relations boards are specialized agencies established under federal or provincial legislation to administer specific aspects of legislation influencing the employee-employer relationship.
3.   Three methods frequently used to delay or prevent work stoppages are conciliation, mediation, and fact-finding. The purpose of these processes is to assist the disputing parties to arrive at an agreement. However, the disputing parties are under no obligation to accept the recommendations.
4.   Arbitration is a substitute for free collective bargaining which imposes a settlement that both parties are obliged to accept.
5.   When negotiating a collective agreement, the parties must be aware of any compensation guidelines which may be in force at the time. The most important aspects of these guidelines are the "maximum" allowable rates of increase in compensation, the rigidity with which these "maximums" are enforced and the procedures which must be complied with prior to or upon the termination of negotiations.
6.   Although no Canadian jurisdiction presently makes use of labour courts, there is some interest in the potential of such institutions.
7.   Future alternatives available to the Canadian public include leaving the collective bargaining system as it is, introducing modifications into the present system such as the abolition of sanctions, or replacing our present adversary system with a Scandinavian type of cooperative system.

References

4.1   *Canada Year Book,* 1973, p. 338.
4.2   Woods, H.D. *Labour Policy in Canada.* Toronto, The Macmillan Company of Canada Ltd., 1973, pp. 339-340.
4.3   Sack, J. and M. Levinson. *Ontario Labour Relations Board Practices.* Toronto, Butterworths, 1973, p. 15.
4.4   Buchanan, A.R. "Letter to Editor", *Financial Post,* July 17, 1971, p. 7.

4.5   Dunlop, J.T. "The Social Utility of Collective Bargaining", in *Challenges to Collective Bargaining,* edited by L. Ulman. Englewood Cliffs, N.J., Prentice-Hall, Inc., 1967, p. 169.

4.6   Labour Relations Law Casebook Group. *Labour Relations Law.* Kingston, Industrial Relations Centre Queen's University, 1974, p. 30.

4.7   *Canadian Industrial Relations, The Report of the Task Force on Labour Relations.* Ottawa, Queen's Printer, 1968, p. 37.

Suggested Reading for Further Study

Anton, F.R. *The Role of the Government in the Settlement of Industrial Disputes.* Toronto, Commerce Clearing House, 1962.

Cunningham, W. B. "Compulsory Boards of Conciliation", in *Canadian Industrial Relations: A Book of Readings,* edited by S.M.A. Hameed. Toronto. Butterworths, 1975.

Issac, J. E. "Compulsory Arbitration in Australia". A Study for the Task Force on Labour Relations. Ottawa, 1970.

Issac, J. E. "Compulsory Arbitration and Collective Bargaining Reconsidered". *Journal of Industrial Relations,* Vol. 16, No. 1 (March, 1974).

Malles, Paul. "Trends in Industrial Relations Systems of Continental Europe". A Study for the Task Force on Labour Relations. Ottawa, 1970.

Palmer, E.E. "Preliminary Report on Constitutional Law Facing the Labour Task Force". A Study For The Task Force On Labour Relations. Ottawa, 1970.

Sack, J. and M. Levinson. *Ontario Labour Relations Board Practices.* Toronto, Butterworths, 1973.

Scott, F. "Federal Jurisdiction over Labour Relations". Paper delivered to the 11th Annual Conference at the McGill University Industrial Relations Centre, September, 1959.

Ulman, Lloyd. *Challenges to Collective Bargaining.* Englewood Cliffs, N.J., Prentice-Hall, 1971.

Woods, H.D. *Labour Policy in Canada.* Toronto, Macmillan of Canada, 1973.

Experiential Assignment

Debate the following issue:
      "RESOLVED: Strikes should be banned in Canada."

Part B: The Negotiation Phase Of The Collective Bargaining Process

We are now ready to consider the fundamentals of negotiating a collective agreement. The basic considerations that are identified in this section will be applicable whether the contract negotiations involve private, public, or professional employees.

An analytical view of collective bargaining relationships is the focus of Chapter 5. This sets the stage for the more practical areas that follow. All negotiations should be preceded by thorough preparations. The areas in which preparations are required are spelled out in Chapter 6. The objective of these preparations is to facilitate the conduct of contract negotiations, which is considered in Chapter 7.

If the parties cannot reach agreement at the bargaining table, they may decide to take their case to arbitration or engage in a work stoppage. The former option is covered in Chapter 8 and the latter in Chapter 9.

Chapter 5

An Analytical View Of Collective Bargaining Negotiations

I   INTRODUCTION:

One labour relations consultant has described the attitude possessed by the typical labour negotiator in the following manner (5.1): "No matter how realistic we are the management will cut our proposal in half. So the thing we have learned to do is to get the membership sold on a really high figure and go to the table with the authority to call a strike. Then we sit there and call on management to make its offers. If they offer enough, we make a deal and tell the members that is all we can get. If management is slow to move, or doesn't move far enough, we take their last offer to the members and ask them to turn it down. This usually brings another offer, and, of course every time this happens, our members know management would have cheated them if it hadn't been for the union."

The stance assumed by a typical management is reflected this way: "Collective bargaining is akin to eastern bazaar haggling. The union comes in with a flock of blue-sky demands, and we put up our best front that no change is called for. We reject accusations that we are offering nothing in return by saying, we are prepared to continue the existing high level of benefits, knowing all the time that we have to do something to keep competitive in the labour market. Later, when we think we know what the union will settle at, we make an offer to get them moving. We always gauge our 'final' offer to leave something for the union committee to demand as a price for their committment to recommend settlement. On the other hand, if we think the mood is for strike regardless, we leave something out of our 'final' prestrike offer to settle the strike". Little wonder people are saying there must be a better way!

The actual negotiation of a collective agreement is a highly complicated process. So far, no single theory provides a complete explanation of the negotiation process. Also, there is no single theory that can be relied upon to generate accurate predictions concerning the outcome of contract negotiations. In spite of these severe limitations, existing theories do provide useful insights into certain aspects of the negotiation process. The discussion that follows presents segments of negotiation theories chosen to improve one's understanding of labour-management interaction at the bargaining table.

II   TRADITIONAL ECONOMIC ANALYSIS OF THE EMPLOYEE-EMPLOYER RELATION

Under traditional economic analysis wages and other terms and conditions of the employment relationship are considered to be determined by the "invisible hand" of the market.

Such analysis is usually divided into three segments:

a) An analysis of the available supply of employee services and how this varies within the range of compensation that might be offered (the supply side).

b) An analysis of the employer's demand for the services of employees and the compensation that he would be willing to pay for varying quantities of such services (the demand side).

c) An analysis of the interaction between the demand side and the supply side which determines the number of employees that will be hired and the compensation that will be paid.

The conclusion that emanates from this analysis is that there is very little room for negotiation between an individual employee and his employer. Any employer that pays "too much" will be forced out of business in a competitive product market, thereby resulting in lost jobs for employees who demand excessive compensation. Employers who do not pay "enough" will lose their employees to competitors and will ultimately be forced out of business.

Such analysis is based upon the assumption of perfect competition *(i.e.,* many buyers and sellers, perfect knowledge of market conditions and complete mobility to act instantly on the basis of that market knowledge), not only in the labour market, but in all markets. Few markets, including the labour market, come close to fulfilling the restrictive requisites of perfect competition. This does not mean traditional economic analysis has no place in bargaining considerations. Rather, supply and demand considerations provide useful information on the upper and lower ranges that will be a part of employee-employer negotiations.

III BEHAVIOURAL ASPECTS OF COLLECTIVE BARGAINING NEGOTIATIONS

Collective bargaining negotiations do not, by definition, involve an individual employee interacting with an individual employer. Instead, the collective bargaining relationship involves representatives of two multi-member institutions which must resolve a series of internal conflicts before commencing negotiations with an adversary institution. A number of models have been formulated to provide an understanding of collective bargaining relationships when two complex institutions are involved. One of the most impressive models is that of Walton and McKersie, which uses a synthesized behavioural science approach. Walton and McKersie identify four subsystems of activities in collective bargaining negotiations (5.2):

a) Intraorganizational bargaining: This refers to the subsystem of activities that is required to achieve consensus *within* a particular organization. Such activities are designed to bring about agreement among the negotiators for a particular organization as well as agreement between the negotiators and the principals they are representing.

b) Attitudinal structuring: This subsystem of activities is designed to change or influence the attitudes and relationships which surround the negotiating parties.

c) Integrative bargaining: This includes activities where there is a perceived area of common concern and the gains of one party do not represent equal sacrifices by the other. Thus, both parties can proceed to increase the size of the joint gain that is available to them.

d) Distributive bargaining: This refers to a pure conflict subprocess in which one party's gain is another party's loss. Prior to the Walton and McKersie analysis, distributive bargaining activities were frequently considered to be the only aspects of bargaining worthy of consideration. Since the publication of their analysis, the three other behavioural dimensions of bargaining have received a more reasonable share of attention.

Walton and McKersie also developed the internal logic for each subsystem and provided an analysis of the interrelationships between these subprocesses. Although this work has been criticized as being "badly written, oversimple, and as ignoring important relevant research" (5.3), it does provide a useful analytical framework for dealing with negotiations between complex institutions.

IV THE CONTRACT ZONE IN COLLECTIVE BARGAINING NEGOTIATIONS

Professor Reynolds has provided an interesting framework for understanding the range of offers and demands that will be acceptable to both parties (5.4):

1. Strike Points and Contract Zones

Assume that at the outset of bargaining:

a) the management negotiating team determines a point M_s at which they will take a strike rather than offer more to the employees;

b) the employee's negotiating team sets a point E_S at which they will strike rather than accept less from management;

c) neither side knows the strike point of the other party.

Figure 5.1(a) represents a hypothetical case where the minimum amount employees will accept without striking (E_S) is, say, $4 per hour. The maximum offer management will grant to avoid a strike (M_S) is say $8 per hour. Here, we find a positive contract zone, $E_S M_S$ (*i.e.*, between $4 per hour and $8 per hour), in which there exists a series of offers and demands acceptable to both parties.

In Figure 5.1(b) it is assumed that the strike points of the parties are identical (*i.e.*, both E_S and M_S are equal to $6). Since agreement is possible at one point only, this situation is referred to as a point contract zone.

Figure 5.1(c) shows a situation where management is unwilling to offer more than $4 per hour ($M_S$) while the employees are unwilling to accept less than $8 per hour ($E_S$). In this case we have a negative contract zone that will require one or both parties to modify their positions if there is to be an agreement.

2. Offers and Contract Zones

Now, assume that neither party initially puts forward its true offers or demands so that:

a) M_O represents the initial offer made by management;

b) E_D represents the initial demand put forward by the employees.

The offer of management (M_O = $5) could be less than the demand of employees (E_D = $7) but within a positive contract zone (E_S to M_S = $4 to $8) as shown in Figure 5.2(a). The length of time it will take the parties to come to an agreement will depend on the size of the gap between the initial offers and the relative willingness of the parties to back down from their initial offers.

Figure 5.2(b) illustrates a similar set of offers made when a point contract zone exists. Once again there is room for potential agreement.

Figure 5.2(c) shows a negative contract zone. Even if both parties reveal their true positions, there is no possiblity of a mutual settlement without some revision in one or both strike points.

Figure 5.2(d) illustrates why most negotiations are initiated with a demand by employees that is well in excess of their strike point and a reciprocally low offer by management. If the employees demands were presented first, and they requested $5 per hour ($E_D$) they would have no way of knowing that management was already prepared to offer $6 per hour ($M_O$). Similarly, if management presented an offer without knowing the employees' initial request, management would be offering $6 per hour ($M_O$) when the employees were ready to accept $5 per hour. This also explains why management is usually content to sit back quietly until the employees have presented their initial demands.

V BARGAINING POWER

Many attempts have been made to develop a theory that will explain the final outcome within the contract zone. Most of this work is related to the study of the concept called bargaining power, which is most easily thought of as the "ability to hurt someone".

A typical example of the models that have been developed to determine the bargaining power of the parties to collective bargaining relationships is that proposed by C.F. Smythe.

Smythe's model, which is shown schematically in Figure 5.3, has three basic elements (5.5):

Figure 5.1

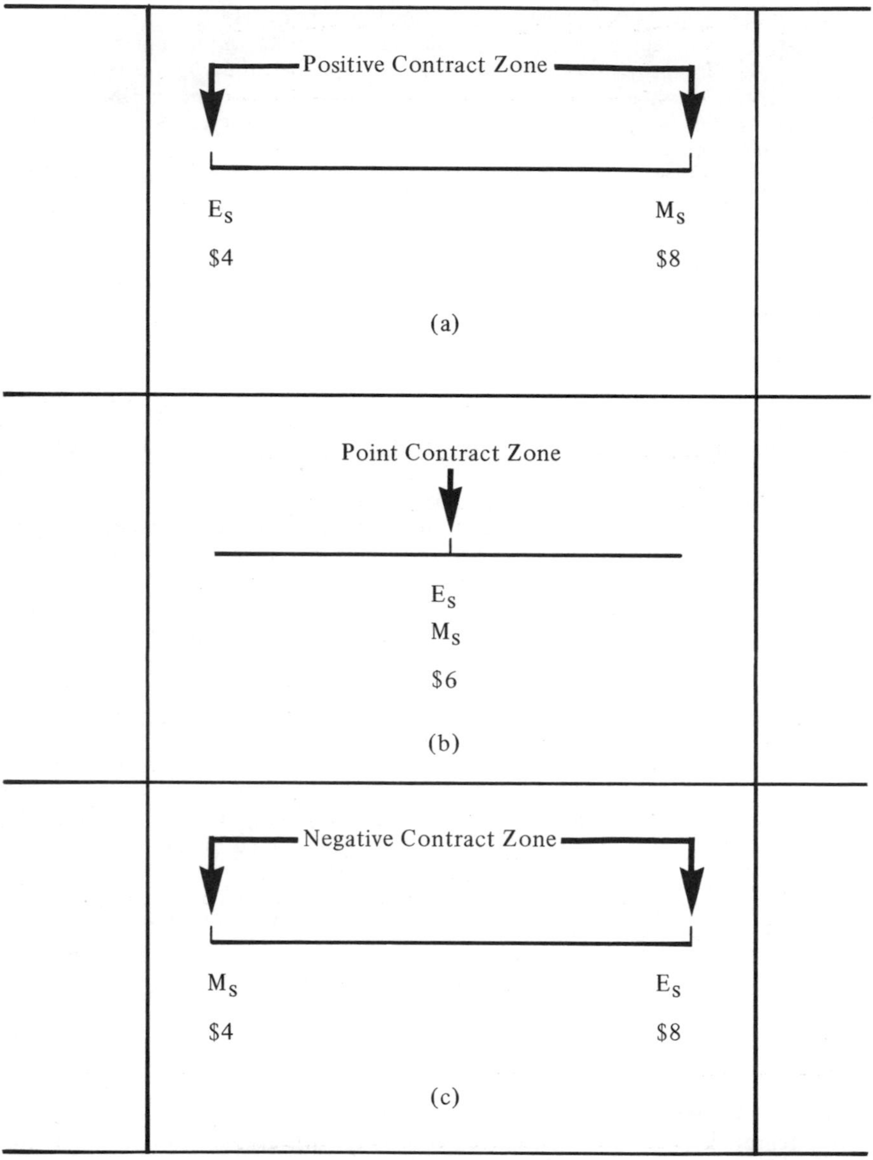

Positive Contract Zone

E_S M_S

$4 $8

(a)

Point Contract Zone

E_S
M_S
$6

(b)

Negative Contract Zone

M_S E_S

$4 $8

(c)

1.   Bargaining Power (Economic Variables)

Bargaining power is derived from two economic variables, critical need and irreplaceability in the labour market. "Critical need" refers to the degree to which the employer cannot produce goods or services without the services of the striking work group. The greater the critical need for employees in the productive process, the greater will be the bargaining power of the employees.

"Irreplaceability" refers to the degree to which an employee can effectively cut off an employer's access to the labour market. The greater the

Figure 5.2

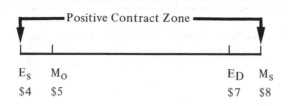

E_S M_O E_D M_S
$4 $5 $7 $8

(a)

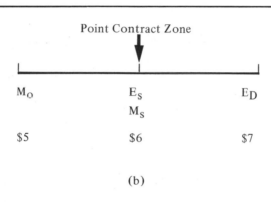

M_O E_S E_D
                    M_S

$5 $6 $7

(b)

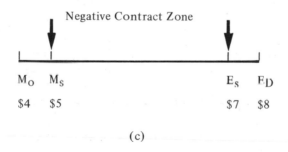

M_O M_S E_S F_D
$4 $5 $7 $8

(c)

E_S E_D M_O M_S
$4 $5 $6 $7

(d)

ability to deprive employers of sources of labour, the greater will be the
bargaining power of the employee organization.

2.   Use of Bargaining Power (Psychological Variables)

The parties to collective bargaining relationships must not just possess bargaining
power to effectively achieve their objectives. They must also perceive the true
extent of their bargaining power and be willing and able to use it. The better a
party perceives its bargaining power in an appropriate way and at an appropriate
time and place, the greater will be the bargaining power of that party.

Figure 5.3

The Smythe Model of Bargaining Power

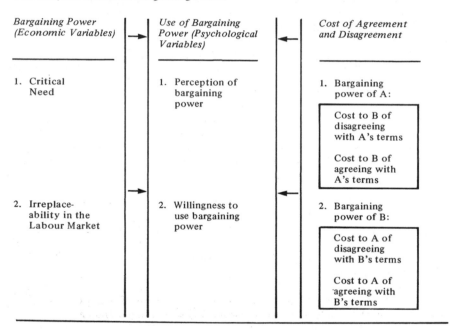

Source: Adapted from Jonathan S. Monat, "Determination of Bargaining Power",
Personnel Journal, Vol. 50, No. 7, July 1971, p. 519.

3.   The Measurement of Bargaining Power

This third element of Smythe's model incorporates Chamberlain's construction
of the costs of agreement and disagreement as measures of bargaining power.
According to Chamberlain, management's (A's) bargaining power is related to
the ratio of the cost to the union (B), of _disagreeing_ with management's (A's)
terms to the cost to the union (B), of _agreeing_ with management's (A's)
terms, as assessed by the union (B). The union's (B's) bargaining power is the
ratio of the cost to management (A) of _disagreeing_ with the union's (B's) terms
to the cost to management (A) of _agreeing_ with the union's (B's) terms, as
assessed by management (A).

Thus, if each party converts all sets of bargaining demands into dollar
equivalents, it is possible to derive a comparable set of the net dollar advantages
or disadvantages of various potential agreements.

In general, this model demonstrates that each party has a number of options available to achieve its objectives. These include:

    i) lowering the other party's economic power (or augmenting its own economic power);

    ii) lowering the other party's psychological bargaining power (or augmenting its own psychological power);

    iii) lowering the other party's ratio of the costs of disagreement to the costs of agreement.

There are in existence many other highly sophisticated bargaining power models which draw upon ideas developed for the study of game theory and the social sciences. Although the details of these theories are beyond the scope of this book, the reader should be aware of three significant shortcomings of such theories:

    a) Bargaining power theories rarely consider the total situation surrounding the parties. Any productive analysis of collective bargaining must take into account not only the striking or resistance capacities of the parties, but the economic, political and social circumstances as well (5.6).

    b) Bargaining power theories are usually static, but to be meaningful, such theories must be dynamic in the sense of allowing for the possibility that bargaining power may shift over time. Even within brief periods of time, relative positions may change considerably.

    c) Bargaining power theories generally neglect the skill of the negotiator as an important element of power. Other things being equal, a "skilled" negotiator will tend to gain more than an "unskilled" negotiator.

    The true significance of these shortcomings will become apparent after one becomes familiar with the following chapters on negotiation practices.

Summary

1. Traditional economic theory analyzes the relationship between an individual employer and an individual employee in terms of demand and supply considerations.

2. Walton and McKersie have identified four subsystems of behavioural activities that are a part of negotiations between complex employer and employee institutions: intraorganizational bargaining, attitudinal structuring, integrative bargaining and distributive bargaining.

3. The contract zone refers to that range of offers and demands that will be acceptable to both negotiating parties. There is always the possibility that no contract zone exists.

4. Bargaining power refers to the ability to hurt someone. Complex bargaining power theories have been developed in an attempt to predict the outcome of particular types of bargaining relationships.

References

5.1   Hemsworth, L. "Letter to Editor". *Labour Gazette*. Ottawa, Canada Department of Labour, July 1975, p. 456.

5.2   Walton, R., and R. McKersie. *A Behavioural Theory of Labour Negotiations*. New York, McGraw-Hill, 1965.

5.3   Strauss, G. "Organizational Behaviour and Personnel Relations", in *A Review of Industrial Relations Research, Vol. I.* Madison, Wisc., Industrial Relations Research Association, 1970, p. 175.
5.4   Reynolds, R. G. *Labour Economics and Labour Relations.* Englewood Cliffs, New Jersey, Prentice-Hall, 1970, p. 431.
5.5   Smythe, C. F. *Teacher-Administrator.* Minneapolis, University of Minnesota, January, 1967, pp. 1-3.
5.6   Chamberlain, N.W. and J.W. Kuhn. *Collective Bargaining.* New York, McGraw-Hill, 1965, p. 172.

Suggested Readings for Further Study

Bishop, R. "Game Theoretic Analyses of Bargaining". *Quarterly Journal of Economics,* Vol. LXXVII, November, 1963 pp. 449-602.

Cheng, P. "Wage Negotiation and Bargaining Power". *Industrial and Labour Relations Review,* Vol. 21, January 1968, pp. 168-82.

Compini, B. "The Value of Time In Bargaining Negotiations: Some Experimental Evidence". *The American Economic Review,* Vol. VIII, June 1968, pp. 374-393.

Livernash, E. Robert. "The Relation of Power to the Structure and Process of Collective Bargaining". *The Journal of Law and Economics* VI, October 1963.

Mabry, B. "The Pure Theory of Bargaining". *Industrial and Labour Relations Review,* Vol. 18. July 1965, pp. 479-502.

Nash, J. "The Bargaining Problem" *Econometrica,* Vol. 18, April 1950, pp. 155-162.

Pen, J. "A General Theory of Bargaining" *The American Economic Review,* Vol. XLII, March 1952, pp. 24-42.

Somers, G. G. "Bargaining Power and Industrial Relations Theory", in *Essays in Industrial Relations Theory,* edited by G.G. Somers. Ames, Iowa, Iowa State University Press, 1969.

Stevens, Carl M. *Strategy and Collective Bargaining Negotiation.* New York, McGraw-Hill, 1963.

Walton, R. and Robert McKersie. *A Behavioural Theory of Labour Negotiations.* New York, McGraw-Hill, 1965.

Experiential Assignment

Turn to Chapter 17, Section V and prepare the "Assignment on Contract Negotiations".

Chapter 6

Preparing To Negotiate
A Collective Agreement

I   INTRODUCTION

Each year a number of Canada's 20,000 collective agreements expire and must be renewed. Canadian laws and agencies exist to encourage the interested parties to listen, respond and accept the necessity for compromise – that is, to negotiate.

The form that these negotiations may take is dependent on the integration which characterizes the "actual bargaining unit" or "negotiating unit". Negotiations may vary in terms of employer representation (by plant, company, or employer associations); union representation (by locals, national or international unions, or groups of unions); occupations involved (single trades, or groups of trades); and geographical areas covered (local, provincial, national or international). Negotiations may also vary in the extent to which they influence or are influenced by other negotiations. The results of some negotiations may serve as a "master" agreement for numerous local negotiations. The results of other negotiations may serve as a "pattern" for other sectors of the industry or economy.

In view of these complexities, there is obviously no "best" way to prepare for negotiating a collective agreement. However, it is possible to describe specific guidelines that are applicable in a wide variety of circumstances.

II   INTRAORGANIZATIONAL NEGOTIATIONS

Union contracts in all Canadian jurisdictions must run for a specified time period of no less than one year. As the expirations date draws near, representatives of both the employees and the employer begin to prepare for another round of negotiations. Initially, both parties must determine what offers and demands should be put forward

1.   Establishing employee demands

When an independent local union represents employees, potential demands are usually discussed at a general membership meeting. A committee is then appointed to draft a detailed set of demands and facts which justify the reasonableness of such demands. These detailed demands are taken back to another membership meeting, discussed, modified, and finally ratified.

In negotiations which involve an international union, proposed demands may be agreed upon by executives of the international and submitted to a conference of representatives of local unions. These demands are then discussed, modified and, eventually approved.

2.   Establishing the employer's position

The contract proposals and counterproposals of employers may be formulated by a wide range of individuals. Usually, any potential offers that necessitate a departure from established company policies or involve significant financial outlays must receive the approval of top level management.

Where an employer association is involved, representatives of the member companies will work out proposals for negotiations. Once a policy is agreed upon, negotiations are delegated to a working committee of company representatives.

The importance of such intraorganizational activities is frequently overlooked. Irresponsible or uninformed decisions at this stage of the negotiation process can lead to serious problems later.

III   THE COMPOSITION OF THE NEGOTIATING COMMITTEE

Once the parties have agreed upon a range of demands to be presented, a negotiating committee must be selected to meet with the opposition. Decisions have to be made concerning the number of committee members needed, the personal attributes of committee members that are most desirable, and who should serve as committee spokesman.

1. The Number of Committee Members

The size of the negotiating committee can be an important determinant of the final outcome of negotiations. The number of members on the negotiating team depends on the size and resources of the organization being represented. In general, many experts feel that committees composed of more than five individuals tend to become unwieldy and are not conducive to promoting a sound agreement.

The committee representing the interests of employees frequently includes the president, secretary, chief steward and business agent of the local organization. If the local is affiliated with a national or international organization, the parent organization may send a professional negotiator to provide specialized skills and advice to the local committee.

Employers show much less uniformity in the size of their negotiating teams. In some cases a single owner may handle all the negotiations while in others a specialized team of internal managers, labour relations specialists, and outside consultants may negotiate with the opposition. In addition, members of employers' associations may be provided with advisors or spokesmen for the bargaining team.

2. The Personal Attributes of Committee Members

The quantity of members on a negotiating committee is not nearly as decisive a factor as the quality of the members selected. In fact, the quality of potential members may influence the quantity of members actually needed.

Contract negotiation is more an art than a science and depends heavily on the value system, sense of judgment and skills possessed by the individual negotiators. The "ideal" negotiator might be characterized as possessing the following attributes:

a) A value system that includes:
- personal integrity and courage
- genuine belief in collective bargaining as a workable method of joint decision-making and reconciling conflicting values.

b) A sound sense of judgment derived from a thorough knowledge of:
- the essential facts relevant to the position of both opposing parties
- the pressures and compulsions influencing both parties.

c) Specific skills that include the ability to:
- speak and write with clarity of expression
- be a patient listener
- be creative
- inspire confidence by making sound decisions.

Obviously, few individuals possess all of these attributes. However, it is frequently possible to choose a team of individuals which possesses an optimal number of these characteristsics.

Keeping these personal attributes in mind, it is also useful to include on the committee individuals who:
- a) are representative of the organization which will be affected by the bargain;
- b) have enough authority to be credible;

c)   will have a direct role in administering the agreement;

d)   are promising trainees and will be available to bargain in the future.

3.   Selection of a Committee Spokesmen

The selection of a committee spokesman is the next decision that has to be made after the composition of the committee has been determined. The spokesman must be capable of coordinating his committee's presentation, dealing effectively and decisively with the opposition and keeping his own side under control at all times. Disagreement among committee members in the presence of the opposition can prove to be disastrous. To be effective, the spokesman should know how far he can go and have the authority to deal with members of the opposition committee on an informal basis if the opportunity arises.

IV   INFORMATION FOR NEGOTIATIONS

Information and knowledge constitute a source of power which every skilled negotiator should endeavor to exploit. Intelligent and thorough preparation for bargaining requires an understanding of at least four vital topics:

1.   The Employing Entity

To negotiate effectively, it is essential to be knowledgeable about the firm's objectives, facilities, strengths and weaknesses. More specifically, this includes:

a) General historical data about the relevant organization: The negotiator must be aware of the organization's scope of operations, growth, problems and objectives.

b) The physical and technical characteristics of the organization: Some of the most significant characteristics that can influence present and potential agreements include:

- product characteristics
- the nature of the production process
- the type of employees needed
- the state of available facilities
- the product market
- the quality of management.

c) A history of employee-employer relations in the organization: The historical pattern of negotiations in an organization has a considerable influence on existing relationships. Such information can provide some useful insights into the present environment for negotiations.

2.   The Existing Agreement

An analysis of the strengths and weaknesses of the existing agreement should constitute an important part of the preparation for negotiations. In this context, a "bargaining book" can be a valuable aid to both parties. Such a book breaks down the existing contract into its component clauses and contains all proposals and counter proposals that have ever been put forward concerning each clause. The fate of these proposals and others that were put forward in the past, but have not yet been introduced into the present agreement, are also included in a typical bargaining book. It is equally important that all negotiators should be well informed about agreements that pertain to other companies and industries.

3.   Your Present Objectives and Limits

Before entering into negotiations the parties should categorize all proposals and counter proposals as being unconditionally acceptable, unconditionally unacceptable, or negotiable. Those proposals that fit into the "negotiable" category should then be classified as to their relative importance and bolstered with logical arguments, facts, figures and charts.

4.   The Opposing Negotiators and the Group they Represent
To negotiate effectively, the personal characteristics and attitudes of your opposition should be understood. This information can throw light on what the opposition is willing to accept, the motivation for various proposals and the pressures under which the opposition is operating. In addition, this type of information should ensure that members of the team are not startled or caught off balance by the actions of their opponents.

V   WAGE CRITERIA IN CONTRACT NEGOTIATIONS
Wages constitute one of the basic issues upon which the negotiating parties must agree. In practice, both parties use a wide variety of criteria to justify a particular wage increase. Professor Dunlop has broken these criteria down into four convenient categories (6.1):

1.   Comparable Wage Rates
Wage comparisons require the parties to look at what is being paid elsewhere in order to ensure "equal pay for equal work". Unfortunately, the problems associated with securing agreement from the parties as to which particular comparisons are valid and which are not are by no means easy to resolve. As Dunlop points out:

   a)   The content of job classifications designated by the same job title varies widely among different employers.

   b)   Comparability in wage rates is impaired by variations in the method of wage payment.

   c)   The influence of regularity of employment must be assessed in defining comparable wages.

   d)   The terms and conditions of employment typically include a variety of fringes in addition to the stated wage rate.

   e)   There are always geographical implications that must be considered.

2.   Productivity
Like wage comparisons, productivity (output per person-hour) is frequently used to generate emotional appeal during wage negotiations. In fact, there are those who advocate that productivity alone should provide the basis for establishing wage increases.

   Attempts to use changes in productivity to justify a particular change in wages are generally fraught with the following types of complications:

   a)   The rate of change in productivity in our economic system varies widely among the component segments.

   b)   The measurement of productivity presents one of the more difficult problems of economic analysis, econometrics and statistical measurement.

   c)   Between any two periods output per person-hour may vary as a result of a great many factors, some of which are quite distinct from the services provided by employees.

3.   Ability to Pay
Both parties have frequently found it useful to justify their positions on the basis of the employer's ability or inability to pay. The application of this criterion is highly subjective, raising a host of questions such as:

   a)   What is the period during which one is concerned with ability to pay?

b)   How should one estimate the effect of wage-rate changes on costs?

c)   How does the character of competition in the markets in which the products must be sold affect the ability to pay wage increases?

d)   What constitutes a reasonable rate of return on investment for a particular company?

e)   Is it appropriate to use before-tax or after-tax income in defining ability to pay?

4.   Cost of living

Those negotiating on behalf of a company's employees will frequently argue that compensation for the other three criteria previously described should come *after* wages have been adjusted to reflect changes in the purchasing power of the dollar. In practice, the cost-of-living criteria present certain difficulties:

a)   There are many problems associated with the accurate measurement of changes in the cost of living.

b)   The selection of an appropriate base period or starting point for adjusting wages is a controversial subject. Disagreement will likely arise over the issue of whether or not prior wages were properly adjusted.

c)   Automatic adjustment of certain wage rates for changes in the cost of living may be inappropriate where prior wages were "overadjusted", productivity has been falling, or a particular company no longer has the ability to pay for such an adjustment.

VI   COSTING THE PROPOSALS (6.2)

There is presently no standard methodology or terminology for costing contract proposals, but it is becoming a common practice to delineate two separate categories of costs:

a) Direct costs: This refers to the costs which are directly attributable to some negotiated item. For example, the direct cost of wage increase is the increase in wage payments resulting from it.

b) Impact or rollup costs: This refers to other costs that must be incurred as a result of any negotiated increase in direct costs. For instance, the increase in vacation costs that results from any wage increase would be classified as an impact cost.

When the objective of costing is to provide factual information that is conducive to meaningful negotiations, the following details should be kept in mind:

1.   The costing method used should be kept as simple as possible. Whenever value judgments are involved, any assumptions that have been used to facilitate computations should be clearly spelled out.

2.   A fully costed position statement should be presented quite early in the negotiations. The purpose at this stage should be to achieve some consistency between the two parties on terminology and methodology.

3.   Although many of the initial costs can be estimated, greater precision should be used as negotiations progress.

4.   In the crucial stages of negotiations, a clear understanding of the language and methodology of the costing procedure being used should prevail. This will enable the parties to concentrate almost exclusively upon substantive bargaining issues.

Unfortunately, there are factions within both the employer and union ranks who strongly oppose constructive costing procedures. Many Canadian employers are reluctant to make relevant company data available to unions, fearing that this could lead to further encroachments on the rights of management. Similarly, representatives of some powerful Canadian unions still look upon the costing of contract proposals as a sophisticated management device used to deprive workers of a fair and just settlement.

Gilbert Levine of the Canadian Union of Public Employees has predicted that (6.3):

"... unions will remain very cautious about costing proposed or actual settlement packages. Unions will continue to look upon the costing technique as a management negotiating tool to inflate and distort the real cost of a union's bargaining proposals. Effective unions will bargain for *benefits* instead of bargaining on the basis of *costs*. They will bargain for collective agreement provisions and benefits on their merits and on the needs of their members, regardless of some distorted management cost estimates."

Summary

1.   Before meeting at the bargaining table, both parties must obtain the views of their constituents as to what should be requested and offered during negotiations.

2.   Decisions must be made also on such matters as the optimal number of committee members, the necessary personal attributes of committee members and the selection of a committee spokesman.

3.   Negotiators should be well informed about the employing entity, the existing collective agreement, present objectives and limits, and the opposing negotiators and the group they represent.

4.   Criteria that are commonly used to justify particular wage demands and offers include comparable wage rates elsewhere, productivity, the employer's ability or inability to pay and changes in the cost of living.

5.   There is a great deal of controversy surrounding the usefulness and methodology of costing demands and counteroffers presented at the bargaining table.

References:

6.1   Dunlop, J.T. "Criteria For Wage Dispute Settlement", in *Unions, Management and the Public,* edited by E. Bakke, *et. al.* New York, Harcourt, Brace & World, Inc., 1967, pp. 571-577.

6.2   The discussion in this section is based on the material contained in "Collective Agreement Costing", *Relations Industrielles,* Volume 28, No. 4, pp. 787-824.

6.3   Levine, G. "Assessing the Costs and Benefits of Collective Bargaining: The Potential Use of Costing". *Relations Industrielles,* Volume 28, No. 4, p. 824.

Experiential Assignment

Turn to Chapter 17, Section V and prepare the "Assignment on Contract Negotiations".

APPENDIX TO CHAPTER 6

PRINCIPAL PUBLISHED SOURCES OF DATA
INDUSTRIAL RELATIONS AND PERSONNEL – CANADA

I   THE ECONOMY

1. *Annual Review.* Ottawa, Economic Council of Canada.
2. *Bank Newsletters.* Most Canadian banks release periodic newsletters or reports on various aspects of the Canadian economy. The *Commercial Letter* of the Canadian Imperial Bank of Commerce presents an annual review of the Canadian economy together with a statistical supplement in one issue each year.
3. *Bank of Canada Review.* Ottawa, Bank of Canada, monthly.
4. *Budget Papers,* presented by the Minister of Finance with his annual budget. Ottawa, Department of Finance, annual.
5. *Canada Year Book.* Ottawa, Statistics Canada, annual.
6. *Canadian Business Review.* Ottawa, The Conference Board, quarterly.
7. *Canadian Business Trends.* Ottawa, The Conference Board, monthly.
8. *Canadian Statistical Review.* Ottawa, Statistics Canada, monthly and annual supplement.
9. *Canadian Tax Journal.* Toronto, Canadian Tax Foundation, bi-monthly.
10. *Canadian Tax Journal.* Toronto, Canadian Tax Foundation, occasional.
11. *Corporation Financial Statistics.* Ottawa, Statistics Canada, annual.
12. *Index of Industrial Production.* Ottawa, Statistics Canada, monthly.
13. *Industrial Corporations.* Ottawa, Statistics Canada, quarterly.
14. *Monthly Bulletin of Business Activity.* Victoria, B.C., Department of Industrial Development, Trade and Commerce.
15. *National Income and Expenditure Accounts.* Ottawa, Statistics Canada, quarterly and annual.
16. *Private and Public Investment in Canada.* Ottawa, Statistics Canada, annual.
17. *Quarterly Canadian Forecasts.* Ottawa, The Conference Board.

II   LABOUR FORCE AND EMPLOYMENT

1. *Canada Manpower Review.* Ottawa, Department of Manpower and Immigration, quarterly.
2. *Employment, Earnings and Hours.* Ottawa, Statistics Canada, monthly.
3. *Review of Employment and Average Weekly Wages and Salaries.* Ottawa, Statistics Canada, annual.
4. *Estimates of Employees by Province and Industry.* Ottawa, Statistics Canada, irregular.
5. *Federal Government Employment.* Ottawa, Statistics Canada, quarterly.
6. *Historical Labour Force Statistics.* Ottawa, Statistics Canada, annual.
7. *The Labour Force.* Ottawa, Statistics Canada, monthly.
8. *The Labour Gazette.* Ottawa, Labour Canada, monthly.
9. *Local Government Employment.* Ottawa, Statistics Canada, quarterly.
10. *Manpower Review (Atlantic Region).* Halifax, Department of Manpower and Immigration, quarterly.
11. *Manpower Review (Ontario Region).* Toronto, Department of Manpower and Immigration, quarterly.
12. *Manpower review (Quebec Region).* Montreal, Department of Manpower and Immigration, quarterly.
13. *New Brunswick Labour Force Review.* Fredericton, N.B., Department

of Labour, bi-monthly.
14. *Notes on Labour Statistics.* Ottawa, Statistics Canada, annual.
15. *Provincial Government Employment.* Ottawa, Statistics Canada, quarterly.
16. *Quarterly Immigration Report.* Ottawa, Department of Manpower and Immigration, quarterly.
17. *Quarterly Report on Job Vacancies.* Ottawa, Statistics Canada, quarterly.
18. *Saskatchewan Labour Report.* Regina, Department of Labour, monthly.
19. *Selected Labour Statistics for Nova Scotia.* Halifax, N.S., Department of Labour, semi-annual.
20. *Women in the Labour Force: Facts and Figures.* Ottawa, Labour Canada, annual.

III   WAGES, SALARIES, HOURS AND PRODUCTIVITY

1. *Aggregate Productivity Trends.* Ottawa, Statistics Canada, annual.
2. *B.C. Wage Settlements.* Victoria, B.C., Department of Labour, annual.
3. *Base Rate Increases.* Ottawa, Labour Canada, quarterly.
4. *Earnings and Hours of Work in Manufacturing.* Ottawa, Statistics Canada, annual.
5. *Employment, Earnings and Hours.* Ottawa, Statistics Canada, monthly.
6. *Estimates of Labour Income.* Ottawa, Statstics Canada, monthly.
7. *Farm Wages in Canada.* Ottawa, Statistics Canada, three issues a year.
8. *Fringe Benefit Costs in Canada.* Toronto, The Thorne Group Limited, bi-annual.
9. *Hours, Wages and Related Payments in the Ontario Construction Industry.* Toronto, Ontario Department of Labour, annual.
10. *Labour Costs in Manufacturing.* Ottawa, Statistics Canada, occasional.
11. *Labour Costs in Mines, Quarries and Oil Wells.* Ottawa, Statistics Canada, occasional.
12. *Negotiated Wages and Working Conditions in Ontario Hospitals.* Toronto, Ministry of Labour, annual.
13. *Principal Wage Settlements.* Vancouver, Employers' Council of British Columbia, annual.
14. *Review of Employment and Average Wages and Salaries.* Ottawa, Statistics Canada, annual.
15. *Review of Man-Hours and Hourly Earnings.* Ottawa, Statistics Canada, annual.
16. *Salary and Wage Rate Survey.* Edmonton, Alberta Department of Industry and Commerce, annual.
17. *Survey of Wage and Salary Rates.* Fredericton, New Brunswick Department of Labour, annual.
18. *Survey of Working Conditions.* Fredericton, New Brunswick Department of Labour, annual.
19. *Wage Adjustments in Collective Bargaining Agreements in Saskatchewan.* Regina, Saskatchewan Deaprtment of Labour, semi-annual.
20. *Wage and Salary Survey.* Winnipeg, Manitoba Department of Labour, annual.
21. *Wage Developments* (Research Bulletin). Ottawa, Labour Canada, quarterly.
22. *Wage Developments in Collective Bargaining Settlements in Ontario.* Toronto, Ontario Department of Labour, quarterly.

23.   *Wage Rates and Hours of Labour in Nova Scotia.* Halifax, N.S. Department of Labour, annual
24   *Wage Rates, Salaries and Hours of Labour.* Ottawa, Labour Canada, annual.
25.   *Working Conditions and Fringe Benefit Plans Survey.* Edmonton, Alberta Department of the Treasury, annual.
26.   *Working Conditions in British Columbia Industry.* Victoria, B.C. Department of Labour, annual.
27.   *Working Conditions in Canadian Industry.* Ottawa, Labour Canada, annual.
28.   *Working Conditions in Nova Scotia.* Halifax, N.S. Department of Labour, annual.

IV   TRADE UNION ORGANIZATION AND ACTIVITIES

1.   *Annual Report of the Minister of Industry, Trade and Commerce under the Corporations and Labour Unions Returns Act. Part II.* Ottawa, Statistics Canada, annual.
2.   *Canadian Labour.* Ottawa, Canadian Labour Congress, monthly.
3.   *Labour Gazette.* Ottawa, Labour Canada, annual.
4.   *Labour Organizations in Canada.* Ottawa, Labour Canada, annual.
5.   *Le Travail.* Montreal, Confederation of National Trade Unions, monthly.

NOTE: Most provincial labour federations and many unions also issue periodic publications.

V   INDUSTRIAL RELATIONS AND PERSONNEL ADMINISTRATION

1.   *Analysis of Canadian Public Service Collective Agreements.* Ottawa, Pay Research Bureau, irregular updating.
2.   *Annual Conference Proceedings.* McGill University Industrial Relations Centre, Laval University Department of Industrial Relations and the Canadian Manufacturers' Association publish the proceedings of their annual industrial relations conferences.
3.   *Annual Report.* Ottawa, Labour Canada, annual.
4.   *Annual Reports.* Most provincial Departments of Labour release annual reports.
5.   *Business Quarterly.* London, University of Western Ontario, quarterly.
6.   *CLV Reports.* Toronto, Canadian Labour Views Co. Ltd., weekly.
7.   *Calendar of Expiring Collective Agreements.* Victoria, B.C. Department of Labour, annual.
8.   *Calendar of Expiring Collective Agreements Covering 500 Employees or More, but Excluding the Construction Industry.* Ottawa, Labour Canada, annual.
9.   *Canadian Business.* Montreal, Canadian Chamber of Commerce, monthly.
10.   *Canadian Labour Relations Board Reports.* Scarborough, Butterworths.
11.   *Canadian Personnel and Industrial Relations Journal.* Toronto, Council of Canadian Personnel Associations, bi-monthly.
12.   *Collective Agreements Expiring in New Brunswick.* Fredericton, N.B. Department of Labour, annual.
13.   *Collective Agreement Survey in ....* Halifax, N.S. Department of Labour, annual. (Issues one volume for each of the following: Manufacturing

Industry, Public Administration, Trade Industry, and Transportation, Communications and Other Utilities.)

14. *Collective Bargaining in Ontario.* Toronto, Ontario Department of Labour, annual.
15. *Collective Bargaining Provisions in Ontario Municipal Agreements.* Toronto, Ontario Department of Labour, annual.
16. *Collective Bargaining Settlements in Ontario.* Canada Department of Labour and Ontario Department of Labour, monthly.
17. *Collective Bargaining Review.* Ottawa, Labour Canada, monthly.
18. *Conciliation Board Reports.* Ottawa, Labour Canada, irregular.
19. *Current Labour Developments and Labour Law News.* Toronto, Golden, Levinson.
20. *Executive.* Don Mills, Southam Maclean, monthly.
21. *Industrial Canada.* Toronto, Canadian Manufacturers' Association, monthly.
22. *Industrial Relations Bulletin.* Vancouver, Employers' Council of British Columbia, weekly.
23. *Canadian Industrial Relations and Personnel Developments.* Don Mills, CCH Canadian Ltd., weekly.
24. *Labour Arbitration Cases.* Toronto, Canada Law Book Ltd., monthly.
25. *Labour Arbitration News.* Toronto, monthly.
26. *Labour Board Reports.* The Federal and Provincial Labour Boards release periodic reports.
27. *Labour Case Reporter.* Ottawa, Labour Canada, monthly.
28. *Labour Legislation in Nova Scotia.* Halifax, N.S. Department of Labour, annual.
29. *Labour Research Bulletin.* Victoria, B.C. Department of Labour, monthly.
30. *Legislative Review.* Ottawa, Labour Canada, occasional.
31. *Canadian Labour Law Reports and Labour Notes.* Don Mills, CCH Canadian Ltd., bi-monthly.
32. *Labour Legislation in Nova Scotia.* Halifax, Nova Scotia Department of Labour, annual.
33. *Labour Standards in Canada.* Ottawa, Labour Canada, annual.
34. *Mercer Actuarial Bulletin.* Vancouver, William M. Mercer Ltd., monthly.
35. *Nova Scotia Department of Labour Bulletin.* Halifax, quarterly.
36. *Ontario Collective Agreement Expirations.* Toronto, Ontario Department of Labour, annual.
37. *Principal Contracts Expiring in British Columbia.* Vancouver, Employers' Council of British Columbia, annual.
38. *Provincial Labour Standards.* Ottawa, Labour Canada, annual.
39. *Relations Industrielles.* Quebec, Department of Industrial Relations, Laval University, quarterly.
40. *Saskatchewan Collective Agreement Expiration Calendar.* Regina, Sask. Department of Labour, annual.
41. *View From Ottawa.* Ottawa, CCH Canadian Ltd., weekly.
42. *Work Stoppages* (Research Bulletin). Ottawa, Labour Canada, monthly.

VI BIBLIOGRAPHY AND GENERAL REFERENCES

1. *Abstracts and Abstracting Services,* by Robert L. Collison. Santa

    Barbara, California and Oxford, England, Clio Press.

2.   *Avenues of Research: A Businessman's Guide to Sources of Business
     Information.* Montreal, Canadian Chamber of Commerce.

3.   *Canadian Almanac and Directory.* Toronto, Copp Clark, annual.

4.   *Canadian Business Handbook.* Toronto, McGraw-Hill.

5.   *Canadian Graduate Theses, 1919-1967: An Annotated
     Bibliography,* by W.D. Wood, L.A. Kelly and P. Kumar. Kingston,
     Industrial Relations Centre, Queen's University, 1970.

6.   *Canadian Labour Law Reporter.* Don Mills, CCH Canadian Ltd.

7.   *Corpus Almanac of Canada.* Toronto, Corpus, annual.

8.   *Director of Canadian Labour Statistics.* Canadian Studies, No. 6.
     Montreal, National Industrial Conference Board, 1963.

9.   *Glossary of Terms Used in Industrial Relations* (English-French), by
     Gerard Dion. Quebec, Department of Industrial Relations, Laval
     University, 1972.

10. *Historical Statistics of Canada,* by M.C. Urquhart. Toronto,
     Macmillan, 1965.

11. *Industrial and Labour Relations in Canada: A Selected Bibliography,*
     by A.F. Isbester, D. Coates and C.B. Williams, Kingston, Industrial
     Relations Centre, Queen's University, 1965.

12. *Industrial and Labour Relations Terms,* by R.E. Doherty and G.A.
     DeMarchi, Ithaca, Cornell University.

13. *Labour Relations Law: Cases, Materials, and Commentary,* by The
     Labour Relations Law Casebook Group. 2nd Ed. Kingston,
     Industrial Relations Centre, Queen's University, 1974.

14. *McGraw-Hill Dictionary of Modern Economics*, by Douglas
     Greenwald. Toronto, McGraw-Hill Publications.

15. *Manpower Management in Canada: A Selected Bibliography,* by C.B.
     Williams. Kingston, Industrial Relations Centre, Queen's University,
     1969.

16. *Roberts' Dictionary of Industrial Relations,* by Harold S. Roberts.
     Washington, Bureau of National Affairs, 1966.

17. *The Use of Economics Literature,* by J. Fletcher. Connecticut,
     Archon Books, 1971.

SOURCE: Wood, W.D. *The Current Industrial Relations Scene in Canada 1974.*
            Kingston, Industrial Relations Centre, Queen's University, 1974.

Chapter 7

The Conduct Of
Contract Negotiations

I   INTRODUCTION

Certain procedural matters should be worked out before the negotiation sessions begin if order is to prevail. The time and place for the meetings, an appointment of a chairman, rules governing recognition to speak, recesses, acceptable conduct and adjournment must all be considered beforehand. In addition, a decision has to be made by both parties as to which members of the bargaining committee should be assigned the task of presenting certain information and replying to opposition demands. It is hazardous to generalize, but some considerations that have been proposed include:

a) persuasiveness — which committee members are most gifted in the verbal and logical skills necessary for effective bargaining?

b) facts — which committee members are most knowledgeable about particular demands and their broader ramifications?

c) experience — which committee members have acquired the most negotiating experience and skills directly on the firing line?

d) respect — which committee members are deemed by the opposition to possess the most integrity and sincerity?

e) personality — which committee members tend to be even tempered, firm (but not inflexible), and easy to get along with?

II   THE PRESENTATION OF PROPOSALS

The decision as to who should present the proposals determines to a certain extent how the proposals will be advanced. Each individual has his own style and manner of presentation. The following are some of the common strategies frequently encountered in bargaining sessions:

1.   Aggressive vs. Conciliatory Strategies

Some negotiators attempt to browbeat their opponents into submission with loud noises, uncompromising attitudes and threats of dire consequences if their proposals are not accepted. Although aggressive behaviour may simply elicit a similar type of response from the opposition, there are cases where such an approach has proved successful.

A conciliatory strategy involves the introduction of serious proposals for change, listening to the counterproposals and reasoning of the opposition, and attempting to arrive at a mutually acceptable set of proposals. In this approach logic is substituted for noise, facts are substituted for insinuations, and flexibility is substituted for dogmatism.

2.   Bluffing vs. A Candid Strategy

A bluff is an attempt to mislead the opposition into believing certain threats will be carried out when a particular party really has no intention or capability of doing so. Explicit and implicit bluffs are a part of most negotiations and every negotiator should be capable of assessing the credibility and level of commitment associated with any threat that is made. There are dangers associated with any attempt to bluff. Present negotiations could be impeded by bluffs that lock either party into an undesirable course of action. Future problems often result from the hostility that may be generated when the opposition becomes aware that it has been "bluffed".

A candid strategy does not imply giving the opposition all the relevant facts. It means, instead, that a party refrains from providing false or misleading statements of interest to the opposition. Initial demands should still differ from the most favorable point of agreement for each of the parties. But the negotiators know this and are prepared for future discussions that will narrow the gap between initial offers and counteroffers. Neither party attempts to imply that the initial proposal is a take-it-or-leave-it proposition.

3. Piecemeal Acceptance vs. A Package Acceptance Strategy
The philosophy underlying a piecemeal acceptance strategy presupposes that there is a better chance of arriving at a final agreement through a series of small pacts than through a single complex agreement. Most practitioners agree that certain issues can be negotiated individually and formally accepted before proceeding to other issues. However, few negotiators use such an approach.

Both parties tend to favour a "package acceptance" strategy whereby formal or legalistic commitment on any one issue is deferred until tentative agreement has been reached on all issues. Such a procedure enables each party to determine the overall dimensions of the final package before any formal commitment is made. Thus, neither party locks itself into an untenable position during the early stages of the negotiation process. In actual practice, negotiators seldom withdraw a tentative agreement when the final package is considered.

4. Using Subcommittees
Negotiating teams often find it useful to separate into smaller subcommittees, each of which studies a specific category of demands. The meetings of these subcommittees, which are looked upon strictly as information sessions, offer certain advantages where the negotiation units are large. First, negotiators are able to search out tradeoffs, counterproposals and compromises without being forced to adopt a rigid position. Also, negotiators are in better positions to watch the reaction of specific members of the opposition to certain types of proposals. This should assist the negotiators in assessing the limits and objectives of the opposition.

5. Procrastination
After the original positions of the parties are stated and explained, experienced negotiators will attempt to preserve flexibility and continuity in the negotiation process by suggesting that the parties "save certain items for later". The decision to pass over an item for the time being is usually adopted after it becomes clear that there are other issues which must be resolved before any agreement can be reached on this issue, or further discussion will serve to harden existing positions and threaten agreement on other issues. Gradually, a pattern of agreement will emerge and generate a variety of concessions, compromises and counter-proposals.

6. Calling a Caucus
When the opposition suggests a significant concession, compromise, or counterproposal, the spokesman may call a caucus or recess. Such an action usually implies that the proposal is receiving serious consideration and there is a good probability that a tentative agreement is close at hand.

7. Joint Study Sessions
Settlement of the easy problems frequently facilitates agreement on more difficult issues. However, some of the issues may be so complicated that they cannot be resolved during the normal negotiation process. In such cases, the parties may choose to delegate these issues to a joint study group composed of employer and employee representatives. The primary function of such a group is to concisely diagnose the problem and identify a range of feasible alternative solutions. Such alternatives are communicated back to the bargaining committee which is then required to make a choice. If no agreement can be reached, the issue will reappear in the next set of contract negotiations.

Generally, the research and discussion that has been carried out by the joint study group often lays the foundation for a reasonable settlement during present or future negotiations.

8.   Deadlines

An important aspect of negotiations is the constant pressure exerted by a deadline. Obviously, without a deadline both parties would be reluctant to settle until they had achieved an optimal result. One party may often conclude that no agreement is more advantageous than a suboptimal agreement.

A deadline implies that beyond a certain time limit one party will attempt to hurt the other party in some way. As this deadline approaches each side is compelled to weigh the costs and uncertain implications of disagreement against the costs and calculable implications of agreement. As it becomes more and more certain that one party has no intention of accepting the present offer, the opposition often reassesses its conditions of settlement and starts making more realistic offers to the other side.

III   PHASES OF THE NEGOTIATION PROCESS

No two negotiations proceed in exactly the same manner. In spite of this, it is possible to make some general observations about the various phases of the negotiation process.

1.   The Initial Demands

The first phase of the negotiation process is characterized by a wide gap between the positions of the parties. The long and ambitious list of initial demands is probably the most misunderstood aspect of the bargaining relationship. There are some very compelling reasons for this ritual (7.1):

a)   It is often politically dangerous to be held responsible for rejecting the demands of the individuals you represent. A wiser strategy is to take frivolous demands into the negotiation session and allow the opposition to quickly dispose of them. This shifts any antagonism towards one's adversaries at the bargaining table.

b)   An ambitious list of demands provides a useful lever for "trading" and concession granting.

c)   A large number of demands makes it easier to conceal one's true position while an attempt is being made to ascertain the "real" position of the other party.

d)   Some demands are included so that the opposition will become familiar with them and be more favourably disposed towards them in future years. It is unlikely that the opposition will concede a new demand the first time it is presented. However, in a few years time such proposals gradually appear to be less radical and more feasible.

e)   Large initial demands may eliminate the necessity for introducing new demands during the negotiation period. Many negotiations take place over a long period of time during which conditions can change quite drastically. Any attempt to increase demands after one's initial position has been presented is generally regarded as "bad faith" by the opposition and can endanger the entire negotiating process. But reason must prevail on this issue. If too much is demanded at the outset, individuals outside the negotiations may not concur with the proposed agreement. Thus, the initial demands should provide sufficient scope for bargaining, yet insufficient scope for branding any compromise a failure.

2. Preliminary Questioning and Testing of Strengths

At this stage some of the less controversial issues are dealt with and the more frivolous demands are set aside with the understanding that they may be reintroduced at a later stage. Each party questions the other regarding the meaning, justification and feasibility of each proposal and counterproposal.

3. The Clarification of Positions

During this stage there is a concerted effort by both parties to ascertain the negotiability of various issues. Also, each side distinguishes certain combinations of items or "packages" which would be considered acceptable. Much of the discussion at this stage takes the form of, "If we did this, would you be willing to do that?"

4. The Approach of the Deadline

A phenomenon that is common to many negotiations is referred to as "crisis bargaining". What this means is that one or both parties make a tactical decision not to offer realistic packages that could bring about a settlement until certain sanctions are imminent. At this point discussions begin in earnest with subcommittees and informal meetings producing proposals, concessions and packages that have not been suggested previously. Eventually, a package will emerge that the negotiators believe will be a basis for settlement.

5. The Ratification of the Agreement

No agreement is final until it is approved by the individuals whom the negotiators represent.

Employer ratification is much more automatic than employee ratification. Although the employer's representatives may find it necessary to "sell" the final package to their superiors, the suggested terms are usually accepted in total. Employee representatives, on the other hand, have been encountering a growing trend for members not to ratify agreements. A study conducted in Ontario by the Industrial Relations Centre at Queen's University indicated that in 1974 over 20 percent of the tentative settlements surveyed were rejected by union members. Such refusals may be spontaneous, but it is not uncommon for union representatives to secretly urge their members to reject a proposed agreement as a bargaining ploy. When ratification is not forthcoming, the negotiators are required to spend more time and effort in the negotiation process.

6. The Duration of Negotiations

Figure 7.1 shows that the collective bargaining process does require a considerable amount of time. During the 1963-70 period the average duration of negotiations was around 6 months. Since 1970 there has been a reduction in the proportion of settlements concluded after negotiations of 3 months or less and an increase in the proportion requiring 10 months or more of negotiations.

IV SOME LEGAL ASPECTS OF CONTRACT NEGOTIATIONS

There are three legal issues that frequently arise during the course of contract negotiations.

1. The Duty to Bargain

All Canadian jurisdictions require that an employer must bargain collectively with the certified representatives of his employees within a specified period of time (sixty days in Ontario) after one of the parties has given notice of its desire to bargain.

Figure 7.1

Major Collective Bargaining Settlements* by Duration of Negotiations, Canada: Selected Years, 1963-74

Duration of Negotiations (in months)	1963		1966		1969		1972		1974	
	Agreements	Employees in Thousands	Agreements	Employees in Thousands	Agreements	Employees in Thousands	Agreements	Employees in Thousands	Agreements	Employees in Thousands
3 months or less	60	101.2	44	115.4	94	255.9	61	77.5	88	215.6
4-6 months	66	77.6	88	144.6	122	197.6	145	263.1	177	325.0
7-9 months	47	53.6	39	106.6	74	124.4	81	152.3	89	185.9
10 months and over	40	66.6	20	25.0	51	205.4	67	302.4	56	185.7
Total	213	299.0	191	391.6	341	783.3	354	795.3	410	912.2
Percentage Distribution										
3 months or less	28.2	33.8	23.0	29.5	27.6	32.7	17.2	9.7	21.5	23.6
4-6 months	31.0	26.0	46.1	36.9	35.8	25.2	41.0	33.1	43.2	35.6
7-9 months	22.0	17.9	20.4	27.2	21.7	15.9	22.9	19.2	21.7	20.4
10 months and over	18.8	22.3	10.5	6.4	14.9	26.2	18.9	38.0	13.6	20.4
Total	100.0	100.0	100.0	100.0	100.0	100.0	100.0	100.0	100.0	100.0

* Settlements involving 500 or more employees in all industries, excluding construction.

Source: Canada Department of Labour, *Collective Bargaining Review.*

2. "Good Faith" in Collective Bargaining

"Good faith" in collective bargaining is an extremely obscure concept. According to one expert on the subject, the concept causes problems in three major areas (7.2):

i) Problems centering around the extent to which subjective attitudes towards collective bargaining conflict with "good faith". In many cases management has refused to bargain with unions on the basis that the union no longer had the support of the majority of employees, that the bargaining committee was not represented by employees of the company involved, or that management strongly distrusted unions. Boards have generally ruled against management for the objective act of refusing the bargain, but *not* for reasons of "bad faith" associated with their subjective attitudes.

ii) Problems of when objective activity at the bargaining table constitutes "bad faith". Canadian boards have generally ruled that, at one extreme, it is the duty of the employer to advise his employees what terms he is willing to accept. At the other extreme, making excessively "unreasonable" demands may also constitute bargaining in bad faith. Any attempt to force an illegal clause on the other party or a refusal to discuss new factors relevant to the current negotiations, such as the recommendations of a conciliation board, are almost certain to be ruled as acts of "bad faith".

iii) Problems associated with the use of economic power. The use of illegal economic pressure (such as unilateral changes in employment conditions by the employer or pre-conciliation work stoppages), is obviously incompatible with "good faith" bargaining. However, there are very few guidelines in Canada which govern the use of legal economic pressures.

The opinion expressed by the Task Force on Labour Relations summarizes the situation that prevails in most Canadian jurisdictions: "We do not think it is useful to industrial relations in Canada to put the issue of good faith bargaining into such an elaborate jurisprudential container (as does the United States). The duty to bargain is not a duty to agree; nor does the right to bargain grant a right to a particular bargain. We see no reason why the subject matter of bargaining should not include anything that is not contrary to law. As to tactics, the highest duty that should reasonably be placed on either party to a bargaining situation, in which each has a claim to preserve its freedom respecting its bargaining position, is to state its position on matters put in issue. But we cannot envisage such a duty being amenable to legal enforcement, except perhaps to the extent of an obligation to meet and exchange positions." (7.3)

However, recent amendments to the Ontario Labour Relations Act may set the stage for a dramatic change of philosophy on the question of "bargaining in good faith".

The Ontario Labour Relations Act now provides for the Ontario Labour Relations Board to investigate complaints and give directions where the duty to bargain in good faith is alleged to have been contravened.

One of the earliest applications of this provision came in 1976 when the Ontario Labour Relations Board ruled on a dispute between Local 13704 of the United Steelworkers of America and Canadian Industries Limited. The union complained that the company had not bargained in good faith because it refused to discuss proposals in excess of what it considered was permitted by the Anti-Inflation Act guidelines. The union had taken the position that negotiations should take place without any reference to the guidelines. The Board cited both parties for failure to bargain in good faith. According to the Board, an employer must bargain on union proposals that in the company's opinion exceed the Anti-Inflation Act guidelines. On the other hand, a union must not refuse to discuss the impact of the guidelines during negotiations.

3.   The Compulsion to Divulge Full Information

There are no legal requirements in Canada that the employer must divulge relevant company data. Such a requirement has been in effect in the United States for many years and is currently being examined more closely in Canada.

Summary:

1.   Each negotiating team should devise a strategy regarding the conduct of contract negotiations. Such a strategy will determine whether the team members will be aggressive or conciliatory, deceptive or candid. Also, a decision must be made as to whether agreement will be made on a piecemeal or package basis, and the use that will be made of subcommittees. While negotiations are in progress, the usefulness of procrastination, caucuses and extended deadlines must all be considered.

2.   Most negotiations contain a number of phases, which include the initial presentation of ambitious demands and conservative offers, the asking of questions and testing of strengths, the clarification of positions, and crisis bargaining. Eventually, an agreement is hammered out and ratified by the constituents of both teams.

3.   Canadian laws require that employers must bargain "in good faith" with duly certified representatives of employees. But "good faith" remains an extremely elusive concept. At present, Canadian employers are not legally obligated to provide company data to members of the opposing negotiating team.

References:

7.1   Dunlop, J.T. and J.J. Healy. *Collective Bargaining.* Homewood, Ill., Irwin, 1953, pp. 54-56.

7.2   Palmer, E.E. "The Myth of Good Faith In Collective Bargaining", *Alberta Law Review,* Vol. 4, 1966.

7.3   *Canadian Industrial Relations.* The Report of the Task Force on Labour Relations. Ottawa, Queen's Printer, 1969, p. 163.

Suggested Readings for Further Study

Allan, A.D. "A Systems View of Labour Negotiations", *Personnel Journal,* February 1971, pp. 103-14.

Backman, Jules. *Wage Determination: An Analysis of Wage Criteria.* Princeton, D. Van Nostrand, 1959.

David, L. and Victer Scheifer. "Estimating the Cost of Collective Bargaining Settlements" Vol. XCII, *Monthly Labour Review.* May, 1969, pp. 16-26.

Healy, James J., ed., *Creative Collective Bargaining.* Englewood Cliffs, N.J., Prentice-Hall, 1965.

The Labour Relations Law Case Book Group. *Labour Relations Law.* Kingston, Ontario, Industrial Relations Centre, Queen's University, 1974, pp. 184-237.

Morse, B. *How to Negotiate the Labour Agreement.* Detroit, Trends Publishing, 1971.

Ryder, M., Charles Rehmus and Sandord Cohen. *Management Preparation for Collective Bargaining.* Homewood, Ill., Dow Jones – Irwin Inc., 1966.

Experiential Assignment

Turn to Chapter 17, Section V and prepare the "Assignment on Contract Negotiations".

Chapter 8

Interest (Contract) Arbitration

I   INTRODUCTION

There are two basic types of union-management disputes. First, there are "rights" disputes that generally arise over the interpretation, application, administration, or alleged violations of the existing collective agreement. Secondly, there are "interest" disputes which involve wages, hours of work, or working conditions that should be included in a new agreement. The former are concerned with rights accrued in the past, while the latter are concerned with the acquisition of rights for the future. This chapter is primarily concerned with providing a general overview of the arbitration of interest disputes. The nature of rights disputes and related arbitration procedures will be discussed in Chapter 11 in the context of contract administration.

When the negotiating parties cannot agree on the terms of a collective agreement, a variety of courses of action are open to them, including carrying on negotiations as before, invoking some type of sanction, or submitting the dispute to a third party for determination. This latter option is referred to as contract or interest arbitration. In Canada there has been relatively limited use of arbitration in settling contract or "interest" disputes. However, in times of heavy strike experience there is often a dramatic growth of interest in contract arbitration by the "innocent bystanders" who are required to suffer some inconvenience and the government officials whom they elect.

II   TYPES OF ARBITRATION PANELS

The decision to resort to contract arbitration may result from the mutual agreement of the negotiating parties or from legislation which invokes arbitration at the request of one party or some outside agency such as the Ministry of Labour. Where the decision to arbitrate is voluntary, the selection of the arbitrator, procedural aspects of the hearing and the issues that will be discussed may all be determined by the disputing parties. However, the responsibility and authority for a final decision rests strictly with the arbitrator whom the parties have chosen. Where arbitration has been invoked by compulsory legislation, the disputing parties may lack influence over the procedures and relevant issues, as well as the final decision.

Under both voluntary and compulsory arbitration the arbitrator may be chosen on an *ad hoc* basis, a permanent basis, or on a tripartite basis.

1.   Ad Hoc Arbitration

Ad hoc arbitration refers to the situation where a single arbitrator is selected on a case-by-case basis by agreement of the parties, or, failing this, the decision is made by a previously specified agency. It is argued that this approach results in less partisanship and a more neutral decision than under the tripartite approach.

2.   A Permanent Arbitrator

Under the "permanent" chairman approach, the parties specify an arbitrator for all disputes which occur during a certain time period. It has been suggested that this approach enables the arbitrator to become sufficiently knowledgeable about the disputants and thereby able to render more consistent decisions than would be possible under the other approaches to arbitration.

3.   The Tripartite Approach

In the tripartite approach the disputing parties each select their own representative on an arbitration committee. The two representatives then pick a neutral chairman. If they are unable to do so within a specified time, a previously specified agency may, on request, appoint a chairman. After hearing the evidence, the chairman may request that his colleagues submit their decisions to him in writing. Alternatively, the chairman may issue his report to his colleagues for their consideration. The final result may be a unanimous decision, a majority report (where the chairman supports the opinion of one of his colleagues), or a decision of the chairman which is unsupported by either of his colleagues. Unless legislation provides otherwise, the decision of the chairman prevails. Any member of the committee who disagrees with the majority finding (or the finding of the chairman), may issue a minority report which could tend to weaken the precedential value of the final outcome. The primary merit of the tripartite approach is the assurance that both disputing parties will have their viewpoints considered during the hearing and in the final report.

III   CRITERIA USED IN THE ARBITRATION OF INTEREST DISPUTES

The task involved in interest arbitration is the same as the task carried out by collective bargaining in Canada. Normally, the arbitrator is required to rely solely upon the haphazard data and arguments presented by the disputing parties as a basis for arriving at an award. Such arguments and data frequently centre around five general issues: comparative wage rates, productivity, ability to pay, cost of living and "special" circumstances. This latter issue of "special circumstances" frequently determines whether an arbitrator will simply "split the difference" or favour either management or the union. Therefore, both parties tend to devote a significant proportion of their efforts to developing sound, logical statements which explain how and why their case is somehow "special".

The following excerpt from an arbitration award for Ontario hospital employees exemplifies some of the factors that may influence an arbitrator's decision on what constitutes an appropriate settlement.

"While the list is not complete, and while no single item is conclusive, we would give the following comparative factors great weight:

1.   Wage paid in 'comparable hospitals', *i.e.,* those of similar type in communities enjoying a similar cost of living and average wage level.

2.   Trends in cost of living and average wages in the locality where the hospital is located.

3   Trends in comparable hospitals.

We would also consider the following factors to be relevant:

1   Difficulties encountered by the hospital in recruiting and holding staff (some evidence of the hospital's failure to pay a level of wages high enough to attract workers on local labour market).

2   Trends in non-comparable hospitals and in non-hospital occupations, where deserving of special consideration.

3   Trends in hospital wages generally.

We would accord little weight to the following factors:

1   Wage level in non-comparable hospitals.

2   Wage levels in non-hospital occupations, where there is not substantial identity of working conditions (*e.g.,* hospital

tradesmen cannot be compared with construction
workers).
3   Abstract appeals to 'justice'.
By looking at various appropriate trends as well as existing
wage levels, an element of flexibility and movement is
preserved which should help to reflect shifts in general
community prosperity and in the relative position of
hospital workers within the community. It is by
reference to these factors that the impact of any
decision to make hospital work more attractive can
be felt." (8.1)

In British Columbia, a board of arbitration recently suggested that the
following criteria be used in interest arbitration awards (8.2).

1. *Public sector employees should not be required to subsidize the
community by accepting substandard wages and working conditions.* "On
balance, the total community which requires the service should shoulder the
financial loss and not expect the employees of the industry to bear an unfair
burden by accepting wages and working conditions which are substandard;
that is not to say that the public sector employer ought to be the best
employer in the community – it need not. Rather, it should be a good
employer and also be seen as a fair employer."

2. *Cost of living.* "It is important to consider the cost of living
standard as a maintenance standard. It is intended to maintain the position of
the employees relative to the balance of the economy. In many respects it
keeps jobs at a stationary level rather than advancing them. To put it simply,
a position valued at $10,000.00 in any economy where the cost of living is
increasing by 10 per cent annually should be valued at $11,000.00 in the
subsequent year."

3. *Productivity.* "A problem arises in public sector situations which are
essentially of a service nature because it is not feasible to assess productivity;
or to put it another way, when productivity cannot be quantified and
documented with respect to a particular group of employees, they should not
be precluded from consideration for productivity increases. Merely because
no scientific or empirical evaluation can be made as to the productivity of a
group of employees does not mean that they should not share in the
productivity of the general community. For this type of situation, statistics
are available which demonstrate the increases in the Gross National Product
and public and quasi-public sector employees should not be denied the
benefits of such productivity advances."

4. *Internal Comparisons.* The Board felt that it was necessary to ensure
that those employees doing work of comparable skill and ability receive
comparable salaries.

"As a practical matter where one employee is doing work which
compares in skill and ability to the work of another employee it will
create a considerable dissatisfaction and create a disruption if those
equivalent positions do not receive equivalent compensation.
In the long run it serves the best interest of all parties to have a system of
job evaluation where comparisons may be made and challenged through

a grievance procedure or other procedure rather than attempt to negotiate these matters, because negotiations constitute an arena where job disputes may be resolved in unscientific trade offs which may have undesirable long-term effects on the total job structure.
In conclusion, internal differentials and internal comparisons must be considered as a factor in interest disputes."

5. *External comparisons in the same industry.* "The external comparison to the same jobs in the industry ensures that the same relationship is maintained among employees who work in the industry and who may be considered to be doing work in similar conditions and thus similar considerations must prevail. Not only can comparisons be more readily made between jobs in the same industry, but there is some virtue in maintaining a competitive position between employers. The inability to compete because of a particular wage structure may result in a diminution of jobs and may cause serious repercussions."

6. *External comparisons using work of a similar nature in different industries.* "The Board stated that it was also appropriate to look beyond a particular industry or public sector situation to determine the patterns set in similar occupations or positions in order to prevent the process from becoming too internalized. Dissatisfaction could arise if unequal rates were paid for the same work in different industries. Accordingly, it is appropriate to compare the wages and working conditions in the public sector against the external employment market as a measure as to the appropriate rates in the public service."
After outlining these criteria, the Board concluded:
"In conclusion, I am of the view that the above criteria may be used in whole or in part in interest disputes and that varying weight may be given to each of the criteria as the individual situation demands. The criteria should enable a form of adjudication based on a more scientific analysis and should also permit the parties to properly prepare for the interest arbitration."

IV   "ACCOMMODATIVE" vs. "NORMATIVE" ARBITRATION
There are two schools of thought as to what the main objective of interest arbitration should be. One school of thought supports the concept of accommodative arbitration. This implies that the arbitrator should strive to make his award approximate the type of solution the parties would have reached on their own in the context of the existing balance of power. The other school of thought supports the concept of normative arbitration. This implies that the arbitrator should make a "just" award based entirely on the merits of the case rather than on the balance of power or the biases of the disputing parties.
There is a tendency for most Canadian arbitrators to shy away from normative arbitration for at least three reasons:
1.   Arbitrators are reluctant to award less than management's last offer or more than the union's last demand. Yet normative bargaining may require them to do so.
2.   Few arbitrators have access to sufficient "objective" information concerning a given situation in the context of a particular industry and region. The best they can do is arrive at a compromise on the basis of the conflicting data provided by the disputing parties.
3.   Most arbitrators wish to avoid the possible legal and financial repercussions that could result from "normative" awards.

V FINAL OFFER SELECTION

The "final offer selection" technique (FOS) represents a creative variation of the traditional methods of contract or interest arbitration. The essence of this approach is that an arbitrator or "selection officer" is given the power to select and impose upon both parties the final negotiating position of one party. The knowledge that one party's final offer is going to be imposed on the other is supposed to stimulate the parties to bargain in good faith, to narrow the issues separating them and to formulate a realistic final position that is supported by sound statistics and reasoning.

In recent years, the use of this technique has expanded considerably, especially among those defined as "essential" employees and newly organized professional groups such as engineers and professors. The experience that has been gained has demonstrated the significance of the following factors in final offer selection (8.3):

1. *What type of panel should make the selection?* Examples are available of cases which involve one or three selectors. Those favouring a single selector indicate that this promotes objectivity, fewer delays and lower expenses. Those favouring a tripartite panel point out the valuable assistance which the side members (the union and management representatives) can provide in dealing with the complexities of the two offers.

2. *Should the selection panel provide written reasons for selecting a particular offer?* Some individuals feel that a written statement of the selection panel's logic should be made available as a guideline for future cases. Others point out that such a requirement can cause delays and have a damaging effect on the spokesmen for either party.

3. *Should mediation form part of the process?* The "sophisticated" format of final offer selection that was originally introduced into Canada consisted of four phases:

a) Preliminary Phases: 1) Before the commencement of negotiations, both parties would agree on a list of potential selection officers who, in turn, would indicate a willingness to serve if so requested, at a convenient time. 2) Negotiations would begin six months before the expiry date of any existing contract, with a list of items drawn up as a result of an exchange of negotiating agendas. 3) Items could be negotiated separately and settled independently. When agreement was reached on any given item or items, such agreement would be contained in a document signed by both sides and the item or items removed from the negotiating agenda.

b) Obtaining the Services of a Selection Officer: 1) At some time prior to two months before contract termination, a selection officer could be brought in at the joint request and expense of both negotiating parties. 2) If all items had not been voluntarily settled two months before the contract expired, either side could elect to bring in a selection officer to help reach a voluntary settlement on the remaining items. 3) The choice of a selection officer could be made by mutual agreement of the negotiating parties and the person chosen or, if after one week agreement could not be reached, through random selection from a predetermined list of names.

c) Mediation Phase: 1) Within three days of the choice of a selection officer, both sides would submit their positions on all outstanding items in writing to the selection officer and to each other. 2) The selection officer would arrange the agenda for discussions. 3) At convenient times during a three-week period, the selection officer would hold hearings, giving equal time to both parties. He would not receive representations from outside parties, but could receive information and evidence concerning the contract in force, the results of the current negotiations to date, comparative benefits of workers and comparative profits of companies. 4) During this three-week period, the selection officer would try to assist the parties to reach agreement, possibly through a trading-off process. Any agreements reached with the assistance of the selection officer during this period would be binding and could not be changed except through agreement of both parties. 5) If all items had not been settled at the end of the three-week mediation period, the negotiating parties would be given one week to put their final positions in writing and submit them to each other and to the selection officer for his final judgment.

   d) Judgment Phase: 1) The selection officer would consider each submission as a package offer and would decide totally in favour of the one he considered the more reasonable. If one side did not have its position submitted in time, the other side would automatically receive the award. 2) The selection officer could call in either party for clarification of its submission, but could not accept any changes in its final offer. 3) The selection officer would submit his decision in writing to both parties and to the Minister of Labour before the expiry date of any existing contract. His decision would be final and binding, forming, with all previously settled items, the contract between the parties. This contract would come into force, retroactively where necessary, at the formal renewal date of the contract. The selection officer would not be required to justify his decision beyond stating that all evidence presented had been considered. 4) Throughout this whole mediation-judgment process there could be no extension of the deadlines without the agreement of both sides.

   During the third phase, the selection panel would be required to assist the parties to reach agreement through a trading-off process. The advocates of this approach believe that mediation tends to lessen the number of issues placed before the selection panel for final adjudication. Those who oppose this modification argue that it simply leads to a delay in the finalization of offers and detracts from the objectivity of the process.

   4. Should the selection panel be permitted the option of choosing between the positions of the two sides on individual items in an offer? A number of selection officers have felt uncomfortable about having to accept a package which contains the "least lousy offer". Consequently, the suggestion has been made that the selection officer should be able to compromise and combine the two offers into an acceptable "final position". However, there is much opposition to this modification of the process because it could encourage parties to leave low priority items in their final offer and would ignore the interdependence of the individual items which make up an offer. In effect, all the disadvantages of normal arbitration would be introduced into the process.

   5. What leeway should the parties be granted with respect to the presentation of evidence to the selection panel? Some individuals advocate that once the selection panel has been constituted, its only contact with the negotiating parties should be the receipt of the final offers and written briefs. In most cases, however, the selection panel finds it necessary to call a hearing to clarify various aspects of the offers and briefs. Ground rules for such hearings should be set out before the selection process begins.

Some individuals also advocate that a selection panel should make its decision only on the basis of the evidence presented to them by the negotiating parties. However, it is difficult to find cases where selection officers have not attempted to obtain some "supplemental" outside evidence to help arrive at a more "rational" decision.

6. *How many offers should the parties be permitted to make?* There are some cases on record in which the selection panel has encouraged the parties to change their positions before a final decision was made. Although this may tend to narrow the issues which must be resolved by final offer selection, it also tends to remove the "finality" which is an integral part of the final offer selection process.

The following is an account provided by a selection officer of the procedures used to deal with a recent teacher-school board dispute (8.4):

"I was selected by the parties in a situation where I encountered substantial sophistication on the part of the representatives of the parties and this permitted the adoption of procedures which were free of conflict and which were expeditious. In this matter the parties, by a written memorandum, set precise time limits. Initially, the parties agreed to carry on negotiations for the purpose of reducing the issues which were to be referred in the form of one final offer from each party. Through this process four of the nine matters which were originally to be incorporated in the final offers were settled. Therefore, there were five remaining matters which were dealt with in each final proposal which was submitted in writing and supported by comprehensive briefs. I was then instructed to exchange these briefs. The parties' were given an opportunity to submit a written response to the brief of the other party. These responses were also exchanged. A hearing date was established when the parties could make their representations and call evidence. While the parties were provided the option of agreeing to not conducting a hearing, in this case a hearing was conducted. At the hearing conducted by me the parties were permitted to "up-date" any statistics which they had included in their final offers. They were also permitted to adduce evidence on other public settlements and to call expert witnesses on what conclusions I should draw from the statistical information already supplied. The procedure went smoothly. Shortly after the hearing the award was made. In accordance with the request of the parties reasons were given for my acceptance of the teachers' final offer. All of the "time locks" imposed by the parties on themselves and on me were satisfied. I was able to study the comprehensive proposals and responses prior to the hearing, but there was no delay and I hope the parties concluded that the cost was reasonable."

Summary

1.   Interest disputes involve future employee rights with respect to wages, hours of work, or working conditions.
2.   Arbitrators for interest disputes can be selected on an *ad hoc* basis, a permanent basis, or a tripartite basis.
3.   There are no universally accepted criteria that can be used in the arbitration of interest disputes. However, such factors as comparative wage

rates, productivity, ability to pay, cost of living and "special circumstances" normally influence the decision of the arbitrator.

4.   Most Canadian arbitrators attempt to provide "accommodative" awards that the parties would have been expected to reach given the realities of the existing environment. Normative awards that seek to establish a "just" settlement tend to be rare in Canada.

5.   Final offer selection is a form of arbitration in which the arbitrator or "selection officer" has the power to designate one party's final offer as a final and binding settlement.

References

8.1   The Labour Relations Law Casebook Group. *Labour Relations Law.* Kingston, Ontario, Industrial Relations Centre, Queen's University, 1974, pp. 28-29.

8.2   Labour Law News. Toronto, June, 1976.

8.3   Ferguson, G.S. "Final Offer Selection". *Canada Labour Views,* March 27, 1975.

8.4   *Ibid.*

Suggested Readings for Further Study

Brown, D. "Interest Arbitration". A Study for the Task Force on Labour Relations. Ottawa, 1970.

Carrothers, A.W.R. *Labour Arbitration In Canada.* Toronto, Butterworths, 1961.

Craig A.W. "Arbitration of Labour-Management Disputes In Canada". *Labour Law Journal,* 1961.

Experiential Assignment

Turn to Chapter 17, Section V 8 and prepare the assignment on "Final Offer Selection".

Chapter 9

Work Stoppages

I   INTRODUCTION

Some degree of employer-employee conflict prevails in every industrialized nation. This conflict can manifest itself in a variety of forms, such as violations of shop rules, lateness and absenteeism, careless job performance, dramatic increases in grievances requiring binding arbitration, wilful destruction of company property and violent mob behavior.

In Canada, the most widely recognized form of employer-employee conflict is the work stoppage. A profound mix of feelings and thoughts can be found among the parties affected by work stoppages. The employees may view work stoppages in a number of ways ranging from a normal part of the bargaining ritual to a visible protest against unsuitable conditions. The union may regard a work stoppage as a symbolic demonstration of power or as part of a planned strategy to undermine a disliked enemy. The employers may think of work stoppages as an unavoidable part of operating a business, or as an unreasonable and uncalled-for interference with the legitimate rights of management. The general public may view work stoppages as the salvation of the working man, or as the greatest shortcoming of the modern industrial relations system.

II   STRIKES AND LOCKOUTS

Although strikes are still the most widely recognized symbol of industrial unrest in Canada, it is presently becoming fashionable in statistical documents to use the general term "work stoppages" rather than "lockouts" or "strikes". This practice avoids the implicit assignment of responsibility for the stoppage to one of the parties.

1.   Defining "Lockouts" and "Strikes"

A "lockout" refers to those situations in which the employer refuses work to employees or closes an establishment in order to force the settlement of a dispute.

A "strike" is an intentional withdrawal of services by a group of employees. Usually, it is regarded as a union's ultimate weapon that is to be used only as a last resort. Strikes may be categorized according to the way they are conducted, by whom they are conducted, and the reasons why they are conducted.

a) Ways of Conducting Strikes
i)   Walk-out strikes
   This is the most common form of strike. It is undertaken by employees who cease work in order to gain economic concessions or to protest certain actions of management.
ii)   Slowdown strikes
   Slowdowns represent situations where employees remain on their jobs but restrict their output. Under such circumstances, employers often retaliate with a lockout.
iii)   Sitdown strikes
   These are work stoppages in which employees remain at their jobs but refuse to carry out the tasks assigned them. This technique makes it virtually impossible for the employer to use strikebreakers or supervisory personnel to keep the plant in operation during a strike. Sitdown strikes often lead to violence and have been made illegal in most jurisdictions.
b) The Employees Involved in Strikes
i)   Wildcat strikes
   These are strikes called without the authorization of the union. Such

strikes will be illegal if they violate the union constitution or existing collective agreement and can result in severe penalties being inflicted on the participants.

ii) Sympathy strikes (not encouraged now)

In a sympathy strike employees cease work to demonstrate moral support for strikers from another bargaining unit. At present, the legality of sympathy strikes is being questioned seriously in most jurisdictions. The traditional union justification for absentee workers, "fear of bodily harm", is no longer readily accepted by employers. Instead, employers are becoming more determined to have the courts declare sympathy strikes to be concerted, organized efforts by the union to break an existing collective agreement with the company.

iii) General strikes

A general strike includes most of the organized employees in a geographical area. It is usually designed to protest rules or practices imposed by the federal or provincial government. Canada's first general strike, the violent Winnipeg General Strike of 1919, has been well documented in Canadian history books. In recent years there has been growing support within the labour movement to again make use of this weapon as a protest against governmental actions which are not in the best interests of labour.

c) Reasons for Strikes

i) Contract strikes

This refers to work stoppages that take place to force the employer to grant certain concessions to employees.

ii) Unfair labour practice strikes

Strikes that are designed to protest the actions of management during the organization of a union, or while a collective agreement is in effect have, for the most part, been outlawed in Canada. Alternative institutions, such as labour relations boards and grievance arbitration, appear to have lessened the need for these types of strikes.

iii) Jurisdictional strikes

Jurisdictional strikes generally involve disputes among competing unions over the rights to represent certain employees and to fill certain jobs. Labour relations boards have been gradually accorded sufficient legal power to eliminate the need for such strikes.

2. The Legality of Work Stoppages

The "timeliness" or legality of a strike depends on whether or not the following conditions apply:

1. *Have bargaining rights been acquired by the union?* All Canadian jurisdictions (except Saskatchewan) require that a union must have acquired bargaining rights either through certification or voluntary recognition before it can legally engage in a strike. The purpose of this requirement is to prevent employees from bypassing statutory procedures which are designed to eliminate recognition disputes.

2. *Is a collective agreement in effect?* In all jurisdictions (except Saskatchewan) strikes are prohibited during the term of a collective agreement.

3. *Have required conciliation procedures been followed?* In many jurisdictions a strike is prohibited until after a government-appointed conciliation officer and/or a conciliation board has investigated a dispute and submitted a report to the Minister of Labour. Specific time limits are set out for this process.

4. *Has the necessary majority of employees in the bargaining unit voted to authorize strike action?* A strike vote is a statutory requirement in some jurisdictions. Even where such a vote is not legally required, it is a common practice for unions to take a vote of employees prior to any strike action to gauge the probable reaction of members to a breakdown of negotiations.

Where an illegal strike does occur and the employer wishes to prosecute the strikers, he is normally required by law to:

1.   Apply to the labour relations board for confirmation that a strike is illegal.
2.   Apply to the labour relations board for permission to prosecute the offending union.
3.   Apply to the courts for an appropriate remedy.

Some jurisdictions, Ontario for example, have revised their laws so that the labour relations board can issue injunctions directly against any union engaging in an illegal strike. Violation of the injunction places the union in contempt of court and makes it liable to severe penalties involving heavy fines and possible imprisonment of its officers.

3.   The Rights and Obligations of Employees Engaged in a Legal Work Stoppage

The rights and obligations of the parties engaged in a legal work stoppage have never been clearly defined in any Canadian jurisdiction. Some of the most important questions that have arisen in this respect include:

1. *The employee's right to his job after the strike is settled.* All Canadian labour statutes offer striking employees protection against losing their jobs or benefits as a result of actions taken in support of a strike. However, an employer can legitimately discharge an employee after a strike if it can be demonstrated that the job has been eliminated for reasons that are unrelated to anti-unionism.

2. *The right of the employer to hire replacements during a strike.* In most Canadian jurisdictions, the employer has the right to replace striking employees. While this still remains a contentious topic for debate, increasing numbers of violent incidents seem to be generating a growing sympathy for a ban on professional strikebreakers.

3. *Employees' rights to benefits during the strike period.* The entitlement of a striker to employment-related benefits and his eligibility for various forms of public assistance are important considerations. At present, only a minority of labour statutes offer striking workers any protection of benefits while on strike. In addition, striking workers are not eligible for benefits under the Unemployment Insurance Act or the Canada Assistance Plan.

4. *The obligations of striking employees to their employer.* There is no clear cut legislation which specifies what obligations striking employees must fulfil during a strike. For the most part, as long as an employee does not participate in violent or destructive actions and does not accept employment elsewhere, there are few specific grounds that will warrant discharge on the grounds of "employee negligence" while a work stoppage is in progress.

5. *The obligations of striking employees to the public.* In some cases, however, employees and unions may be deemed to owe specific obligations to the general public. The Government of British Columbia recently took what it deemed to be appropriate action in the face of a withdrawal of services by the

non-professional staff of a large Vancouver hospital. The Labour Minister ordered the British Columbia Labour Relations Board to designate facilities and services essential to the prevention of immediate danger to life, health, or safety. The Board complied and instructed the hospital to keep a specific number of beds available and ordered certain "essential" union members to stay on the job. In addition, the Board required the union to allow ambulances, blood delivery, oxygen, medical supplies and "essential" food services through the picket line. Officers of the Board were dispatched to maintain a continuous surveillance over safety standards and to deal with disputes that arose over the duties of the designated union workers.

4. Picketing During Work Stoppages

Once the union has chosen to incur the costs of a strike, employees will be called off their jobs and an attempt will be made to shut down the plant. A strike will not be effective in situations where the employer can split the ranks of strikers by getting some to work during the strike, by replacing striking workers, or by farming out work to other plants. The primary means for avoiding these situations is the picket line.

Picketing refers to the conveyance of information by union members to fellow workers and to members of the public. Usually, the gist of the information is "Do not cross the picket line". In many cases, the peaceful communication of information by carrying signs and by word of mouth is sufficient to elicit a cooperative response. Where it does not, those on strike may decide to issue verbal and physical threats to intimidate and prevent persons and goods from crossing the picket line.

There is a wide variation amongst Canada's eleven labour relations jurisdictions as to what employees may or may not do while picketing. In general, the following practices are frequently discouraged or prohibited:

1. Allowing the situation to reach a point where there is a strong possibility of serious violence.
2. Secondary picketing where employees picket at the premises of suppliers or customers of the employer.
3. Assaulting persons attempting to enter the organization being struck.
4. Damaging company property.
5. Obstructing a highway or roadway to prevent vehicles from going in and out.

Where these sorts of practices prevail, the employer may call upon the courts to issue an injunction or restraining order which may limit, or even prohibit, picketing for a certain time period.

5. Employer Activities During Work Stoppages

The employer has to decide whether or not it is feasible to continue operating during a work stoppage. If the employer does not feel he can operate, he must be prepared to shut down his plant, secure his property and continue bargaining.

Employers who choose to operate during a work stoppage should obtain the following information:

1. Will there be a sufficient supply of workers available to continue operations from:
   - supervisory personnel?
   - employees not represented by the striking union?
   - strike replacements?
   - unionized employees unsympathetic to the strike?
2. Will all legislative requirements governing safety be complied with?

3.   Are there sufficient numbers of security personnel to protect operating employees and property?
4.   What type of pay system will govern employees that work during the strike?
5.   Will it be worthwhile to document improper activities on the picket line by using photographs, detailed notes and, perhaps, the services of special investigators?
6.   What alterations can be expected in relationships with contractors, suppliers, customers and carriers of shipments?

A handbook prepared by the Canadian Manufacturers' Association suggests that any company choosing to remain in operation should be prepared to take the following actions:
1.   Move essential records to another location.
2.   Prepare accommodation in the plant where necessary for those who will be working.
3.   Make it clear to nonstrikers that they are expected to cross the picket lines and can do so legally. However, such employees are not expected to take undue personal risks.
4.   Never negotiate with the union over which employees may enter the plant, since all employees have the legal right to enter the plant whenever they are scheduled to perform work.
5.   Advise supervisors to refrain from any words or actions which might suggest that an employee will be discriminated against or coerced in any way either because he goes on strike or because he elects to report for work.

III   BOYCOTTS

In situations where the union becomes involved in a work stoppage, an effort is often made to gain the cooperation of those who are not directly involved in the dispute. A common strategy to gain such cooperation is to use a boycott.

A boycott refers to any refusal by employees to handle, transport, sell, or purchase particular goods or services. Where such actions are directed against the employer of the participants, the situation is described as a primary boycott. Primary boycotts tend to be ineffective because employees seldom have sufficient purchasing power to be of any great significance. Actions which are directed against someone with whom an employer does business are described as secondary boycotts. In order to augment the bargaining power of individuals outside their bargaining unit, employees may refuse to handle the products or services of another company and attempt to force their employer to obtain such goods or services elsewhere (or even do without such goods or services).

IV   THE COSTS OF WORK STOPPAGES

1.   Work Stoppage Statistics (9.1)

The recent history of work stoppages in Canada is summarized in the statistical appendix to this chapter. These quantitative reports reflect the fact that although the number of work stoppages is important, the number of employees involved and the number of days lost must also be considered. Therefore, a "man-days lost" figure is often calculated as a rough indicator of the seriousness of work stoppages during a particular time period.

The statistics demonstrate that both the number of work stoppages and the number of man-days lost have been rapidly escalating during the 1970's. An international survey of strikes in a number of industrialized nations showed that Canada was among the top three nations in terms of man-days lost during the decade 1962-1971. A recent report of the International Labour Organization indicates that Canada was second in the world in 1974 in man-days lost through strikes and related work stoppages.

However, when making international comparisons, one should keep in mind the results of a study by Malcom Fisher, entitled *Measurement of Labour Disputes and Their Economic Effects* (9.2). This study points out that there are too many differences in the way statistics are gathered and reported in different countries for any reliable comparisons to be made. Specifically, countries vary in terms of:

1.   The minimum amount of time a work stoppage must last in order to be recorded (for instance, in Finland it is two hours, in the U.S. it is a shift, in certain other countries it is a day).

2.   The minimum number of man-days lost before anything is recorded (for example, 10 man-days lost in Australia, Canada, West Germany and Ireland, but 100 in Denmark).

3.   The inclusion of information on workers indirectly laid off because of labour disputes.

4.   The types of strikes that are reported (for example, Ireland, Italy, Britain and the United States report only industrial and sympathy strikes, while other countries include political strikes in their statistics).

On a jurisdictional breakdown, considerably more than one-half of all work stoppages occur in Ontario and Quebec. Both the federal jurisdiction and British Columbia are not far behind in terms of the number of work stoppages and man-days lost. Industrially, a high proportion of the work stoppages usually take place in manufacturing, construction, transportation and mining. However, work stoppages have increased dramatically in public administration, education and health and welfare sectors. It is also interesting to observe that a few unions seem to consistently account for a relatively high proportion of the total number of work stoppages in some parts of the country.

Finally, it is worth noting that a significant proportion of negotiations do not result in a settlement until work stoppages have occured.

Some of the main causes that have been suggested for these trends include:

1.   The extension of the collective bargaining process to the public and para-public sectors.

2.   Increasing unionization in general.

3.   More young people in the labour force.

4.   The uncertainties associated with "double-digit" inflation.

Although these trends are of real significance to everyone interested in labour relations, it is not possible to analyze them adequately in the context of the topics covered in this book.

2.   Indirect Costs and Benefits of Work Stoppages

The true costs of work stoppages are not easily quantified. Any attempt to do so must somehow take into consideration the following issues:

a) The "offset factor theory" (9.3) — Some individuals argue that certain strikes do not cost the economy anything in terms of lost production. Their reasoning draws attention to the fact that in some industries, especially where durable goods are involved, the production that is lost during a work stoppage can be recouped in a number of ways including:
- increased output prior to a strike
- increased production of competitors during a strike

- increased production at other plants during a strike
- increased production levels after the strike is over.

b) Secondary idleness — Many work stoppages result in shortages of materials, services, or clientele in other sectors of the economy. Consequently, a significant number of individuals may find themselves subjected to layoffs as a result of work stoppages being conducted elsewhere.

c) Psychological factors — It has been found in certain instances that post-strike productivity levels greatly exceed those which prevailed prior to a work stoppage. This result has been attributed to the release of tension and feelings of inferiority that prevailed before the strike period. However, examples can also be found of decreased productivity after prolonged disputes. Internal frictions between supervisory and production personnel may be magnified during the strike period and are not easily forgotten when employees return to their jobs (9.4).

d) Future bargaining power — The basic issue behind some work stoppages is not so much the terms of the new contract as it is the balance of power between the two parties in future years. The threat of a strike may lose its effectiveness unless it is occasionally carried out. Also, items negotiated in the new contract can set a pattern for other employee groups and for future years. Obviously, these futuristic considerations are almost impossible to quantify.

V   CONCLUSION

The work stoppage must be viewed as an integral part of our system that encourages unionism and collective bargaining. As Bakke has noted:
>". . . the strike itself is not the conflict, but a symptom of it. Trying merely to end strikes is like trying to end fevers and ignoring the cause of the fever" (9.5).

Bakke goes on to compare many of the proposals to eliminate strikes with decapitation which, he claims "will cure a headache but can scarcely be considered a rational remedy".

With this perspective in mind a continuing effort must be made to lessen the frequency and impact of work stoppages by systematically eliminating their causes. Unfortunately, as the years pass many related accomplishments in this respect go unrecognized. The violence once associated with jurisdictional disputes, the battles for union recognition and the work stoppages attributed to grievance disputes have, to a great extent, become relics of the past. It is usually forgotten that none of these practices was eliminated overnight. Patience and persistence were necessary to discover workable procedures that the disputing parties would accept. The same patience and persistence will be a necessary prerequisite for any future solution to the problems associated with work stoppages in Canada.

Summary

1.   Work stoppages may be initiated by the employer (lockouts) or the union (strikes) for a variety of reasons.

2.   For a work stoppage to be legal, the union must have legally acquired

bargaining rights, no collective agreement between the parties should be in effect and stipulated conciliation procedures must have been adhered to.

3.   In most jurisdictions employees cannot be deprived of their jobs as a result of supporting a strike, employers have the legal right to hire replacements during a strike and employees have few obligations to their employers during a strike period.

4.   Picketing is used by those on strike to prevent fellow workers and members of the public from entering the struck plant for the purpose of performing the duties of striking workers.

5.   A boycott is a refusal by company employees to handle, transport, sell, or purchase particular goods or services. Such actions may be directed against the employer or the participants in the boycott (a primary boycott), or against someone with whom the employer does business (a secondary boycott).

6.   Work stoppage statistics usually provide information on the number of work stoppages, the number of employees involved and the duration of work stoppages.

7.   The effect of "offset factors", secondary idleness, psychological factors and future bargaining considerations must all be evaluated in assessing the costs of work stoppages.

References

9.1   Beaucage, A. *An Outline of the Canadian Industrial Relations System.* Ottawa, Canada Department of Labour, 1976.

9.2   *Labour Gazette.* March, 1976, p. 123.

9.3   Christenson, C.L. "The Theory of the Offset Factor: The Impact of Labour Disputes upon Coal Production". *The American Economic Review,* XLIII, September, 1953, pp. 513-547.

9.4   Morris, J. "The Psychoanalysis of Labour Strikes". *Labour Law Journal,* December, 1959, pp. 833-844.

9.5   Bakke, E.W. *et al. Unions, Management and the Public.* New York, Harcourt Brace & World, Inc., 1967, p. 278.

Suggested Readings for Further Study

Anton, F.R. *Government Supervised Strike Voting.* Toronto, CCH Canadian Ltd., 1961.

Arthurs, H.W. "Labour Disputes in Essential Industries", A Study for the Task Force on Labour Relations. Ottawa, 1970.

Jamieson, Stuart. "Times of Trouble. Labour Unrest and Industrial Conflict in Canada, 1900-66". A Study for the Task Force on Labour Relations. Ottawa, 1968.

Kerr and Seigal. "The Inter Industry Propensity to Strike — An International Comparison". In A. Kornhauser, *The Industrial Conflict.* New York, McGraw-Hill, 1956.

The Labour Relations Law Case Book Group. *Labour Relations Law.* Kingston, Ontario, Industrial Relations Centre, Queen's University, 1974, pp. 400-495.

Masters, D.C. *The Winnipeg General Strike.* Toronto, University of Toronto Press, 1950.

Rand, Hon. Ivan C. "Ontario Royal Commission Inquiry Into Labour Disputes - The Rand Report". Toronto, CCH Canada Limited, 1968.

Vanderkamp, John. "The Time Pattern of Industrial Conflict in Canada, 1901-1966". A Study for the Task Force on Labour Relations, Ottawa, 1970.

Experiential Assignment

A.   As a member of the Yourtown Public Library System Board (see Chapter 17), how would you prepare for a strike to be conducted by Professional Librarians?

B.   As the president of the Canadian Union of Public Librarians, Local 100 (see Chapter 17), how would you prepare for a strike to be conducted by your membership?

STATISTICAL APPENDIX TO CHAPTER 9

Figure A.9.1

Work Stoppages in Selected Countries — 1955-1974

Country	Number of industrial disputes	Workers involved[1] (thousands)	Working days lost (thousands)	Days lost per thousand employees[2]
UNITED STATES[3]				
1955	4,320	2,650	28,200	571
1956	3,825	1,900	33,100	648
1957	3,673	1,390	16,500	320
1958	3,694	2,060	23,900	471
1959	3,708	1,880	69,000	1,320
1960	3,333	1,320	19,100	358
1961	3,367	1,450	16,300	304
1962	3,614	1,230	18,600	338
1963	3,362	941	16,100	286
1964	3,655	1,640	22,900	395
1965	3,963	1,550	23,300	388
1966	4,405	1,960	25,400	407
1967	4,595	2,870	42,100	649
1968	5,045	2,650	49,018	737
1969	5,700	2,481	42,869	626
1970	5,716	3,305	66,414	956
1971	5,138	3,280	47,589	681
1972	5,010	1,714	27,066	374
1973	5,353	2,251	27,948	373
1974	5,900	2,700	48,000	629
CANADA[4]				
1955	159	60	1,875	466
1956	229	89	1,246	291
1957	245	81	1,477	333
1958	259	111	2,817	631
1959	216	95	2,227	482
1960	274	49	739	156
1961	287	98	1,335	278
1962	311	74	1,418	285
1963	332	83	917	178
1964	343	101	1,581	295
1965	501	172	2,350	416
1966	617	411	5,178	803
1967	522	252	3,975	641
1968	582	224	5,083	787
1969	595	307	7,752	1,170
1970	542	262	6,540	970
1971	569	240	2,867	414
1972	598	706	7,754	1,075
1973	724	318	5,776	754
1974	1,216	592	9,255	1,156
FRANCE				
1955	2,672	1,061	3,079	277
1956	2,440	982	1,423	125
1957	2,623	2,964	4,121	353
1958	954	1,112	1,138	96
1959	1,512	940	1,938	163
1960	1,494	1,072	1,070	89
1961	1,963	2,552	2,601	213
1962	1,884	1,472	1,901	151
1963	2,382	2,646	5,991	460
1964	2,281	2,603	2,497	185
1965	1,674	1,237	980	71
1966	1,711	3,341	2,524	180
1967	1,675	2,824	4,204	295
1968	1,103	464	423	29
1969	2,480	1,444	2,224	150
1970	3,319	1,160	1,742	114
1971	4,358	3,235	4,388	282
1972	3,464	2,721	3,755	237
1973	3,731	2,246	3,915	241
1974	3,984	1,714	3,377	208

Figure A.9.1 (Continued)

Country	Number of industrial disputes	Workers involved[1] (thousands)	Working days lost (thousands)	Days lost per thousand employees[2]
GERMANY[6]				
1955	(7)	600	857	52
1956	(7)	52	1,580	93
1957	(7)	45	1,072	61
1958	(7)	203	782	44
1959	(7)	22	62	3
1960	(7)	17	38	2
1961	(7)	20	61	3
1962	(7)	79	451	22
1963	(7)	316	1,846	90
1964	(7)	6	17	1
1965	(7)	6	49	2
1966	(7)	196	27	1
1967	(7)	60	390	19
1968	(7)	25	25	1
1969	(7)	90	249	12
1970	(7)	184	93	4
1971	(7)	536	4,484	207
1972	(7)	23	66	3
1973	(7)	185	563	26
1974	(7)	250	1,051	49
ITALY[8]				
1955	1,864	1,186	3,497	400
1956	1,781	1,240	1,937	216
1957	1,646	1,117	3,287	355
1958	1,756	1,147	2,606	278
1959	1,800	1,464	7,282	762
1960	2,348	1,754	4,254	427
1961	3,388	2,408	7,880	766
1962	3,532	2,652	19,045	1,800
1963	4,003	3,398	10,075	928
1964	3,727	3,063	11,328	1,045
1965	3,061	2,075	5,945	567
1966	2,299	1,690	13,620	1,307
1967	2,554	1,987	7,294	683
1968	3,272	4,414	8,299	763
1969	3,698	6,752	35,325	3,186
1970	4,065	3,520	17,861	1,560
1971	5,482	3,452	10,699	924
1972	4,699	4,078	15,591	1,347
1973	4,063	9,620	20,402	1,723
JAPAN[9]				
1955	659	1,033	3,467	204
1956	646	1,098	4,562	249
1957	827	1,557	5,634	287
1958	903	1,279	6,052	293
1959	887	1,216	6,020	278
1960	1,063	918	4,912	216
1961	1,401	1,680	6,150	257
1962	1,299	1,518	5,400	214
1963	1,079	1,183	2,770	106
1964	1,234	1,050	3,165	117
1965	1,542	1,682	5,669	201
1966	1,252	1,132	2,742	93
1967	1,214	733	1,830	60
1968	1,546	1,163	2,841	91
1969	1,783	1,412	3,634	115
1970	2,260	1,720	3,915	120
1971	2,527	1,896	6,029	178
1972	2,498	2,544	5,147	149
1973	3,326	2,236	4,604	129
1974	6,100	4,055	9,684	270

Country	Number of industrial disputes	Workers involved[1] (thousands)	Working days lost (thousands)	Days lost per thousands[2] employees[2]
SWEDEN				
1955	18	3.9	158.8	65 [9]
1956	12	1.6	4.0	2 [9]
1957	17	1.6	53.0	21 [9]
1958	10	0.1	15.0	6 [9]
1959	17	1.2	23.9	9 [9]
1960	31	1.5	18.5	7 [9]
1961	12	0.1	2.1	1
1962	10	3.5	5.0	2
1963	24	2.8	25.0	8
1964	14	1.9	34.0	11
1965	8	0.2	4.1	1
1966	26	29.4	351.6	112
1967	7	0.1	0.4	(10)
1968	7	0.4	1.2	(10)
1969	41	9.0	112.4	35
1970	134	26.7	155.7	48
1971	60	62.9	839.0	250
1972	44	7.1	10.5	3
1973	48	5.0	12.4	4
1974	---	25.8	59.1	17
UNITED KINGDOM[11]				
1955	2,419	671	3,781	180
1956	2,648	508	2,083	98
1957	2,859	1,359	8,412	394
1958	2,629	524	3,462	163
1959	2,093	646	5,270	247
1960	2,832	819	3,024	138
1961	2,686	779	3,046	137
1962	2,449	4,423	5,798	258
1963	2,068	593	1,755	78
1964	2,524	883	2,277	100
1965	2,354	876	2,925	127
1966	1,937	544	2,398	103
1967	2,116	734	2,787	122
1968	2,378	2,258	4,690	207
1969	3,116	1,665	6,846	302
1970	3,906	1,801	10,980	488
1971	2,228	1,178	13,551	625
1972	2,497	1,734	23,909	1,102
1973	2,873	1,528	7,197	324
1974	2,882	1,605	14,740	664

[1] Workers are counted more than once if they were involved in more than 1 stoppage during the year.

[2] Per thousand persons with paid hours in nonagricultural industries. Days lost include all stoppages in effect.

[3] The number of stoppages and workers relate to those stoppages beginning in the year. Excludes disputes involving fewer than 6 workers and those lasting less than 1 full day or shift.

[4] Excludes disputes in which the time lost is less than 10 man-days. Excludes workers indirectly affected.

[5] May and June, the period of the national strike, excluded.

[6] Excludes the Saar for 1955-56 and includes West Berlin beginning 1961. Excludes disputes lasting less than 1 day, except those involving a loss of more than 100 working days.

[7] Not available.

[8] Excludes strikes in the agriculture sector, political strikes, and workers indirectly affected, except for 1973 which includes agriculture.

[9] Excludes workers indirectly affected and disputes lasting less than 4 hours.

[10] Less than 0.5 days.

[11] Excludes disputes (a) not connected with terms of employment or conditions of labor, and (b) involving fewer than 10 workers or lasting less than 1 day, unless a loss of more than 100 working days is involved.

SOURCE: *Year Book of Labour Statistics* (Geneva, International Labour Office), various issues, and national publications.

SOURCE: U.S. Department of Labor, Bureau of Labor Statistics, *Handbook of Labor Statistics 1975 — Reference Edition.*

Figure A.9.2

Strikes and Lockouts in Canada / Grèves et lock-out au Canada

Year / Année	Number Beginning During Year / Nombre déclaré dans l'année	Strikes and Lockouts in Existence During Year Grèves et lock-out en cours durant l'année			
				Duration in Man-Days Durée en jours-hommes	
		Number / Nombre	Workers Involved / Travailleurs en cause	Man-Days/ Jours-hommes	% of Estimated Working Time / % du temps de travail estimatif
1901	97	99	24,089	737,808	—
1902	124	125	12,709	203,301	—
1903	171	175	38,408	858,959	—
1904	103	103	11,420	192,890	—
1905	95	96	12,513	246,138	—
1906	149	150	23,382	378,276	—
1907	183	188	34,060	520,142	—
1908	72	76	26,071	703,571	—
1909	88	90	18,114	880,663	—
1910	94	101	22,203	731,324	—
1911	99	100	29,285	1,821,084	—
1912	179	181	42,860	1,135,786	—
1913	143	152	40,519	1,036,254	—
1914	58	63	9,717	490,850	—
1915	62	63	11,395	95,042	—
1916	118	120	26,538	236,814	—
1917	158	160	50,255	1,123,515	—
1918	228	230	79,748	647,942	—
1919	332	336	148,915	3,400,942	0.60
1920	310	322	60,327	799,524	0.14
1921	159	168	28,257	1,048,914	0.22
1922	89	104	43,775	1,528,661	0.32
1923	77	86	34,261	671,750	0.13
1924	64	70	34,310	1,295,065	0.26
1925	86	87	28,949	1,193,281	0.23
1926	75	77	23,834	266,601	0.05
1927	72	74	22,299	152,570	0.03
1928	96	98	17,581	224,212	0.04
1929	88	90	12,946	152,080	0.02
1930	67	67	13,768	91,797	0.01
1931	86	88	10,738	204,238	0.04
1932	111	116	23,390	255,000	0.05
1933	122	125	20,558	317,547	0.07
1934	189	191	45,800	574,519	0.11
1935	120	120	33,269	288,703	0.05
1936	155	156	34,812	276,997	0.05
1937	274	278	71,905	886,393	0.15
1938	142	147	20,399	148,678	0.02
1939	120	122	47,038	224,588	0.04
1940	166	168	60,619	266,318	0.04

Figure A.9.2 (continued)

Strikes and Lockouts in Existence During Year
Grèves et lock-out en cours durant l'année

Year / Année	Number Beginning During Year / Nombre déclaré dans l'année	Number/ Nombre	Workers Involved / Travailleurs en cause	Duration in Man-Days Durée en jours-hommes	
				Man-Days / Jours-hommes	% of Estimated Working Time / % du temps de travail estimatif
1941	´ 229	231	87,091	433,914	0.06
1942	352	354	113,916	450,202	0.05
1943	401	402	218,404	1,041,198	0.12
1944	195	199	75,290	490,139	0.06
1945	196	197	96,068	1,457,420	0.19
1946	223	226	138,914	4,515,030	0.54
1947	231	234	103,370	2,366,340	0.27
1948	147	154	42,820	885,790	0.10
1949	130	135	46,867	1,036,820	0.11
1950	158	160	192,083	1,387,500	0.15
1951	256	258	102,793	901,620	0.09
1952	213	219	112,273	2,765,510	0.29
1953	166	173	54,488	1,312,720	0.14
1954	155	173	56,630	1,430,300	0.15
1955	149	159	60,090	1,875,400	0.19
1956	221	229	88,680	1,246,000	0.11
1957	238	245	80,695	1,477,100	0.13
1958	251	259	111,475	2,816,850	0.25
1959	201	216	95,120	2,226,890	0.19
1960	268	274	49,408	738,700	0.06
1961	272	287	97,959	1,335,080	0.11
1962	290	311	74,382	1,417,900	0.11
1963	318	332	83,428	917,140	0.07
1964	327	343	100,535	1,580,550	0.11
1965	478	501	171,870	2,349,870	0.17
1966	582	617	411,459	5,178,170	0.34
1967	498	522	252,018	3,974,760	0.25
1968	559	582	223,562	5,082,732	0.32
1969	566	595	306,799	7,751,880	0.46
1970	503	542	261,706	6,539,560	0.39
1971	547	569	239,631	2,866,590	0.16
1972	556	598	706,474	7,753,530	0.43
1973	677	724	348,470	5,776,080	0.30
1974	1170	1216	592,220	9,255,120	0.46

Source: *Strikes and Lockouts in Canada/Grèves et lock-out au Canada.*
Labour Canada — Travail Canada, Ottawa.

Figure A.9.3

Work Stoppages in Canada by Jurisdiction, 1968-1973

Jurisdiction	1968	1969	1970	1971	1972*	1973*
			Number of Strikes and Lockouts			
Federal	22	20	20	30	30	43
Newfoundland	9	8	8	29	31	31
Prince Edward Island	1	–	1	5	1	2
Nova Scotia	32	60	63	33	21	23
New Brunswick	13	17	17	17	17	13
Quebec	128	141	126	134	119	132
Ontario	286	238	215	202	168	176
Manitoba	6	6	6	10	11	17
Saskatchewan	18	20	12	6	17	10
Alberta	10	15	10	19	8	22
British Columbia	57	70	64	84	55	74
TOTAL	582	595	542	569	478	543
			Number of Man-Days Lost			
Federal	498,960	472,960	341,600	152,030	297,620	1,011,170
Newfoundland	24,490	168,130	2,630	158,200	252,110	201,910
Prince Edward Island	10	–	1,960	3,820	20	140
Nova Scotia	18,660	86,840	257,240	117,580	86,320	109,970
New Brunswick	20,020	13,230	48,240	29,780	41,910	86,690
Quebec	1,003,440	1,259,030	1,417,560	603,120	2,824,630	1,600,130
Ontario	2,922,090	5,318,770	2,547,210	1,366,750	2,160,140	1,685,790
Manitoba	13,900	11,180	54,230	82,760	53,990	113,840
Saskatchewan	36,140	34,010	56,450	1,910	80,800	23,460
Alberta	58,622	64,000	37,160	83,020	24,600	182,990
British Columbia	486,400	323,730	1,775,280	267,620	2,182,150	589,920
TOTAL	5,082,732	7,751,880	6,539,560	2,866,590	8,004,290	5,606,010

* Preliminary total estimates calculated from the monthly research bulletins published by Labour Canada, Economic and Research Branch, in *Research Bulletin: Work Stoppages.*

Figure A.9.4

Work Stoppages in Canada by Industry, 1968-1973

Industry	1968	1969	1970	1971	1972*	1973*
	Number of Strikes and Lockouts					
Forestry, Fishing	6	12	5	28	11	5
Mining	21	27	15	19	24	29
Manufacturing	342	284	263	278	243	283
Construction	103	118	109	72	52	51
Transportation and Utilities	40	46	48	55	52	58
Trade	31	44	42	46	39	48
Finance	–	–	–	1	2	–
Service	21	51	47	43	24	47
Public Administration	16	13	13	27	31	22
TOTAL	582	595	542	569	478	543
	Number of Man-Days Lost					
Forestry, Fishing	9,740	8,100	2,010	89,980	71,620	37,000
Mining	100,800	2,087,490	53,680	193,490	425,080	247,160
Manufacturing	3,746,190	2,690,260	3,630,670	1,541,520	2,203,310	3,271,150
Construction	275,510	1,981,300	2,156,890	400,990	1,440,090	449,440
Transportation and Utilities	490,090	559,460	379,990	254,270	1,317,650	1,049,660
Trade	366,712	270,930	46,220	81,040	62,360	195,120
Finance	–	–	–	1,140	1,770	–
Service	26,000	141,250	239,440	220,440	138,230	261,030
Public Administration	67,540	13,090	130,660	83,720	2,344,180	95,450
TOTAL	5,082,732	7,751,880	6,539,560	2,866,590	8,004,290	5,606,010

* Preliminary total estimates calculated from the monthly research bulletins published by Labour Canada, Economics and Research Branch, in *Research Bulletin: Work Stoppages*.

Figure A.9.5

**Work stoppages in public administration,
education, health and welfare**

Period	Number of stoppages	* %	Number of workers involved	* %	Man-days lost in these sectors	* %
1960-64	43	2.8	8,600	2.1	6,590	1.0
1965-69	139	4.9	196,358	14.4	1,401,000	5.8
1970-74	345	9.5	604,953	28.2	3,393,390	10.5

* percentage of the whole economy

Source: *Strikes and Lockouts in Canada,* Labour Canada, Ottawa

Figure A.9.6

Settlements and Work Stoppages, Selected Unions*
Ontario, 1974

	Number of Settlements	Number of Work Stoppages
Auto Workers	43	13
Carpenters	11	2
Chemical Workers	9	3
CUPE	56	2
United Electrical Workers	6	3
Food Workers	10	4
Machinists	13	5
Public Service Alliance	15	0
Rubber Workers	12	6
Service Employees	24	0
Steelworkers	60	14
Textile Workers	12	1
Wood Workers	11	2

* Unions with 10 or more settlements or 3 or more work stoppages.

Collective Bargaining Settlements* By Method of Settlement,
Canada: Selected Years, 1963-74

Method of Settlement	1963 Agreements	1963 Employees in Thousands	1966 Agreements	1966 Employees in Thousands	1969 Agreements	1969 Employees in Thousands	1972 Agreements	1972 Employees in Thousands	1974 Agreements	1974 Employees in Thousands
Direct Bargaining	130	185.2	77	139.4	152	345.4	146	231.3	171	406.9
Conciliation, mediation etc.	62	85.7	81	133.8	134	321.6	140	227.4	148	248.7
Arbitration	12	15.7	3	3.8	15	23.1	19	45.6	27	138.9
Work Stoppages	9	12.4	23	75.0	40	93.2	46	216.3	64	117.7
Others**	–	–	7	39.6	–	–	3	74.7	–	–
Total	213	299.0	191	391.6	341	783.3	354	795.3	410	912.1

Percentage Distribution

Method of Settlement	1963 Agreements	1963 Employees in Thousands	1966 Agreements	1966 Employees in Thousands	1969 Agreements	1969 Employees in Thousands	1972 Agreements	1972 Employees in Thousands	1974 Agreements	1974 Employees in Thousands
Direct Bargaining	61.0	61.9	40.3	35.6	44.6	44.1	41.2	29.1	41.7	44.6
Conciliation, mediation etc.	29.2	28.7	42.4	34.2	39.3	41.1	39.5	28.6	36.1	27.3
Arbitration	5.6	5.3	1.6	1.0	4.4	2.9	5.4	5.7	6.6	15.2
Work Stoppages	4.2	4.1	12.0	19.1	11.7	11.9	13.0	27.2	15.6	12.9
Others	–	–	3.7	10.1	–	–	0.9	9.4	–	–
Total	100.0	100.0	100.0	100.0	100.0	100.0	100.0	100.0	100.0	100.0

* Includes settlements covering 500 or more employees, excluding construction.
** Includes settlements by Government Decree.
Source: Canada Department of Labour, *Collective Bargaining Review.*

Chapter 10

Organizing
And
Maintaining A Union

Part C: Collective Bargaining In The Canadian Private Sector

Up to this point, our analysis has been of sufficient generality to apply to most types of long-term employee associations found in Canada. However, there are some topics that should be discussed with reference to specific sectors of the Canadian economy. The topics in Part C will be examined almost exclusively in the context of the Canadian private industrial sector.

Chapter 10 focuses on the definitional and organizational problems that are encountered in forming and maintaining a union in the private industrial sector. Chapters 11 and 12 discuss the provisions of collective agreements and what can be done to facilitate the administration of such provisions.

I   INTRODUCTION

Canadian "employees" have the legal right to form, join, or assist labour organizations selected by a majority of workers in a defined bargaining unit. To ensure that neither the employer nor the employee engages in actions to undermine this right, all Canadian labour statutes delineate specific regulations for the organization and recognition of·a union. Employees may lose or be refused bargaining rights if they fail to comply with these regulations, while employers may be forced to recognize a specific bargaining agent if they engage in activities contrary to the legislated regulations.

II   WHO IS INCLUDED IN THE DEFINITION OF AN "EMPLOYEE"?

Legislation in all Canadian jurisdictions provides "employees" with the right to organize for the purpose of bargaining collectively. However, there are a number of technicalities that make it difficult to define who is an "employee" under such legislation.

1.   Distinguishing Employees From Employers

Anyone who is carrying on a business for himself is usually excluded from the "employee" category. One set of criteria that has been used to distinguish between an "employment" relationship and a "business" relationship involves three questions:

   a)   What degree of control does one party exercise over the other?
   b)   Who owns the property necessary to carry out the relevant tasks?
   c)   With whom does the chance of profit and risk of loss reside?

Many individuals who could not be classified as employees on the basis of these criteria are heavily dependent upon a particular enterprise for their regular income. Consequently, they share the need of the common law employee to organize for the purposes of collective bargaining without fear of prosecution for conspiracy or breach of the Canada Competition Act. Recently, special legislation has been enacted in a number of Canadian jurisdictions that provides certain types of "dependent contractors" (contractors dependent upon a particular enterprise) with collective bargaining rights.

2.   Individuals Employed In a Managerial or Confidential Capacity

Most Canadian jurisdictions deny collective bargaining rights to individuals exercising functions that are of a managerial or confidential nature. However, most cases are so complex that labour relations boards often find it necessary to appoint an examiner to inquire into the duties and responsibilities of certain persons whose status as an employee is in question. The boards then use the information supplied by the examiner and the testimony of the concerned parties as the basis for certain "tests" to arrive at a logical decision.

The tests most fequently used by labour relations boards to determine whether or not a person's function is managerial, include:

i) Supervision and control exercised over others. Here the board is concerned with whether the employee:

   — has the right to direct the work force
   — has the power to hire or fire or to make effective recommendations in that respect
   — has the right to grant or effectively recommend wage increases

and promotions.
— participates on behalf of the employer in the grievance procedure.
— disciplines employees.
— attends managerial meetings at which labour relations are discussed and policies formulated.
— generally enjoys management perquisites.

ii) Independent discretion. A test frequently used in conjunction with the preceding one is whether the person has the power to make binding policy decisions involving the exercise of independent judgment and discretion. Such independent discretion can involve budgeting, buying, selling, and so on.

iii) The weight or emphasis attached to different functions. Disputes often arise where there is no clear line of demarcation between managerial personnel and employees. In such cases, the persons in dispute normally perform a number of functions, some of which are bargaining unit functions and others which are of a supervisory nature. The board is concerned basically with the question of whether or not these supervisory functions are merely incidental to the performance of work within the bargaining unit. It must be demonstrated that a person is *primarily* engaged in the supervision and direction of other employees and has effective control over their employment relationship if he is to be covered by the managerial exclusion rule. Thus, even though a person may occasionally perform functions of a supervisory nature when an emergency arises or during ocasional absences of the incumbent, this should in no way detract from his prime function as a member of the bargaining unit.

iv) The distinction between technical or professional expertise and decision-making. The requirement that modern employees must possess sophisticated skills and training in order to perform their jobs makes it difficult to determine whether a person is formulating managerial policy or merely carrying out his duties in the bargaining unit by implementing a predetermined course of action. Normally, a board will consider a variety of criteria in arriving at a decision, including such things as the relative position of a person in the managerial hierarchy and the potentiality of a conflict of interest.

Boards normally follow a similar practice in dealing with confidential exclusions as they do with managerial exclusions. The criteria considered in hearings which pertain to confidential exclusions include:

i) The extent of involvement. The confidential capacity must be part of the employee's regular duties. An isolated involvement in some aspect of labour relations is not sufficient to exclude a person from collective bargaining.

ii) The extent of the "confidentiality" of the matter dealt with. The matters must relate to labour relations and must be such that their disclosure would adversely affect the interest of the employer.

iii) A requirement that the individual must use confidential information relating to labour relations in his regular duties. According to Sack and Levinson:
"If management chooses to hold discussions openly where they can be readily overheard or to keep documents in a place where an unauthorized person may inspect them at will, a person who is affected will not become employed in a confidential capacity in matters relating to labour relations unless he is required to use such confidential information or is required to listen to

confidential discussions as part of his regular duties. Thus, a plant nurse has been excluded where she was required to spend a portion of her time in personnel work, whereas a secretary to a school principal and an assistant clerk to a municipal council have not been excluded where they were not required to be privy to confidential information relating to labour relations. Access to information involved in such matters as labour arbitration proceedings as part of one's regular duties will operate to exclude a person from the Act, but not necessarily access to the executive payroll or to planning and cost information. Also, information may lose its confidential character if the union or other employees have access to it." (10.1)

Such exclusions do possess a certain degree of logic when the activities of upper-level management are considered. However, this inability to bargain collectively places certain individuals who perform the tasks of a supervisory or confidential nature at a distinct disadvantage relative to their upper-level colleagues and their unionized subordinates.

The Task Force on Labour Relations presented the following viewpoint on these issues (10.2):

"In some industries extensive exclusions from bargaining units have been made on the ground that individuals were exercising management functions or were in a confidential capacity respecting labour relations. Some exclusions may be justified to avoid conflicts of interest which are implicit in a situation where a union bargains with management respecting a unit that includes managerial as well as non-managerial personnel. Nevertheless, the exclusions deny these persons access to the normal processes of collective bargaining. In our views, the exclusions should be held to a minimum.

"Employees appropriately excluded on these grounds are effectively denied access to any form of collective bargaining. This is unjust in the case of supervisory and junior managerial employees. We recommend, therefore, that the statutory right of collective bargaining be extended to these employees, subject to their being placed in separate bargaining units and in separate unions, and provided further that these unions not be permitted to affiliate with other unions or labour organizations except those composed exclusively of similar types of employees. We would not extend these formal collective bargaining rights to middle and senior levels of management, on the ground that the extension would be incompatible with efficient management and the economic welfare of the country.

"We recommend that collective bargaining be extended to persons employed in a confidential capacity in matters relating to labour relations, subject to the same provisos for supervisory and junior managerial employees."

3. Other Exclusions

Historically, certain occupational groups in Canada have been denied full collective bargaining rights for a variety of reasons. Some of the most notable exclusions are agricultural workers, domestic servants, private security employees, police and firefighters. As a result of the growing controversy over these exclusions, most jurisdictions are currently re-examining their legislation in this respect.

III   THE LEGALITY OF EMPLOYER OPPOSITION TO UNIONIZATION

Despite the existence of modern collective bargaining legislation which provides "employees" with the right to organize for the purposes of collective bargaining, employer opposition to unionization and collective bargaining still exists. Although the tactics used by employers who are reluctant to engage in collective bargaining are much less violent and more subtle than those used in the past, they still serve and often accomplish the same purposes.

Canadian labour laws generally prohibit employers from engaging in the following types of activities:

1.   *Contributing financial or other support to an existing or potential union.* This restriction is based upon historical experience which has demonstrated that employer-dominated unions rarely act in the best interests of the employees.

2.   *Threatening, intimidating, or coercing employees not to unionize.* In addition, the employer must not make explicit commitments to reward employees for not unionizing, nor alter working conditions after application for certification has been made.

3.   *Instituting a total ban on the discussion of unionization by employees.* However, such discussions may be restricted if it can be demonstrated that they are disrupting normal company operations.

4.   *Making speeches and issuing communications that interfere with the rights of employees to unionize.* As a result of this restriction, many employers have learned the hard way that legal counsel should be sought *before* (not after) a speech or communication is presented to employees.

5.   *Utilizing property rights in a manner that prevents employees from communicating with individuals who desire to provide assistance in the formation of a union.* According to the Ontario Labour Relations Act:
> "Where employees of an employer reside in the property of an employer, or on property to which the employer has the right to control access, the employer shall, upon a direction from the Board, allow the representative of a trade union access to the property on which the employees reside for the purpose of attempting to persuade the employees to join a trade union." (10.3)

IV   ORGANIZING A UNION

Chapter 2 provided a number of reasons why employees may desire to join a union or an employee association. As a general rule, some well established union will be available to organize employees who desire union representation. But there are situations in which employees prefer not to be affiliated with some outside union organization. In either case, extreme care must be exercised in a number of areas if a union is to be certified as the bargaining agent for a particular group of employees.

1.   Determining the Appropriate Bargaining Unit

One of the major initial decisions facing union organizers is what group of employees should be covered by a given contract. This group of employees is referred to as a bargaining unit. A proposed bargaining unit that is in some way contrary to policies of the appropriate labour relations board could seriously complicate the certification process.

Some factors that should be considered in forming a unit is appropriate for collective bargaining include:

a) The form or extent of present self-organization among employees. The desires of the employees affected are always a factor of great importance in evaluating the appropriateness of a proposed bargaining unit. However, other criteria must be considered where a number of competing organizations seek to represent a group of employees.

b) Community of interest. In determining the appropriate bargaining unit, some conclusion must be reached concerning the "community of interest" which exists among employees. This raises a series of questions about the day-to-day relationships among employees, such as:

   — Do the employees perform a similar type of work?

   — Are the skills of employees as a group similar?

   — Are employees subject to similar working conditions and fringe benefits?

   — What is the degree of geographical proximity among the employees?

   — To what degree do the employees intermingle?

c) The comprehensiveness of the bargaining unit. It is often feared that a multiplicity of bargaining units in a particular organization, will lead to inter-group rivalry, jurisdictional disputes and general instability in labour relations. On the other hand, "comprehensive" bargaining units may fail to meet the needs of special interest groups which do not desire to be represented by a particular union. Generally, labour relations boards tend to accept the most comprehensive units unless there are compelling reasons for them to do otherwise. Any union hoping to successfully establish a segmented bargaining unit must be prepared to prove that employees in the proposed unit are functionally distinct *and* that they can be represented effectively as a separate group.

d) The composition of bargaining units which prevail in the same industry or for similar types of employees. Although labour relations boards make decisions concerning the appropriateness of bargaining units on a case-by-case basis, they often consider precedents established in other industries and at other times. Where memberships have been historically confined to special occupational or geographical groups, the "appropriate" bargaining unit is often defined in a similar manner.

e) Statutory limitations on the "appropriate" bargaining unit. Certain occupational classifications (such as security guards) are often required by law to be included in an exclusive bargaining unit. Also, those occupational groups not recognized as "employees" under the law cannot be included in a bargaining unit.

2.   Establishing the Existence of an Employee Association

In order to carry on organizing activities among the appropriate group of employees, someone must accept the responsibility for setting up an initial organizational meeting. At this meeting, plans should be made for the drafting of a constitution which contains the following information:

   — the name of the employee association

- the purposes of the association, one of which must be the
  regulation of relations between the employees and the employer
- procedures for the election of officers and the duties and
  responsibilities of such officers
- the frequency of meetings
- the dues which members must pay.

Several jurisdictions will not grant bargaining rights to unions governed by constitutions which discriminate against members because of race, colour, national origin, sex or religion.

When a constitution has been drawn up, a meeting of all potential members can be called to formally adopt the constitution. It is very important not to take on members officially before the formal adoption of a constitution. If members are admitted prior to this, they would be joining a non-existent organization, giving rise to a host of legal complications.

Once the constitution has been adopted, dues may be collected, membership applications or cards may be handed out, and officers should be elected. In most Canadian jurisdictions there is a stipulated minimum membership fee that must be paid (often $1 or $2). Also, only paid-up members are eligible to vote for executive officers of the association. Detailed, accurate records and minutes should be kept to show that all the technicalities necessary for certification have been fulfilled.

3.   Certification

Once the association has been established, it should seek to obtain a certificate which specifies that it is the legally recognized bargaining agent for a particular group of employees. The procedures by which the association does so is referred to as the certification process.

a) When may certification be sought?   An application for certification may be unsuccessful if it is put forward when there is an existing collective agreement, when a union has recently made a prior application, or when a union has been involved in an illegal strike.

Most jurisdictions attempt to provide some stability for the collective bargaining process by legislating that certified unions cannot be challenged during the life of a collective agreement (provided the life of the agreement does not extend beyond a specified period, such as three years in Ontario, or two years in the Federal jurisdiction). Also, once a union is certified it is generally protected from "raiding" for a prescribed period of time.

b) Ways of obtaining certification.   An employer may choose to voluntarily recognize a union as the bargaining agent for his employees and subsequently negotiate a binding agreement with this union. In this case the union generally will be treated in the same manner as one that has been legally certified.

Where voluntary recognition is not granted, application must be made to the appropriate labour relations board. Here, it will be determined whether or not the association is a trade union within the jurisdiction of the labour relations board and whether or not the proposed bargaining unit is appropriate. If there are no difficulties in this regard, there are two paths to certification:

i) Automatic Certification. If the union can demonstrate that it has signed up more than a certain percentage (*e.g.*, in Ontario, 55%) of the employees in the bargaining unit, the labour relations board may automatically certify the applicant union.

ii) Certification by vote. If the union can show that it has a reasonable number of members (*e.g.*, in Ontario more than 45% of the employees in the bargaining unit), then a vote may be ordered by the labour relations board to satisfy itself that a majority of the union members in the appropriate bargaining unit favour the union making the application. Usually, the majority is based on the number of votes cast rather than the number of eligible votes. Thus, a failure to vote is not classed as a negative vote. However, the vote will generally be nullified if less than a certain percentage (often 35%) of eligible voters actually vote. In addition, a run-off election may be held if more than one union is seeking certification and no single union obtains a clear majority.

The ballot used by the labour relations board can take three forms:

i)   Where a single union is applying for certification in a non-union company, the ballots provide for two choices: "union" or "no union".

ii)   Where two (or more) unions are applying for certification in a non-union company, the ballots contain the names of the two (or more) unions plus a choice of "no union". If none of the choices receives a clear majority, a run-off is held between the two choices that received the most votes.

iii)   Where an existing union is being challenged by another union, the ballots contain only the names of the competing unions.

Where it can be proven that an employer has engaged in certain forms of "unfair practices" during a union's organizational phase, most boards have the power to automatically certify an applicant union. Thus, an employer representative must exercise extreme caution during this period. In Ontario, for instance, the Board has expressed the view that an attempt by an employer representative to present opinions to employees on a one-to-one basis may be considered as coercion. So may attempts by employer representatives to speak to employees during working hours.

Most labour relations boards impose strict waiting periods for unions whose applications for certification have been unsuccessful. A union may have to wait anywhere from three to ten months before it can reapply for certification.

The certification procedure provides an alternative to striking and picketing for recognition. Any strike conducted for the purpose of forcing an employer to recognize the existence of a union is illegal in all Canadian jurisdictions. Applications for certification which are made while a recognition strike is in progress will inevitably be dismissed. However, when proof can be provided that the strike has been terminated, the application may then be reconsidered.

c) Decertification. At some point in time, employees may find it necessary to end the bargaining rights of a particular union. This process, referred to as decertification, normally will be undertaken when a collective agreement has expired, or during the statutory "open" periods in long term contracts. Application is made to the labour relations board, and, if accepted, a vote will be ordered. If a majority of workers in the bargaining unit cast votes favoring the decertification proposal, the existing union will lose its rights as bargaining agent. This will set in motion a new round of organizational activities among unrepresented employees.

4.   Union Security

The success of a union in organizing the workers of a particular bargaining unit may be short-lived if a concerted effort is not made to guard against the apathy of workers, the reintroduction of some degree of individual bargaining by employers and competition from other unions. Activities directed towards the achievement of union security frequently involve the negotiation of specific protective clauses in the collective agreement.

a) Open shop provisions. This is the type of situation that a newly certified union usually faces. Employees are free to choose whether or not they wish to join or cease to be members of a particular union. The only security available to the union in these circumstances is the legal protection for the duration of the agreement against both competition from rival unions and the withdrawal of recognition by employers. Also, the employer is not permitted to make deals with non-union members in the defined bargaining unit which differ from the terms of the negotiated agreement.

b) Maintenance of membership provisions. Such provisions require workers that belong to a union at the beginning of a contract term to remain members through the period of the contract. However, withdrawal from the union is possible during a specified interval close to the time that the contract expires.

c) Agency shop provisions. In this situation, sometimes referred to in Canada as the Rand Formula, employees in a defined bargaining unit are not required to join the union as a condition of continuing employment. However, because non-union members obtain the benefits of union activity, they are required to pay the union the equivalent of initiation fees and dues.

d) Union shop provisions. This form of union security permits the employer to hire non-union employees. Within a specified time after being hired, new employees are required to join the union and remain members in good standing if they wish to continue to be employed.

e) Closed shop provisions. A closed shop provision requires the employer to hire individuals who are already union members in good standing. This is the maximum form of union security in that it gives the union control over the hiring process. When an employer needs additional employees, he is required to apply to the union which controls referrals to the job. Such provisions are legal in Canada, but usually only apply to employees hired after such a provision has been negotiated.

f) Dues checkoff provisions. Checkoff provisions are designed to ensure that members remain in "good financial standing" with the union. The employer agrees to deduct union dues from his employees' wages and transmit them to the union at specified intervals. Most Canadian jurisdictions authorize only voluntary revocable checkoff provisions that require a written authorization from an employee before an employer can check off his dues.

In recent years, a number of jurisdictions have passed legislation that permits a person who objects to union membership on the grounds of religious conviction or belief, to pay the equivalent of union dues to a charitable organization of his choice.

Summary
1.   Canadian workers who fit into the appropriate legislation definition of an "employee" have the legal right to form, join or assist "trade unions".
2.   Technicalities that must be considered in defining who is and who is not an "employee" include:
   — distinguishing employees from employers
   — separating individuals employed in a managerial or confidential capacity
   — excluded occupational groups.

3.   All jurisdictions have placed legal restrictions on the employer's right to oppose unionization.

4.   In organizing a union, care must be taken to see that all legal regulations are adhered to. This includes:
  — ensuring that the defined bargaining unit is "appropriate".
  — ensuring that a legally acceptable employee association exists.

5.   An application to the labour relations board for certification must be put forward to an appropriate time. Certification may be obtained by:
  — seeking voluntary recognition from the employer
  — signing up a sufficient number of members to qualify for automatic certification by the labour relations board
  — signing up a specified minimal number of members and obtaining majority support in a vote conducted by the labour relations board.

6.   Union security clauses that may be negotiated include open shop, maintenance of membership, agency shop, union shop, and closed shop provisions. Many unions have also negotiated for dues check-off provisions.

References

10.1   Sack, J. and M. Levinson. *Ontario Labour Relations Board Practice.* Toronto, Butterworths, 1973, p. 37.
10.2   Canadian Industrial Relations. *The Report of the Task Force on Labour Relations.* Ottawa, Queen's Printer, 1968, p. 139.
10.3   *Ontario Labour Relations Act.* Revised Statutes of Ontario 1970, Section 10.

Suggested Readings for Further Study

Carrothers, A.W.R. *Collective Bargaining Law in Canada.* Toronto, Butterworths, 1965.
Christie, Innis and Morley Gorsky. "Unfair Labour Practices". Task Force Study No. 10. Ottawa, 1968.
Herman, Edward E. *Determination of the Appropriate Bargaining Unit by Labour Relations Boards in Canada,* Ottawa, Canada Department of Labour, 1967.
Herman, E. "The Size and Composition of Bargaining Units". A Study for the Task Force on Labour Relations. Ottawa, 1970.
The Labour Relations Law Case Book Group. *Labour Relations Law.* Kingston, Ontario, Industrial Relations Centre, Queen's University, 1974, pp. 43 - 183.

Experiential Assignment

Turn to Chapter 17, Section III and prepare the "Assignment On Certification".

Chapter 11

The Administration
Of The
Collective Agreement

I   INTRODUCTION

Preceding chapters have described methods of establishing a bargaining relationship and reaching an agreement through collective negotiations. The participants in this process are also concerned with the interpretation and application of the collective agreement. In fact, whether or not a collective agreement is successful is determined in part by how well that agreement is administered. The purpose of this chapter is to provide an insight into the complexities of contract administration and an awareness of the interdependent relationships within the agreement.

II   MANAGEMENT RIGHTS

"Management rights" are an extremely controversial aspect of contract administration. Professor F. Young has provided the following summary of this controversy:

"There are two opposing theories of management rights. The residual rights theory put forward by management asserts that all the pre-existing rights and privileges of an employer are reserved to him except when they have been specifically surrendered or limited in the agreement. The bargaining theory or limited view of management rights put forward by the trade unions, holds that the establishment of collective bargaining eliminates earlier rights, practices and precedents. If a matter arises which is not covered by the collective agreement, it must be dealt with by mutual agreement, or by following practices established since collective bargaining began, or by exercising an exclusive management right found in the agreement." (11.1)

For many years the overwhelming majority of Canadian arbitration decisions reflected a bias towards the "residual rights" theory. Consequently, there was a tendency for management to press for collective agreements that remained silent on the issue of management rights or covered the topic with a cryptic, catch-all clause like the following:

"The management of the business in all its phases and details shall remain vested in the Employer. The rights of the Employer and the employees shall be respected and the provisions of this contract for the orderly settlement of all questions regarding such rights shall be observed."

Unions tended to press for the following type of management rights clauses:

"The Union recognizes that it is the right of the Employer to exercise the regular and customary function of management and to direct the working forces, subject to the terms of this agreement. The question of whether any of these rights is limited by this agreement shall be decided through the grievance and arbitration procedure."

A growing number of arbitration awards rendered in the late 1960's and early 1970's appear to indicate that arbitrators are becoming more flexible with respect to the interpretation that should be given to the concept of "management rights", As a result, it is becoming more and more common for collective agreements to contain a very detailed, explicit section on management rights, such as:

"The Union acknowledges that it is the exclusive function of the Company, subject always to the provisions of this Agreement, to hire, promote, demote, transfer, suspend, discharge or otherwise discipline any employee for cause, provided that a claim by an employee that he has been discharged or disciplined without reasonable cause may be the subject of a grievance and dealt with as herein provided.

"The Union also acknowledges that the Company has certain other rights prominent among which, but by no means wholly inclusive, are the rights to decide the number and location of its plants, their machines and tool equipment, the products to be manufactured, the method of manufacture, the schedules of products and the general control and direction of the business of the Company. It is further recognized by the Union that the Company may from time to time apply rules and regulations to be observed by the employees so as to assure proper direction, discipline and safety for the working forces."

Once management has made the decision to rigidly define the meaning of "management rights" in the context of a particular agreement, it then becomes extremely important that no "basic" rights are left out.

III   GRIEVANCE PROCEDURES AND ARBITRATION

1.   Types of Grievances

The success with which any collective agreement is administered is influenced by the grievance procedure contained within that agreement. A grievance is usually defined as a complaint by an employee or employer which alleges that some aspect of a collective agreement has been violated. Most grievances fall into one of the following categories:

a) Clear violations of the agreement: This category of violations pertains to those instances where ignorance or carelessness results in the failure of a party to comply with some unambiguous regulation contained in the agreement.

b) Disagreements over the facts of a particular situation: This refers to disputes which arise when a party is accused of agreement violations that he denies having committed.

c) Disputes over the meaning of an agreement: It is not uncommon to find collective agreements which are deliberately left ambiguous in the interests of achieving a "quick" settlement. Such ambiguities give rise to a multitude of disputes over what specific clauses mean in various situations.

d) Disagreements over methods of applying the agreement: Few agreements contain detailed procedures for implementing every clause. As a result, both parties may offer conflicting opinions on the most appropriate method of applying the agreement.

e) Disagreements over the reasonableness or fairness of various standards or penalties: Cases arise where individuals openly admit they have violated some part of the collective agreement. However, such individuals may claim they were justified in doing so because they were being evaluated against "unreasonable" standards or by "unfair" methods. They may also grieve against "harsh" or "unjust" disciplinary measures being applied to them.

2.   The Content of Grievance Procedure Clauses

Today, almost every collective agreement contains some type of formalized procedure to deal with grievances that arise during the life of the agreement. Although there is a wide variation in the steps that can be followed for handling grievances, each procedure involves a systematic consideration of the problem by union and management representatives at increasingly higher levels of authority. If the problem cannot be settled at one of these levels, all Canadian labour jurisdictions (except Saskatchewan) require that the grievance be submitted to an arbitrator whose decision will be final and binding.

In general, the first step in a grievance procedure involves the relationship between the employee and his immediate supervisor and is normally dealt with verbally. If the employee is not satisfied with the supervisor's answer and decides to pursue the case, the grievance machinery is set in motion.

The union usually provides a standardized form that must be completed by the employee to take the grievance into the second step. Such forms request information on the employee (name, department, etc.), the date, the article and section allegedly violated, the nature of the grievance, the desired adjustment, and signatures of the employee, witnesses and the appropriate steward. The completed form is then presented to the appropriate department head.

The department head will normally set up a meeting with the department steward and the employee. Both parties usually keep thorough records of what transpires during this meeting. The department head may decide to conclude this meeting with a carefully worded response such as (11.2):

"From the evidence presented, it is my opinion that there is no violation of the collective agreement."

or:

"In order to resolve this grievance prior to arbitration, management is prepared to settle on the following basis without prejudice or precedent . . . . "

If the department head is not prepared to move on the grievance a third step may be set in motion which involves the grievance committee and higher level management representatives. The management representatives should make sure that all relevant information has been brought out and checked for reliability before any formal response is provided.

Time limits may be carefully specified in some grievance procedures so that "justice delayed is not justice denied". Some grievance procedure clauses may also impose specific penalties on the party responsible for the delay. For example:

". . . either party to this agreement who violates the time periods provided herein or fails to request an extension of the time period will be recognized as having yielded and must concede the case to the other party."

No single type of grievance procedure will be applicable in every situation. Figure 11.1 illustrates a relatively uncomplicated grievance procedure which has operated effectively for a large Canadian paper company. It is interesting to note that this clause applies to all categories of complaints whether or not they allege that the collective agreement has been violated.

Figure 11.2 demonstrates the complexity of some grievance clauses. In this particular example grievances are rigorously defined and a five-step procedure precedes arbitration. Two significant elements of this procedure include:

a) Shop stewards (committeemen): Most collective agreements allow employee representatives, called shop stewards or committeemen, to be elected by the union members of a particular work unit. The role of the shop steward is to make certain that the supervisor observes and enforces the rules

---

Figure 11.1

20. ADJUSTMENTS OF COMPLAINTS

In the event that grievances or complaints arise in a Department of The Great Lakes Paper Company, Limited, these shall be reported by the officials of the local Union to the Mill Manager, preferably in writing, and the Mill Manager shall make a report, preferably in writing, stating the adjustment made of the matter. If the Mill Manager fails to adjust the complaint in a satisfactory manner, it may be taken up in conference by the General Manager or President of The Great Lakes Paper Company, Limited and the International President or Representatives of the Union. If these two fail to reach an understanding, the matter may be referred to arbitration. The Company will have the privilege of selecting an arbitrator; the Union will have the same privilege and the two thus chosen may select a third arbitrator. If these two arbitrators cannot agree upon a third arbitrator, the Minister of Labour for Ontario shall appoint a third arbitrator and this Board of Arbitration shall convene and render a decision which shall be final and binding upon both parties to this Agreement. If an employee should be discharged, in a manner he considers unjust, it shall be reported to the Mill Manager within 48 hours. If, after going through the above procedure, such an employee should prove that he was unjustly discharged, he shall be reinstated and receive pay for lost time.

Figure 11.2

THE HANDLING OF GRIEVANCES

Definition of Grievance

A grievance shall be defined as any difference arising out of interpretation, application, administration, or alleged violation of the collective agreement or a case where the Employer has acted unjustly or improperly.

Settling of Grievances

An earnest effort shall be made to settle grievances fairly and promptly in the following manner:

Step 1

The aggrieved employee(s) will submit the grievance to his Steward. If the employee's Steward is absent, he may submit his grievance to the Chief Steward and/or another member of the Grievance Committee. At each step of the Grievance procedure the Grievor shall have the right to be present.

Step 2
If the Steward and/or the Grievance Committee consider the grievance to be justified, he/they will first seek to settle the dispute with the employee's Supervisor.

Step 3
Failing satisfactory settlement within two working days after the dispute was submitted under Step 2, the Chief Steward will submit to the Department Head a written statement of the particulars of the grievance and the redress sought. The Department Head shall render his decision within four (4) working days after receipt of such notice.

Step 4
Failing settlement being reached in Step 3, the Grievance Committee will submit the written grievance to the Chief Administrative Officer, who shall render his decision within five (5) working days after receipt of such notice.

Step 5
Failing a satisfactory settlement being reached in Step 4, the Union may refer the dispute to arbitration.

Policy Grievance
Where a dispute involving a question of general application or interpretation occurs, or where a group or employees or the Union or the Employer has a grievance, Steps 1, 2 and 3 of this Article may be by-passed.

Union May Institute Grievances
The Union and its Representatives shall have the right to originate a grievance on behalf of an employee, or group of employees and to seek adjustment with the Employer in the manner provided in the Grievance Procedure. Such a grievance shall commence at Step 2.

Grievance on Safety
An employee, or a group of employees, who is required to work under unsafe or unhealthy conditions shall have the right to file a grievance in the third step of the grievance procedure for preferred handling.

Replies in Writing
Replies to grievances stating reasons shall be in writing at all stages.

Facilities for Grievances
The Employer shall supply the necessary facilities for the grievance meetings.

Mutually Agreed Changes
Any mutually agreed changes to this collective agreement shall form part of this collective agreement and are subject to the grievance and arbitration procedure.

Failure to Act Within Time Limits
If the grievor or the Union fails to process a grievance to the next step in the grievance procedure within the time limits specified, they shall not be deemed to have prejudiced their position in arbitration.

Figure 11.2 continued

Technical Objections to Grievances
No grievance shall be defeated or denied by any formal or technical objection.
An arbitrator shall have the power to allow all necessary amendments to the
grievance and the power to waive formal procedural irregularities in the
processing of a grievance, in order to determine the real matter in dispute and to
render a decision which he deems just and equitable.

that are contained in the collective agreement. If the supervisor fails to do so, it
is the responsibility of the shop steward to set in motion grievance procedures
capable of bringing the supervisor's behaviour into conformity with the rules.

  b) *The grievance committee:* A grievance committee is usually
comprised of a designated union officer, the union's business agent, the chief
steward and a variety of other union officials. Its function is to discuss with
management those grievance issues that:

  1) could not be settled by the shop steward and the supervisor, or
  2) affect more than one work group, or
  3) concern all employees in the bargaining unit.

3. Advantages of Establishing a Formalized Grievance Procedure
A formalized grievance procedure provides some distinct advantages for the
parties affected by the collective agreement.

  a) It recognizes the dynamic nature of the employment relationship.
The grievance procedure provides a vehicle for interpreting how the language of
the agreement applies to problems that were not anticipated when the agreement
was drawn up.

  b) It serves as a safety valve. The grievance procedure enables both the
union and management to recognize potential trouble areas and to take action to
prevent minor areas of discontent from mushrooming into major confrontations.

  c) It promotes smoother future negotiations. The grievances that are
processed suggest to the negotiating parties which aspects of the agreement
require clarification or modification in subsequent negotiations.

  d) It provides a predictable and consistent framework for handling
problems. Few grievance procedures are perfectly "just". However, the mere fact
that the parties know such a procedure exists discourages them from using other
means (such as slowdowns or sabotage) for settling a grievance.

4. Grievance Arbitration
If management and union representatives fail to find an acceptable solution to a
grievance, it becomes necessary to resort to arbitration. Nearly all grievance
disputes in Canada are arbitrable. During 1970, issues that were most frequently
referred to arbitration included:

Discipline and discharge	26%
Pay Issues	20%
Management Rights	12%
Seniority	4%
Other issues:	38%

  — job classification
  — compulsory retirement
  — leave of absence
  — hours
  — composition of bargaining unit
  — layoffs
  — work assignment

There are a number of aspects of the arbitration process that should be given careful attention.

a) Selection of an arbitrator: As a general rule, most parties attempt to select an arbitrator who will give their side the greatest chance of receiving a favorable award in the case. Thus, an extensive investigation of an arbitrator's background and previous awards is usually a more significant factor in the selection of an arbitrator than any "ideal" personal attributes.

There is a tendency for the parties to prefer experienced arbitrators and to avoid arbitrators who develop a reputation for favoring the "other side". As a result, a relatively small proportion of the qualified arbitrators available are actually used. Very little effort has been put forth in Canada to encourage the use of younger, less experienced arbitrators. It is interesting to note in this respect the results of a U.S. study which compared the decisions made by third year law students, inexperienced in labour relations, with those made by professional arbitrators. Seventy-five percent of the students made the "same" decisions as the professional arbitrators. It was concluded that experience in arbitration does not necessarily make a difference in the actual award (11.3).

A federal labour department survey (11.4) published under the title, *The Use of the Arbitration Mechanism in Canada 1972 and 1973,* found that the academic backgrounds of the arbitrators identified in the survey included law (73%), labour relations (14%), business administration (6%), economics (2%) and "other" (5%). The occupational backgrounds of the arbitrators included lawyers (48%), judges (8%), professors (mostly teaching law or labour relations, 20%), businessmen (4%), union representatives (3%), civil servants (1%), consultants (1%), "other" (2%). Occupational information was not available for the remaining 13%.

b) Gathering relevant facts for grievance arbitration: In preparing a case for grievance arbitration, it is advisable to follow these suggestions offered by the American Arbitration Association:

1. Study the original statement of the grievance and review its history through every step of the grievance machinery.

2. Examine carefully the initiating papers (Submission or Demand) to determine the authority of the arbitrator. It might be found, for instance, that while the original grievance contains many elements, the arbitrator under the contract is restricted to resolving only certain aspects.

3. Review the collective bargaining agreement from beginning to end. Often, clauses which at first glance seems to be unrelated to the grievance will be found to have some bearing on it.

4. Assemble all documents and papers you will need at the hearing. Where feasible, make photostatic copies for the arbitrator and the other party. If some of the documents you need are in the possession of the other party, ask that they be brought to the arbitration. Under some arbitration laws, the arbitrator has authority to subpoena documents and witnesses if they cannot be made available in any other way.

5. If you think it will be necessary for the arbitrator to visit the plant for on-the-spot investigation, make plans in advance. The arbitrator will have to be accompanied by representatives of both parties; it is also preferable that the Tribunal Clerk be present.

6. Interview all witnesses. Make certain they understand the whole case and particularly the importance of their own testimony within it.

7. Make a written summary of what each witness will prove. This will be useful as a checklist at the hearing, to make certain nothing is overlooked.

8. Study the case from the other side's point of view. Be prepared to answer the opposing evidence and arguments.

9. Discuss your outline of the case with others in your organization. A fresh viewpoint will often disclose weak spots or previously overlooked details.

10. Read as many articles and published awards as you can on the general subject matter in dispute. (Awards by other arbitrators for other cases may have precedent value and they may help clarify the thinking of parties and arbitrators alike.) (11.5).

c) Making a presentation at an arbitration hearing: The American Arbitration Association has documented four elements of an effective arbitration presentation:

1. An opening statement which clearly but briefly describes the controversy and indicates what he will set out to prove. The opening statement lays the groundwork for witnesses and helps the arbitrator understand the relevance of testimony. For this reason it is frequently advisable that the opening statement be in writing, with a copy given to the arbitrator. This opening statement should also discuss the remedy sought.

2. Names of all witnesses in the order in which they will be called, together with a list of the points they are to cover. Questions should be brief and to the point, and witnesses should be instructed to direct their answers to the arbitrators.

3. A list of exhibits in the order in which they are to be introduced and a notation of what each is to establish. It speeds up proceedings considerably and never fails to make a good impression on the arbitrator when copies are available for distribution to all parties.

4. A closing statement. This should be a summation of evidence and arguments, and a refutation of what the other side has brought out (11.6).

d) Common pitfalls to avoid: Errors which are frequently made in arbitration presentations include:

1. Overemphasis and exaggeration of the grievance.

2. Reliance on a minimum of facts and a maximum of arguments.

3. Using arguments where witnesses or exhibits would better establish the facts.

4. Concealing essential facts; distorting the truth.

5. Holding back books, records and other supporting documents.

6. Tying up proceedings with legal technicalities.

7. Introducing witnesses who have not been properly instructed on demeanour and on the place of their testimony in the entire case.

8. Withholding full cooperation from the arbitrator.

9. Disregarding the ordinary rules of courtesy and decorum.

10. Becoming involved in arguments with the other side. The time to try to convince the other party was before arbitration, during grievance processing. At the arbitration hearing, all efforts should be concentrated on convincing the arbitrator.

e) Procedural matters in grievance arbitration

1. Order of presentations. As a general rule, presentations follow a sequence that permits a logical development of a case. Thus, in most discharge cases the company will make its presentation first while in most other cases the moving party (the party who advanced the grievance to arbitration) will make its presentation first.

2. Burden of proof. Where the evidence presented by both sides is equal, the moving party is considered to have the burden of proof. Thus, in a situation of "equal evidence", the moving party will normally not have his case sustained by an arbitrator.

3. Precedent in arbitration. Arbitration decisions frequently set precedents that control many cases other than the specific one being considered.

Decisions involving the interpretation of a specific contract provision will normally not be reversed by another arbitrator or the same arbitrator on different occasions unless the agreement has been somehow modified to justify a new award. Also, some arbitrators place a great deal of emphasis on precedents cited by the parties involved. However, it must be stressed that the application of precedent is not universally accepted in arbitration as it is in civil or criminal law.

4. *Interpreting ambiguous clauses.* Where a particular clause is ambiguous, an arbitrator can use at least three criteria to arrive at an interpretation:

i)   Intent

The arbitrator may wish to study available transcripts of the contract negotiations to determine the meaning attached to the clause when the agreement was signed.

ii)   General context

The arbitrator may also choose to examine a specific clause in the context of the entire agreement. Other sections of the contract may provide qualifications and points of clarification that shed light on the interpretation that was intended.

iii)   Past practice

In some instances, the arbitrator may seek to determine whether one or both of the parties have exhibited actions in the past that give meaning to the disputed clause.

f) The decision of the arbitrator: Within a reasonable period of time, the arbitrator will provide the disputing parties with a written award. Normally the arbitrator is required only to provide a statement of findings and recommended actions. However, it is common practice for the arbitrator to submit the reasoning by which he reached a decision for reference in future deliberations on the same or similar issues.

It should be pointed out that in practice a "favorable" award does not always mean winning a case before an arbitrator. Professor Slichter has noted three general explanations that account for parties entering an arbitration hearing with a tacit hope of losing their case: internal union politics, staff line conflicts within management and the possible adverse effect of a victory on future bargaining (11.7).

g) The effectiveness of the arbitration process: A report issued by the Labour Council of Metropolitan Toronto examined all the grievance arbitration awards filed with the Ontario Labour - Management Arbitration Commission between September 1, 1971 and September 1, 1973 (11.8). The report presented the following conclusions:

1. The arbitration process is too lengthy and time consuming. However, a single arbitrator deals with grievances faster than does a tripartite board.

During the two year period under study, 37 percent of the arbitration cases were handled by single arbitrators and 63 percent by tripartite boards. When a single arbitrator was used, the median time between the filing of the grievance and the first arbitration hearing was between 125 and 194 days. When a tripartite board was used, the median time increased to between 175 and 199 days. The median time required to render a decision after the last hearing was 15 to 19 days for a single arbitrator and 35 to 39 days for a tripartite board. The study concludes that the entire grievance-arbitration procedure takes approximately two months longer when a tripartite board is used rather than a single arbitrator.

2. The use of legal counsel tends to lengthen the process and provide the party using legal counsel with a definite advantage. Management tends to use legal counsel more often than unions do.

According to the report, management used legal counsel in 58 percent of all cases studied while unions used legal counsel in 34 percent of all cases studied. However, these percentages increased to 66 percent and 42 percent respectively when only those cases involving a tripartite board were considered.

3. Management tends to "win" a higher proportion of the grievances heard.

The report defined a management "win" as occuring in those cases where the arbitrator dismisses a grievance in its entirety and a union "win" as one in which the arbitrator imposes some change in the penalty or action decided upon by management. The statistics show that unions "won" the grievance in about 40 percent of the cases. In addition, the union is more likely to be successful in discharge cases and least likely to be successful in discipline and job promotion cases.

h) The cost of the arbitration process: The preliminary findings of a federal labour department survey entitled *The Use of the Arbitration Mechanism In Canada 1972 and 1973* indicated that the "common" daily fee for arbitrators was in the $300 to $350 range (11.9). The "common" daily fee being charged in Ontario is likely to be in the $600 to $800 range. Normally, the costs of the arbitrator are shared by the parties to the dispute.

Summary

1. There are two opposing theories of management rights: the residual rights theory and the bargaining theory. Employers tend to support the former theory while unions adhere to the latter.

2. Grievance Provisions:
   a) A grievance refers to a complaint by an employer or employee which alleges that some aspect of a collective agreement has been violated. Five classifications of grievances include:
   - clear violations of the agreement
   - disagreements over the facts of a particular situation
   - disputes over the meaning of an agreement
   - disagreements over methods of applying the agreement
   - disputes over the reasonableness of penalties imposed.

   b) Grievance clauses vary significantly in their scope and complexity. Formalized grievance procedures are advantageous to both unions and management. Such procedures can assist these parties by dealing with problems not anticipated when an agreement was drawn up, serving as a safety valve and promoting smoother future negotiations.
   c) When grievances cannot be resolved by the parties themselves, the arbitration process is usually invoked.

3. Grievance Arbitration:
   a) Those involved in the arbitration process should exercise great care in selecting the arbitrator, gathering the relevant facts and presenting their case.
   b) The arbitration process can be very lengthy and costly for the participants.

References

11.1 Young, F. "Issues in Contracting Out", in *Canadian Labour and Industrial Relations* by H.C. Jain. Toronto, McGraw-Hill, 1975, p. 173.

11.2 Feeley, F. "Grievances Are Best Resolved Without the Use of Arbitration".
       The Financial Post, Feb. 1, 1975, p. 25.
11.3 *Labour Gazette.* December 1975, p. 879.
11.4 *Ibid.* July, 1975, p. 447.
11.5 American Arbitration Association. *Labour Arbitration: Procedures and
       Techniques.* New York, American Arbitration Association, 1947, pp. 17-18.
11.6 *Ibid.* pp. 18-19.
11.7 Slichter, S.H., *et al. The Impact of Collective Bargaining On Management.*
       Washington, D.C., The Brookings Institution, 1970, pp. 800-801.
11.8 *Labour Gazette.* July 1975, p. 444.
11.9 *Ibid.* p. 445.

Suggested Readings for Further Study

Chandler, Margaret K. *Management Rights and Union Interests.* New York,
     McGraw-Hill, 1964.
Curtis, C. *The Development and Enforcement of the Collective Agreement.*
     Kingston, Industrial Relations Centre, Queen's University, 1966.
Freedman, Justice Samuel. "Report of the Industrial Inquiry Commission on
     Canadian National Railway Run-throughs". Ottawa, Queen's Printer,
     1965.
The Labour Relations Law Case Book Group. *Labour Relations Law.*
     Kingston, Industrial Relations Centre, Queen's University, 1974,
     pp. 238-399.
Prasow, P. and Edward Peters. *Arbitration and Collective Bargaining: Conflict
     Resolution In Labour Relations.* New York, McGraw-Hill, 1970.
Schiff, Stanley. "Labour Arbitration Procedures". A Study for the Task Force
     on Labour Relations. Ottawa, 1970.
Slichter, S., James Healy and Robert Livernash. *The Impact of Collective
     Bargaining On Management.* Washington, D.C., Brookings Institution,
     1960.
Trower, C. *Arbitration At A Glance.* Toronto, Labour Research Institute,
     1974.
Young, W.D. *The Contracting Out of Work.* Kingston, Industrial Relations
     Centre, Queen's University, 1964.

Experiential Assignment

Turn to Chapter 17, Section VI and prepare the "Assignment on Grievance
Arbitration".

Chapter 12

The Contents
Of The
Collective Agreement

I   INTRODUCTION

The collective agreement contains clauses which state the rights and obligations of management and union members in their dealings with each other. Care must be taken that these clauses have been carefully worded and fully thought out so that they will be applicable in a variety of situations throughout the duration of the agreement. Otherwise, both parties will be forced to devote an unwarranted amount of time to grievance and arbitration cases that could easily have been avoided if more care had been taken in the negotiation sessions. Anyone who is drafting a union contract can greatly improve its readability by keeping in mind the following suggestions (12.1):

1. Don't use sentences of more than 20 words. An average of 15 words is even better.

2. Cut out the whereases and all other legalisms. Words and phrases like "in lieu of", "instigate," "in their discretion," or "equalization" are not in the working vocabulary of many workers. There is also no reason for using "discharged" for "fired", and so on.

3. Don't use legal terms when speaking of the contracting parties. Wherever possible, avoid calling them "employer" and "employee" (to tell them apart is hard on the eyes). Call the parties: "the company", "the union", and "the workers" (without capitals).

4. Analyze all procedures that are part of the agreement (for example, the settlement of grievances), and describe them step by step. Use subheadings: Step 1, Step 2, and so forth.

5. If rules are stated in abstract terms (seniority rules, for example) provide two or more examples to show their practical application. A single example might be misinterpreted. Be sure to say that all examples are illustrations only and nothing more.

II   COMPENSATION PROVISIONS

A complicated, but extremely important part of any collective agreement involves those provisions which specify the payment of wages and salaries. The following are some of the compensation issues which most agreements must somehow resolve.

1.   Internal Job Structures

Employees are paid to perform specified groupings of tasks, referred to as jobs, which involve a variety of skills, knowledge and conditions. Consequently, different compensation packages are associated with different jobs. The process of determining the relative worth of these jobs is referred to as "establishing an internal job structure". Most employers choose one of the three following methods for establishing their internal job structure:

a) Ad hoc market determination: Many employers feel that, over time, market forces will reflect the relative worth of different jobs. Thus, the employer's continuous response to the changing demand and supply factors in the labour market determines any particular job structure. In practice such a procedure often generates a job structure that is both internally inconsistent and inequitable. Consequently, there is a high probability that organizations will experience numerous confrontations with employees and their organizations over job structures which simply "evolve" over time.

b) Employer designed job evaluations: In recent years there has been wide acceptance by employers of job evaluation as a technique for analyzing differences in job worth. Some of the most important aspects of job evaluation include the following:

i) Job descriptions

Complete job descriptions and specifications are prepared to be used as a basis for analyzing every relevant job.

ii) Evaluation plans

The relative importance of those factors or job elements (such as mental, physical, skill, and educational requirements) that distinguish one job from another must be determined. This is one of the most important steps in the job evaluation process. Care must be taken to ensure that evaluation plans "borrowed" from elsewhere have been properly adapted to meet special conditions prevailing in the adopting organization.

iii) Job rating

A system must be selected to place each job within the job structure. A variety of systems may be used, ranging from unsophisticated ranking and classification methods to complex factor comparison and point methods. In many cases the evaluation results are used to group jobs into a reasonable number of "grades" to make the structure administratively manageable.

Technically speaking, job evaluation is not concerned with the actual determination of wage rates. However, once the job evaluation process has been completed, it is then possible to determine a monetary value for each job and thereby establish an internal wage structure.

c) Negotiated Job Evaluations: Many employers still refuse to permit union participation in the job evaluation process. Also, many unions will not take part in the process, even when invited. In recent years, however, there has been an increasing tendency for unions and management to carry out the job evaluation procedure within a negotiated structure. As a result, employees are more likely to accept the differential rates as being fair because their representatives helped to determine the existing system.

In order to facilitate the day-to-day administration of an established internal job structure, care must be taken to ensure that:

i) Both management and the employees understand how the internal job structure has been developed.

ii) Grievance procedures have been clearly established for those employees who feel they are not receiving the appropriate wage rate for the job they are assigned.

iii) Provisions have been made for adding new jobs and classifications, eliminating existing jobs, and revising the content of established job classifications.

2. Wage and Salary Systems

The collective agreement usually specifies the method by which employees will be paid. Two systems of wage and salary payment that are frequently specified include time rates and incentive rates.

a) Time rates: In Canada the majority of employees are paid in accordance with the amount of time (hours, days, weeks, or months) spent at work. Time rate systems may include a single time rate that applies to everyone in a particular classification or a series of rate ranges within each classification. In the latter case, particular attention must be paid to the wording in the agreement in order to avoid a multiplicity of grievances concerning intra-range wage adjustments. The contract should specify:

— If progression through the classification is to be determined by merit, length of service, or a combination of both

— A workable definition of merit

— What rate is applicable to employees entering a classification from outside the plant or from other classifications within the plant.

b) Incentive systems: Incentive systems are designed to reflect the contributions of individual employees to the productivity of an organization. Ideally, the more an employee contributes to the efficient operation of an organization, the more income he earns. Such systems are most often found in areas of employment characterized by repetitive or standardized operations. For the most part, unions have generally opposed the establishment and operation of most types of incentive systems.

Incentive systems may be set up in a variety of ways. It is very important that whatever system is selected should be of sufficient simplicity so that it can readily be understood by both employers and employees. Two common types of incentive systems include:

i) Piece-rate systems
Under these systems employees are paid a designated price for each unit of production completed. Usually, the employees are guaranteed some minimum amount of pay if production falls below a specified level.

ii) Sharing systems
This variety of incentive requires the employee to participate in both the benefits and losses which result from exceeding or falling short of pre-established production or profit standards.

Either type of system may apply to individual employees or to joint contributions of specified groups of employees.

For an incentive plan to be successful in any organization, these areas must be carefully spelled out in the collective agreement:

i) The establishment of standards
It is obvious that both types of incentive systems require someone to determine the "standard" or "norm" against which the observed production or profit level is compared. The agreement should clearly designate who is responsible for determining these standards and how such "norms" should be identified. Standards that are set too high or too low can be a troublesome source of grievance disputes.

ii) The establishment of dollar values
The collective agreement should also make provision for the individuals and procedures that will determine the dollar value attached to each unit of production or profit above the selected "norm".

iii) Adjustments in the incentive system
All collective agreements should contain provisions which safeguard both parties against any potential inequities created by an incentive system. Thus, procedures should be specified for dealing with substantial changes in the job content, the production process or the product which are beyond the control of an individual employee.

A recent study carried out by the Canada Department of Labour indicated that most Canadian workers are now being paid according to time worked, and that pay systems based on output or performance appear to be on the decline. The reasons that were cited for the abandonment of incentive systems included:

i) the increasing use of capital equipment has made it difficult to relate units of output to the work of individual employees.

ii) the results which were anticipated from incentive systems rarely appeared to materialize within a reasonable period of time.

iii) unions have insisted that incentive systems tend to dehumanize the work force, deprive workers of a regularity of income, and force employees to compete with one another.

3.   Cost-of-Living Allowance (COLA) Clauses

During the course of wage negotiations, employees may be concerned with future changes in the cost of living. The difficulties and uncertainties associated with assessing future trends in the consumer price index have led many unions to opt for cost-of-living adjustment clauses in collective agreements. Although there are a wide range of possible arrangements, the most significant characteristic of such clauses involves *automatic* wage adjustments during the life of the agreement in accordance with changes in some statistical index. Some of the major issues associated with the introduction and administration of such clauses include:

a) The selection of a cost-of-living index to be used: Most cost-of-living provisions are based upon the Canadian Consumer Price Index. This index measures changes in the cost of living based on estimated spending habits of an "average" family. The Consumer Price Index is by no means a perfect measure of changes in the cost of living for all individuals. For instance one of the components of this index, food, represents a much higher share of the income of people earning low wages than those with large families. Thus, changes in the Consumer Price Index may bear little relationship to changes in the cost of living for these and other categories of Canadians.

In spite of these limitations, the Consumer Price Index is presently deemed to be the best proxy presently available for measuring changes in the cost of living. Statistics Canada normally publishes the "All-Canada Consumer Price Index" on or before the fifteenth of the following month. The "Regional Cities Indices" are normally released on or before the twenty-second of the following month.

Most agreements also contain a contingency clause which specifies procedures that will be used if Statistics Canada should cease to publish the Consumer Price Index in its present form.

b) The choice of a base year: A cost-of-living clause should indicate the base year from which changes in the cost of living will be computed. The most common practice is to use the index prevailing at the time the contract becomes effective as the base point for future calculations.

c) The link between the index and wage adjustments: The collective agreement must specify what relationship will be formulated between changes in the index which has been selected and wage or salary adjustments. A wide variety of formula can be found in COLA clauses. Many agreements provide for a cents-per-hour raise per point increase in the Consumer Price Index with the most common range of payment being one cent for every increase in the index of four-tenths to six-tenths of one index point. Agreements that involve weekly or monthly salaries rather than hourly wages generally provide for percentage adjustments based on percentage increases in the index. At present a "one-for-one" formulation is being sought by many unions. Also, most agreements are worded in such a way that adjustments are only made for increases in the Consumer Price Index. Decreases in wages are usually not permitted.

d) The inclusion of triggers, ceilings (or caps) and guarantees: The agreement should be clear as to whether or not the index must increase by some minimum before the formula comes into effect (*i.e.,* the trigger, mechanism), and specify any maximum payments (*i.e.,* ceilings or caps) if limitations are to be placed on wage adjustments. In addition, there should be a statement as to whether or not certain increases (guarantees) will automatically come into effect if the cost-of-living clause has not generated a certain minimum level of adjustment by a specified date.

e) Fold-ins and floats (add-ons): Adjustments resulting from the cost-of-living adjustments may or may not be incorporated in the base rate. A fold-in occurs when the employer incorporates all or part of the cost-of-living adjustment into the employees' base rate. This new base rate is then used to calculate premium rates, fringe benefits and possibly even the new cost-of-living adjustment if a percentage formula applies.

A float (or add-on) results from cost-of-living adjustments which are not incorporated into the base rates. Thus, such adjustments do not change the premium rates or fringe benefits which the employer must pay.

f) The frequency of wage adjustments: Consideration must be given to the timing of cost-of-living adjustments. It is common for agreements to provide for quarterly adjustments. However, at high rates of inflation more frequent adjustments may be sought by unions.

g) The indexing of wage supplements: In some cases, cost-of-living clauses may be applied to certain wage supplements, such as pensions and insurance coverage.

A recent study of 225 COLA clauses by Canada Labour Views showed that:

"Almost half (48.3%) of the open escalators (those without a cap or trigger) operate throughout the term of a contract. A slightly smaller group with open escalators (47.5%) only operate for part of the contract term. The remainder (4.2%) are provisions granted by employers who do not have a collective agreement. In contrast, most (60.0%) of the limited (capped or triggered) escalators are only effective for part of the contract term. Only 37.1% of the limited provisions operate throughout a contract term. A few (2.9%) of the limited provisions are granted to non-union employees. The accompanying bar-graphs illustrate the distribution of employers according to the factor rise in the CPI causing them to grant a 1¢/hr. increase. Among those with open provisions, the factors 0.4 and 0.5 are the most common (22.4% each). Significant numbers of employers use 0.35 (17.5%) 0.45 (11.7%); 0.3 (9.2%); 0.6 (4.1%); and 0.8 (3.3%). A half unit change (0.5) is the most common factor 38.1%) among employers with limited escalators (caps and/or triggers). Significant numbers of employers use 0.45 (18.1%); 0.4 (17.1%); 0.6 (10.5%); and 0.3 (3.8%).

The accompanying pie-chart illustrates the method of limitation. All limited escalators have either a cap or a trigger. Seventy-four point three percent (74.3%) of the limited escalators have at least one cap. Thirty-six point two percent (36.2%) of the limited escalators have at least one trigger. Both caps and triggers occur in 10.5% of the limited escalators. The capped provisions also have a guarantee in 5.7% of the limited cases. The triggered provisions have a guarantee in 0.9% of the limited cases. There were no surveyed employers granting provisions with a cap, a trigger, and a guarantee. Guarantees occur in 6.6% of the limited provisions and in 2.5% of the open provisions." (12.2)

4.   Wage Supplements

Labour costs are made up of a wage rate plus a series of wage supplements. Figure 12.1 shows the prevalence of various wage supplements that were negotiated in collective agreements in 1974. Figures 12.2 and 12.3 demonstrate that these wage supplements constitute a significant part of the wage bargain and represent an important cost burden to the employer. The topic of wage supplements has become far too massive and complex for any definitive coverage in a text of this type. Therefore, the approach that will be taken in this section will be to identify key provisions that should be

included in negotiated wage supplement clauses pertaining to pay for time
not worked, premium pay for time worked, and pension plans. Provisions
for legally required benefits will be dealt with in Chapter 16 in the context
of Labour Standards Legislation.

    a) Pay for time not worked: The most prevalent types of pay for
time not worked include holiday pay, vacation pay, paid sick leave and
paid periods for lunch, wash-up and rest.

    i) Holiday pay

Historically, holiday pay was first provided to salaried workers with the
philosophy that these employees should not suffer a loss in pay
because management closed its business for a legal holiday. As
unions became more powerful, holiday pay provisions were negotiated
for a broader spectrum of employees and modified to include premium
pay for holidays worked.

The following items should be spelled out in any holiday clause:

— The days that should be considered as paid holidays and the arrangements that will be made when paid holidays fall on non-working
days.

— The employees that are eligible for holiday pay and whether or not
"length of service" or "attendance" prerequisites are relevant.

— The compensation that will be paid for holidays worked and holidays
not worked.

— The rights of the employer to require employees to report for work
on a holiday.

    According to Figure 12.1, improvements in the number of paid
holidays were made in 41 percent of the agreements negotiated in
1974. The most common provision has been for 11 paid holidays,
which in some cases includes the addition of a "floater" (12.3).

ii) Vacation pay

Over the years, paid vacations have continued to be liberalized. Figure
12.2 indicates that improvements in vacations with pay were the most
costly type of non-wage adjustment in 1973. Recent trends in this area
indicate a continued lowering of service requirements for vacations
and the increasing prevalence of 5 and 6 week vacations (12.4). When
negotiating issues related to paid vacations, the following items should be
discussed:

— The length of the paid vacation period to which an employee is
entitled and the rights of employees to postpone, carry-over, or
accumulate vacation time.

— The employees that are eligible for vacation pay.

— The compensation paid for vacation time worked or not worked.

— The rights of the employer in scheduling vacations.

iii) Paid sick leave

Paid sick leave provisions normally provide that the employer will
continue to pay full salary for a specified time period. The following
issues should be explicitly dealt with in any paid sick leave provisions:

— The computation of the time limit on payments for sick leave and the
rights of employees to accumulate sick leave.

— The employees that are eligible for paid sick leave and the necessity
for a doctor's certificate.

— The level of compensation during sick leave and the length of waiting
periods prior to payment.

— The review of abuses of sick leave privileges.

iv) Workbreaks: lunch, wash-up, and rest periods

Figure 12.1

PROPORTION OF SETTLEMENTS
PROVIDING FOR SELECTED CONTRACT CHANGES IN 1974, BY INDUSTRY

	Mfg.	Transportation, Communication, Utilities.	Trade	Services	Public Admin.	All Indus- tries
Hours of Work						
(per day)	9%	9%	54%	7%	6%	11%
COLA	54%	41%	50%	14%	7%	32%
Premium Pay	76%	79%	82%	41%	59%	65%
Paid Holidays	63%	41%	43%	23%	20%	41%
Sick Leave	12%	9%	11%	22%	13%	14%
Life Insurance	49%	29%	18%	17%	18%	30%
Supp. Medical	24%	4%	29%	12%	8%	15%
Drug Plan	7%	0	21%	1%	2%	5%
Dental	23%	14%	57%	3%	7%	17%
Long-Term						
Disability	22%	14%	11%	9%	17%	15%
Pension Plan	61%	25%	18%	5%	2%	26%

Source: Wood, W.D. *The Current Scene In Industrial Relations, 1975.* Kingston, Ont., Industrial Relations Centre, Queen's University.

Figure 12.2

Average Cost To Employers of Fringe Benefits By Type Of Fringe Benefits, 1973.

Type of Fringe Benefit	In Dollars Per Employee Per Year	In Cents Per Hour
Vacation Pay	560	27.03
Holidays With Pay	337	16.38
Rest Periods	351	17.28
Bereavement, Jury Duty	12	0.56
Other Time Off	120	5.47
Total Paid Time Off	1330	66.72
Unemployment Insurance	80	3.88
Workmen's Compensation	55	2.63
Canada Pension Plan	101	4.88
Total Payments Required by Law	236	11.39
Pension Plans	392	19.17
Group Life, Medical, etc.	473	26.16
Other (severance, etc.)	63	2.74
Total Security Payments	928	45.07
Bonuses and Profit Sharing	130	7.43
Non-Cash Benefits	100	5.28
Total Bonuses	230	12.71
Total Cumulative Cost For Fringe Benefits	2783	135.89

Source: The Thorne Group Ltd. *Fringe Benefit Costs In Canada,* 1973.

Figure 12.3

Fringe Benefit Costs As A Percentage of Gross Payroll 1953-1973

Year	Manufacturing (%)	Non-Manufacturing (%)
1953	14.30	17.50
1957	16.20	17.20
1959	22.80	20.50
1961	23.40	26.50
1963	25.70	27.20
1965	23.00	22.80
1967	25.30	24.99
1969	27.18	28.58
1971	29.64	28.43
1973	28.30	27.97

Source: The Thorne Group Ltd. *Fringe Benefit Costs In Canada,* 1973.

Employers have traditionally granted employees time off during the work day for lunch, wash-up and rest periods. Such periods have increasingly been included as a part of the paid working schedule of all employees. Two items that should be discussed in negotiating these types of benefits include:
— The amount of time that is permitted for workbreaks for various types of employees.
— The rights of the employer in scheduling workbreaks.

b) Premium pay for time worked: In some situations, an employer may be better off to have his existing staff operate under a system of overtime, or work on unpopular shifts. Unions have negotiated provisions designed to discourage such practices, or at least compensate employees who are required to work under these conditions.

Some of the matters which negotiators should take into account when drafting premium pay provisions include:
— A definition of the "normal workday and workweek."
— Whether the employer or the union has the authority to schedule overtime.
— Whether or not overtime is mandatory for employees.
— Which employees will be given preference for work with premium pay.
— Procedures for the computation of "hours worked".
— The rate of overtime pay and the method by which it will be applied to calculate total overtime earnings.
— Special requirements that are necessary for calculating premium pay for employees hired on an annual wage basis.

Improvements in premium pay provisions ranked high in terms of prevalence in 1974 according to Figure 12.1 These improvements included changes in shift premiums, overtime pay and call-back pay (12.5).

c) Negotiated pension plans: To-day pensions are a prominent element of most collective agreements. The issues that unions and management have to resolve in negotiations pertaining to pensions may be categorized under the following headings:
— What methods will be used to fund and finance the plan?
— What proportion of the costs must employees bear?
— Who will be responsible for administering the plan?

- Who will be eligible for benefits under the plan?
- Should the pension rights be vested (provided to employees upon retirement age if they leave the company before reaching retirement age)?
- Should pension rights be portable (*i.e.*, capable of being transferred from one pension plan to another)?
- Should cost-of-living protection be established for pensions?
- What level of survivor benefits will be provided if an employee dies before or after retirement?

III   SENIORITY PROVISIONS

"Seniority" is defined as an employee's length of service with the company for which he works. In any given collective agreement the word takes on peculiar meanings depending upon the language of the agreement, the practices followed in the administration of the contract and certain arbitration decisions.

Seniority provisions should be well thought out if they are going to provide a workable basis for day-to-day contract administration. Some of the most crucial elements in any seniority provisions include the following:

1.   The Purposes For Which Seniority Is Recognized

Slichter (12.6) makes the distinction between two categories of seniority: competitive status seniority and benefit seniority. The former refers to situations where length of service determines an employee's status in relation to other employees concerning such matters as layoff, recall, transfer and promotion. It is generally not easily moved from one location to another within a company.

Benefit seniority involves "those benefits, rights, or privileges to which a man is entitled either explicitly, as in the case of severance pay, or implicitly, as in the case of partial protection from discharge, just because he has attained a certain number of years of service." (12.7) Benefit seniority is often unimpaired by movements of the employee among different plants of the same company. This latter category of seniority is primarily used in determining the applicability of wage supplement provisions.

2.   The Unit Within Which Seniority Is Recognized

Seniority may accrue within the company, plant, department, occupational group, or job classification. As previously mentioned, the unit of seniority used for "benefit" purposes may differ from that used to determine one's competitive status.

3.   Seniority Versus Merit

Unions typically press for extensive recognition of seniority as the sole basis for determining an employee's economic and social role in the work community. This insistence on seniority is largely based on the desire for some objective rule which eliminates judgment and discretion in particular cases.

Many employers still maintain that merit, rather than seniority, should be the most predominating factor for determining the status of an employee within the unit covered by a collective agreement. They argue that there is no incentive for an employee to use his initiative when he is restricted in advancement by seniority rules. Thus, seniority systems may tend to decrease the productivity within a given enterprise. Most collective agreements contain some combination of these two viewpoints. In any particular company, different combinations will be used for different purposes. For instance, straight seniority criteria may be used for determining layoffs, while both merit factors and seniority may be used as criteria for promotions and lateral transfers.

The use of the word "merit", which has many meanings and many dimensions, can be a source of numerous grievances in the day-to-day administration of the collective agreement. In fact, even in non-union plants, the principle of seniority receives support because it tends to eliminate accusations that management is pursuing policies of favouritism.

4.   The Loss of Seniority
Contract provisions must also deal with events which cause a loss of seniority. A Prentice-Hall study of American labour contracts indicated the following types of provisions giving rise to the loss of seniority (12.8):

Cause	Percent of Contracts Studied
Voluntary quit	81%
Discharge	80%
Failure to return from layoff when called (2-30 days)	68%
Layoff longer than a specified time (6 months – 3 years)	65%
Absence without notice (2 – 7 days)	47%
Failure to return from a leave of absence	38%
Acceptance of employment during leave of absence	11%

5.   Exceptions To The Seniority System
Many collective agreements specify certain exemptions from the agreed upon seniority system. Three common exceptions include:

a) Super-seniority: Some agreements provide certain union officials with a preferred status as long as they hold office. Frequently, this preferred status is applicable only in the event of layoffs.

b) Probationary employees: While employees are serving a probationary period they can often be laid off or transferred without reference to seniority.

c) Bumping rights: Some contracts permit employees to displace workers who have less job seniority and are located in other units of the company. It is common to find many restrictions on bumping rights in collective agreements to avoid in unweildy chain of job reassignments.

IV   DISCIPLINE AND DISCHARGE PROVISIONS
Most collective agreements contain written provisions governing the rights of employers to discipline and discharge workers and the corresponding rights of employees to appeal such actions. Discipline and discharge issues can be a troublesome source of grievances if such clauses do not clearly and unequivocally answer a number of related questions.

1.   Reasons For Discipline or Discharge
In a union situation, the right to discipline or discharge workers still remains in the hands of the employer. However, the employer may be required to demonstrate that he has a "just cause" for ordering the discipline or discharge of an employee. Some of the most common "causes" giving rise to discipline and discharge proceedings include:

a) Conduct on the job that is detrimental to effective job performance, such as absenteeism, tardiness, or negligence.

b) Conduct on or off the job that is detrimental to the employing company, such as theft, or divulging trade secrets.

Where grievance arbitration becomes necessary over the issue of whether or not "just cause" exists for dismissal, it is a general rule that the employer is expected to provide clear and convincing facts that justify such a decision. Also, the employer may be required to demonstrate that the rule has been consistently enforced by the company from the time it was introduced.

2.   Forms of Discipline Imposed

Most agreements specify actions that employees may expect for various offences. The forms of discipline most frequently imposed include oral reprimands, written reprimands, suspension with or without pay, demotion and discharge. Should the severity of an employer's actions become an issue that leads to grievance arbitration, the onus is usually on the union to demonstrate that the penalty is too severe.

3.   Procedure For Discipline And Discharge Cases

Many collective agreements contain detailed procedures that must be followed for discipline and discharge cases. Most procedures deal with the following topics:

a)   Defining employees that can make use of these procedures (probationary employees are usually excluded).
b)   Notification of the employee and union as to the specific charges.
c)   The right of the employee to a hearing.
d)   The right of the employee to appeal through the grievance procedure.
e)   Time limits on the previously mentioned steps.

4.   Rules Introduced Unilaterally By The Employer

Any rule introduced unilaterally by the employer and not subsequently agreed to by the union must satisfy the following requirements if it is to be upheld in an arbitration hearing:

a)   The rule must be clear and unequivocal.
b)   The rule must be consistently enforced from the time it was introduced.
c)   The employee concerned must have been notified that a breach of such a rule could result in his discharge if the rule is used as a foundation for discharge.
d)   The rule must not be inconsistent with the existing collective agreement.
e)   The rule must not be "unreasonable". This requirement provides a great deal of latitude for employees to grieve rules imposed unilaterally by the employer.

Summary

1.   Compensation Provisions

a)   Internal job structures (*i.e.,* the relative worth of different jobs) may be established by the market, the employer, or by employee-employer negotiations.
b)   Wage and salary payments may be based on the amount of time spent on the job (time rates), or the contribution of the employee to the productivity of the organization (incentive rates).
c)   Cost-of-Living Allowance Clauses should specify the appropriate statistical index to be used, the base year to be chosen, the link between the chosen index and wage adjustments, the applicability of triggers and ceilings, and the frequency of wage adjustments.

2. Wage Supplement Provisions

Many potential grievances can be avoided by putting a number of essential details into provisions that regulate pay for time not worked and premium pay for time worked. Many of these details relate to employee eligibility requirements and the discretion residing with the employer.

3. Seniority Provisions

Seniority refers to an employee's length of service with the company for which he works. Seniority provisions in a collective agreement should specify the purposes for which seniority is recognized, the unit within which seniority is recognized, the relative significance of seniority and merit, and conditions giving rise to the loss of seniority.

4. Discipline and Discharge Provisions

Discipline and discharge provisions must provide clear guidelines as to the definition of "just cause" for the employer's actions, the types of actions the employer can take in particular circumstances, and the procedures that must be followed before and after a particular incident has occurred.

References

12.1 Prentice-Hall Editorial Staff. *Manual For Drafting Union Contracts.* Englewood Cliffs, N.J., Prentice-Hall, 1969, p. 52, 103.

12.2 *Canada Labour Views.* Toronto, July 17, 1975.

12.3 Wood, W.D. *The Current Scene In Industrial Relations, 1975.* Kingston, Ont., Industrial Relations Centre, Queen's University, p. S-CB-6.

12.4 *Ibid.*

12.5 *Ibid.*

12.6 Slichter, S.H., *et al. The Impact of Collective Bargaining On Management.* Washington, D.C., The Brookings Institution, 1970, p. 104.

12.7 *Ibid.,* p. 106.

12.8 Prentice-Hall. *Industrial Relations – Union Contracts and Collective Bargaining.* Englewood Cliffs, N.J., Prentice-Hall, p. 404.

Suggested Readings for Further Study

Prentice-Hall Editorial Staff. *Manual For Drafting Union Contracts.* Englewood Cliffs, N.J., Prentice-Hall, 1969.

Slichter, S.H., *et al. The Impact of Collective Bargaining On Management.* Washington, D.C., The Brookings Institution, 1970.

Experiential Assignment

Turn to Chapter 17, Section V (4) and critically examine the wording and contents of the "Current Agreement" between the Yourtown Public Library Board and the Canadian Union of Public Librarians, Local 100.

Part D: Collective Bargaining In The Public And Professional Sectors Of Canada

The first twelve chapters of this book have dealt with collective bargaining in the private sector of the Canadian economy. Here both the employer and the union have established mutually accepted collective bargaining arrangements. The two chapters that make up Part D examine collective bargaining in the public and professional sectors. In these sectors the employer may be a government department, a government-run agency, a government-financed agency, or as is sometimes the case, the question of who the employer really is may be open to serious question. Employees in these sectors were traditionally required to remain outside the realm of collective bargaining. Now, however, such employees are organizing rapidly and adopting a militant attitude.

Chapter 13 examines some of the most significant features of collective bargaining in the federal, provincial and municipal public services. Chapter 14 will provide a similar perspective of collective bargaining by professionals in Canada.

Chapter 13

The Canadian
Public Employment Sector

I INTRODUCTION

The federal, provincial and municipal governments of Canada are the country's largest employers. It has been estimated that between 1965 and 1975 the number of Canadian workers employed directly or indirectly by one of Canada's governments has doubled, so that by 1975 approximately one out of every five workers was a "public" employee.

Certain basic labour relations problems are the same for both private sector and public sector employement. These problems can be summarized as (13.1):

1. *Rule making at the workplace:* Government employees, like their private sector counterparts, are equally concerned with the procedures by which they are chosen for further training and promotion.

2. *Determining the compensation of employees:* Managers, whether operating in the private or public sector, are obliged to keep salaries within "reasonable" limits. Conflict can just as easily arise in the public as the private sector over the meaning that should be attached to the word "reasonable".

3. *Settling grievances:* Public employees are subjected to the same types of complaints and grievances that are so common in the private sector.

It is not surprising then, that public employees would be interested in some form of collective bargaining. Yet in spite of these similar problems, labour relations practices in the public sector have not developed at the same rate nor in the same manner as they have in the private sector.

It has been argued that the following factors have contributed to the relatively slower pace at which collective bargaining has been introduced into the public service:

1. *Essential services.* Many public sector services are of an "essential" nature with few acceptable substitutes. Consequently, politicians have felt "public opinion" would not support legislation which could lead to inconvenience and public hardship for their constituents.

2. *The "discipline of the balance sheet" is lacking in the public sector.* The public sector is not dependent upon a designated profit level for its continued existence. Even though budget considerations cannot be completely neglected, there is more leeway in the public than the private sector for adjusting budgets through the use of political tactics. As a result, the opinion has been expressed that public employee organizations could gain undue power vis-a-vis elected officials and successfully win an undeserved allocation of public resources. Ultimately, the taxpayer could be the loser if public employees were granted extensive bargaining rights.

3. *The "sovereignty issue".* Concern has been expressed on many occasions that governments which engage in collective bargaining with their employees are compromising the principle of "the sovereignty of the state". In other words, elected officials have been granted the authority to manage public affairs on behalf of all citizens and sharing this authority with government employees would be an illegal delegation of power.

4. *"Advantageous" conditions attached to public service employment.* Editorial writers have traditionally been of the opinion that public service employees neither want nor need collective bargaining rights in view of the relative security and other "fringes" which they are alleged to enjoy.

In spite of the truth or falsity of these factors, collective bargaining is now becoming an accepted feature in the Canadian public service. However, there are some parts of the "public service" which have developed more extensive collective bargaining rights than others.

In this book, the term "public service" is used in its broadest sense to include the following categories of "employees":

1. Direct Public Employees: those employees who work for a government department which is specifically under the direction of an elected "cabinet minister" or comparable official (for example, the Department of Health and Welfare). It has been estimated that union membership in the public service has increased from about 75,000 members in 1962 to 380,000 in 1973.

2. Public Agency Employees: those employees who work for government agencies, commissions, or corporations which are run by government appointed administrators. Although no exact data is available, it is a well known fact that a large majority of those employed by liquor boards, hydro-electric companies, Air Canada, and other Crown corporations are now unionized and are often regarded as the "militants" of the public sector.

3. Publicly Subsidized Employees: those individuals who are employed by institutions or clientele that are funded by government. Between 1962 and 1973 the number of union members in education, health and welfare jumped from about 52,000 in the former year to about 453,000 in the latter year.

4. Public Interest Employees: those employees heavily influenced by governmental decrees because it is believed that the general welfare of society could be damaged if a continuous and standard quality of services is not maintained. (It should be noted that this latter category and the previous three are by no means mutually exclusive.)

II   COLLECTIVE BARGAINING BY FEDERAL PUBLIC EMPLOYEES (13.2)

The "employer" of public employees may be a federal, provincial, or municipal government. Each level of government employs large numbers of people and is faced with somewhat different structures of collective action by its employees.

A "true" collective bargaining relationship was introduced into the Canadian federal public service in 1967 when Bills C-170, C-181 and C-182 became law. The following is an outline of certain aspects of the collective bargaining relationship which has been established within the federal public service.

1.   The Employer

Bill C-182 defines two categories of employers:

    a)   The Treasury Board, which is designated as the employer of individuals within the central administration.

    b)   Special agencies (such as the National Research Council, the Economic Council of Canada and the Defence Research Board), which operate as separate entities.

2.   The Public Service Staff Relations Board (PSSRB)

The role of the PSSRB is analogous to that of the various labour relations boards which function in the private sector. However, the PSSRB possesses a wider range of responsibilities than most Canadian labour relations boards.

3.   Organizing and Maintaining a Union Under the Public Service Staff Relations Act (PSSRA)

(a) Who is included in the definition of an "employee?": Legislation which governs labour relations in the private sector usually prohibits certain persons from becoming involved in the "employee" side of the collective bargaining process. The same types of rules apply in the federal public service. Under the PSSRA, the following categories of individuals are excluded from collective

bargaining:
- persons employed in a managerial or confidential capacity (which includes individuals having executive duties and responsibilities in relation to the development and administration of government programs)
- persons whose duties include those of a personnel administrator and persons required to deal formally on behalf of the employer concerning grievances.
- certain types of persons locally engaged outside Canada
- persons paid fees of office
- part-time employees
- casual employees with less than six months of service.

The PSSRB has the final say in any disagreements over whether or not a particular individual is eligible for union membership.

. *b) Employer opposition to unionism:* The PSSRA contains provisions which prohibit certain "unfair labour practices" such as:
- employer participation in employee organizations
- employer interference in the formation or administration of employee organizations (which includes intimidation, threats, bribes, discrimination and refusals to employ individuals involved in union activities)
- the solicitation of union membership on the employer's premises during working hours without the employers' permission.

The PSSRB is authorized to receive complaints relating to these matters, to decide upon the validity of such complaints and to issue restraining and compliance orders if necessary.

(c) Certification: The Federal Public Service Staff Relations Board is responsible for overseeing the certification of unions as bargaining agents for appropriate groups of employees. Certification involves two basic tasks: defining the bargaining unit and determining whether a union has "adequate" employee support.

All "employees" in the federal public service are classified into occupational *categories* set out in the Public Service Staff Relations Act, section 2(r). In addition, each occupational *category* is subdivided into a number of specific occupation *groups.* Typical occupation categories and occupational groups which are identified in the PSSRA include:

Occupational Category	Occupational Group
Scientific and Professional	Chemistry
	Law
	Medicine
	Meteorology
	Nursing
Administrative and Foreign Service	Computer Systems Administration
	Information Services
	Programme Administration
Technical	Electronics
	Photography
	Technical Inspection
Administrative Support	Clerical and Regulatory
	Data Processing
	Secretarial, Stenographic
	Typing

Operational   Firefighters
                                                   General Labour and Trades
                                                   Postal Operations

The PSSRB traditionally respects these categories and groups when defining appropriate bargaining units (unless such a unit does not permit the satisfactory representation of employees). Also, the PSSRB may recognize a unit composed of non-supervisory employees, all supervisory employees, or both supervisory and non-supervisory employees.

The PSSRB will certify an employee association if the applicant employee association can show that the majority of employees in the bargaining unit support the association (no mention is made of requiring such employees to be members of the association), and that the association has been duly authorized.

The PSSRA also sets out procedures for decertification and successor rights very similar to those applicable in the private sector.

(d) Negotiations: Certain subjects are excluded from bargaining by provisions of the PSSRA. For example:

— no term or condition of employment may be included in a collective agreement if it requires legislative implementation (other than the appropriation of moneys).
— bargaining is prevented on subjects falling under the jurisdiction of the Public Service Commission (the administrative agency concerned with public service employment), including recruitment, promotions, transfers, layoffs, discharge for incompetence and the superannuation plan.
— the employer has the sole right to determine such things as the distribution of work, manning of equipment, determination of duties, and job evaluation.

At present, there is a growing feeling among employees and their bargaining agents that these constraints on what is bargainable are excessively restrictive.

(e) Conflict resolution: The PSSRA requires that before giving notice to bargain, a bargaining agent must decide whether a conciliation-strike procedure or an arbitration procedure will be used should an impasse develop. Once this choice is made by the bargaining agent and is communicated to the PSSRB, it must be accepted by the employer. The bargaining agent has the right to make a different choice for each subsequent collective agreement if it so chooses.

If the bargaining agent chooses the strike route, conciliation procedures must be invoked before a strike can occur. The chairman of the PSSRB is responsible for appointing a conciliation officer when requested to do so by either the employer or the bargaining agent. Upon receiving the report of the conciliation officer the chairman of the PSSRB decides whether or not a conciliation board should be appointed. If the chairman makes a "no board" decision, or if the board is unsuccessful in assisting the parties in reaching an agreement, strike action may be taken by the union.

The PSSRA does not guarantee all the members of a bargaining unit the right to strike. When the employer receives notice to bargain, he is required to furnish the PSSRB and the bargaining agent with a written list of designated "essential" employees (*i.e.,* "employees whose duties the performance of which at any particular time or any specified period of time is or will be necessary in the interest of the safety or security of the public"). The fact that employees on this designated list are not allowed to strike is of great concern to the bargaining agent. Consequently, the bargaining agent is given the right to express its objections to the employer's "designated" employee list. Where the bargaining agent challenges the employer's interpretation of essential employees, the

PSSRB is given the power to make a final ruling. This responsibility places the PSSRB in the position of being able to determine whether there will be no strike, a partial strike, or a total strike.

When the PSSRA was passed in 1967, it was anticipated that most employees would choose voluntary arbitration rather than the strike route for resolving impasses in the negotiation of collective agreements. Originally, the PSSRA specified a Public Service Arbitration Tribunal to deal with the arbitration of negotiation disputes. In 1975, the PSSRA was amended and the PSSRB assumed the functions and powers of the Tribunal, except where the chairman of the PSSRB considers it desirable to appoint an outside arbitrator.

When either the employer or bargaining agent petitions the PSSRB for arbitration, the Board will ensure that a properly constituted arbitration committee is formed. This committee is restricted to deliberating upon those issues considered to be within the realm of public service collective bargaining and is required to consider the following criteria:

(i)   the needs of the public service for qualified employees.

(ii)   the conditions of employment in similar occupations outside the public service, including such geographic, industrial, or other variations as the Arbitration Tribunal may consider relevant.

(iii)   the need to maintain appropriate relationships in the conditions of employment as between occupations in the public service.

(iv)   the need to establish terms and conditions of employment that are fair and reasonable in relation to the qualifications required, the work performed, the responsibility assumed and the nature of the services rendered.

(v)   any other factor that to it appears to be relevant to the matter in dispute.

(f) Contract administration: grievances – Grievance handling in the federal public service is characterized by somewhat unique features:

i) The definition of a grievance: The PSSRA defines a "grievance" as a complaint in writing which can extent beyond those matters covered by a collective agreement. Also, the right to grieve is extended to individuals exempted from bargaining units.

ii) Grievance procedures: Employees who are represented by a certified bargaining agent have access to those grievance procedures negotiated in a collective agreement. In addition, the PSSRB has the power to issue directions for the processing of grievances for employees not covered by a collective agreement. Where inconsistencies arise, grievance procedures contained within a collective agreement take precedence over PSSRB grievance procedures.

iii) Adjudication: The concept frequently referred to as "grievance arbitration" in the private sector is called "adjudication" in the federal public service. Only certain types of grievances can be submitted for adjudication:

– first, the grievance must have been presented up to and through the first level in the grievance process.

– second, the grievance must remain unresolved.

– third, the grievance must stem from the interpretation or application of a provision of a collective agreement or disciplinary action resulting in discharge, suspension, or financial penalty.

No other grievances can be presented for adjudication and the decision taken at the final level of the grievance process is binding on all parties involved.

(g) Current trends in federal public service collective bargaining: One significant trend has been the growing number of unions opting for the conciliation-strike route rather than the arbitration route as a means of resolving contract deadlocks. When the PSSRA was passed in 1967, only 21 percent of the union members chose the conciliation-strike route. By 1976, nearly two-

thirds of the union members were working out their differences at the bargaining table even if it required overt strike action. The major reasons for this result include:

- the narrow legalistic approach that has been taken by arbitrators
- the failure of arbitration tribunals to give the criteria underlying their awards.
- the delays in handing down awards (one award took 413 days)
- employee suspicion that the arbitration process has not been completely independent of government influence
- the lack of confidence by employees in the data on which the arbitration process is dependent.

These shortcomings have also been blamed for the increasing tendency of federal employees to engage in illegal work stoppages. Recently, public antipathy towards legal and illegal strikes by government employees has been growing. This fact is reflected in the types of recommendations made in 1976 by the Senate-Commons Committee on employee-employer relations in the public service. Its primary recommendations included:

1) Heavy fines and the threat of suspension from employment for illegal strikes.
2) The extension of the definition of "essential services" to include public health and the security of public property, as well as public safety and security.
3) The scope of collective bargaining should be expanded to include technological change and job classifications, but disagreements on these matters should be resolved by compulsory arbitration rather than by work stoppages.
4) Strike votes should be conducted by secret ballot and all members of the bargaining unit should be eligible to vote, whether or not they belong to the union acting as bargaining agent.

A second trend involves the tendency of management to try and "designate" a large number of employees as "essential" employees so that operations can be successfully carried on, thereby rendering any strikes ineffective. Unions have attempted to counter such actions by encouraging "designated" employees to withdraw their services.

A recent report on collective bargaining in the federal public service has suggested that penalties be imposed on designated employees convicted of wilful withdrawal of services and union officials convicted of inciting such actions. In addition, the report recommends that penalties be imposed on any agent of the employer who requires a designated employee to provide services not required by the terms under which the employee was designated.

III   COLLECTIVE BARGAINING BY PROVINCIAL PUBLIC EMPLOYEES (13.3)

In Canada there has been a tendency for provinces to enact specific laws to govern collective bargaining for public employees. At this point in time there does not appear to be any tendency for uniform legislation to emerge among the provinces. However there is a tendency for each province's public service legislation to grow more and more similar to the existing private sector legislation.

It is the purpose of this section to provide a comparison of provincial and federal statutes (as they existed at June 30, 1975), that govern direct public employees and public agency employees in Canada. This comparison involves four primary aspects of the statutes:

a) the applicable act and the category of public employees covered;
b) certification rights; c) bargaining rights; and d) permissible impasse procedures that may be invoked by public employees.

This comparison, as shown in Table 13.1, documents the following facts:
1. Only one jurisdiction (Saskatchewan) makes absolutely no distinction between the collective bargaining rights that are accorded public and private employees.
2. In five of the remaining ten jurisdictions (New Brunswick, Newfoundland, Ontario, Prince Edward Island and Quebec), the same special legislation applies to direct public employees and public agency employees. One jurisdiction (Alberta) has enacted a special statute which applies only to public agency employees. In three jurisdictions (British Columbia, Manitoba and Nova Scotia) public agency employees are covered by the same statutes that apply to private sector employees.
3. In nine of the eleven jurisdictions, the applicable labour legislation permits the certification of any bargaining agent that represents an appropriate unit of employees. Two jurisdictions (Alberta and Nova Scotia) designate a particular agent to represent employees. One jurisdiction (Ontario) will not certify a union that is affiliated with a political party, thereby ruling out unions affiliated with the Canadian Labour Congress (which supports the New Democratic Party).
4. Two jurisdictions (British Columbia and Quebec) make substantial use of what is referred to as "two-tiered" bargaining. General master agreements are negotiated for all bargaining units and then subsidiary agreements are worked out for the various subgroups. Seven jurisdictions (British Columbia, New Brunswick, Newfoundland, Nova Scotia, Prince Edward Island, Quebec and Saskatchewan) grant public employees the right to bargain on the same issues as their private sector counterparts.
5. Six jurisdictions (British Columbia, New Brunswick, Newfoundland, Quebec, Saskatchewan and the Federal Government) give public employees the right to strike. One of these (Quebec) does not permit arbitration of a contract dispute. Five jurisdictions require binding arbitration when an impasse in negotiations must be resolved.

At present, it is difficult to keep pace with the actual and anticipated changes in public policy which govern labour relations in Canada's public services. It is hoped that the preceding survey of current statutes has provided some perspective on the range of alternative systems that are currently being experimented with in Canada.

Two tentative conclusions seem to emerge from this analysis. One is that there is no pronounced tendency for uniform public service legislation to evolve among the eleven jurisdictions. The second is that there is a tendency for each jurisdiction's public service legislation to more and more closely resemble the legislation which governs collective bargaining in the private sector. This latter trend is not surprising — but the rate at which the convergence has taken place in recent years certainly is.

In an effort to hasten "convergence" even more, the Canadian Labour Congress encouraged the formation of the National Union of Provincial Government Employees (NUPGE) and made membership in this union a prerequisite for any provincial government employee association seeking CLC affiliation. By 1976, six provincial government employee associations (British Columbia, Alberta, Saskatchewan, Manitoba, Prince Edward Island and Newfoundland), with a total of more than 105,000 members, made the NUPGE one of Canada's five largest unions. The public service unions of both Ontario and Nova Scotia have so far refused to endorse the new national union and as a result have been expelled from the CLC. In New Brunswick, the majority of civil servants were represented by the Canadian Union of Public Employees which was already affiliated with the CLC.

Figure 13.1

Laws Regulating Collective Bargaining in the Canadian Public Service

Jurisdiction	Does Private Sector Labor Relations Act Apply?	Applicable Act(s) and Coverage	Certification Rights	Bargaining Rights	Permissible Impasse Procedures
Alberta	No	Public Service Act covers direct public employees	Names Civil Service Association as sole bargaining agent Professional employees have right to opt out of the general bargaining unit	Minister of Labor makes final decision on what is negotiable	An arbitration board makes binding recommendations
		Crown Agencies Employee Relations Act covers public agency employees	Same	Same	Same
British Columbia	No	Public Service Labor Relations Act covers direct public employees	Employees represented by unions certified by Labor Relations Board (same Board as private sector)	Each of 3 designated bargaining units (nurses, licensed professionals, all other public service employees) works out master agreements covering all employees in the unit.	Voluntary mediation and voluntary binding arbitration provisions. Strike possible within 3 months immediately following strike vote.

Jurisdiction	Does Private Sector Labor Relations Act Apply?	Applicable Act(s) and Coverage	Certification Rights	Bargaining Rights	Permissible Impasse Procedures
	Yes	Labor Code covers public agency employees	—	Subsidiary agreements then worked out to cover employees in each occupational group. Pensions are a bargainable item.	—
Manitoba	No	Manitoba Civil Service Act covers direct public employees	Act gives statutory recognition to Manitoba Govt. Employees Union. Civil servants can change bargaining agent if a majority cease to be members of this association	Negotiate compensation and working conditions. A joint council has been set up for discussing "nonnegotiable" issues	Binding arbitration of unresolved disputes
	Yes	Labor Act covers public agency employees	—	—	—

Figure 13.1 (Continued)

Jurisdiction	Does Private Sector Labor Relations Act Apply?	Applicable Act(s) and Coverage	Certification Rights	Bargaining Rights	Permissible Impasse Procedures
New Brunswick	No	Public Service Labor Relations Act covers direct public employees, public agency employees, and publicly subsidized employees (schools and hospitals)	No special restrictions on bargaining agents that may be certified by Public Service Labor Relations Board. Bargaining units determined on the basis of a statutory classification system which resembles that of federal system. Permits the organization of supervisory and nonsupervisory staff in the same bargaining unit.	There is a 45-day statutory time limit on public sector negotiations unless the parties agree otherwise	Bargaining agent may choose binding arbitration or a conciliation strike route to dispute settlement
Newfoundland	No	Public Service (Collective Bargaining) Act covers direct public employees and public agency employees	Free to associate in unions of their choice certified by same Labor Relations Board that deals with private sector	Traditional collective bargaining rights	Right to strike. But wide discretionary power in the hands of the Lieutenant-Governor-in-Council to limit this right to strike. Labor Relations Board may request employer to supply a list of "essential" employees.

Figure 13.1 (Continued)

Jurisdiction	Does Private Sector Labor Relations Act Apply?	Applicable Act(s) and Coverage	Certification Rights	Bargaining Rights	Permissible Impasse Procedures
Nova Scotia	No	Civil Service Joint Council Act covers direct public employees	Gives statutory recognition to the Civil Service Association of Nova Scotia		Use of binding arbitration. Strike forbidden
	Yes	Trade Union Act covers public agency employees			Right to strike available but must wait 30 days longer than in private sector to use this right
Ontario	No	Ontario Crown Employees Coll. Bargaining Act covers direct public employees and public agency employees	Ontario Public Service Labor Relations Tribunal grants representation rights to employee organizations that represent an appropriate unit of employees. Similar to private sector (but excludes employee organizations that support a political party)	Act outlines in detail issues that are and are not to be subject of bargaining or arbitration	Strikes and lockouts are forbidden and disputes must be referred to binding arbitration

Figure 13.1 (Continued)

Jurisdiction	Does Private Sector Labor Relations Act Apply?	Applicable Act(s) and Coverage	Certification Rights	Bargaining Rights	Permissible Impasse Procedures
Prince Edward Island	No	Civil Service Act covers direct public employees and public agency employees	After a prescribed transitional period ends, any organization of civil servants may apply and be designated as bargaining agent if it represents more than 50 per cent of the civil servants	Parties must meet 6 months before expiration date of agreement to determine data needed by other party. They must meet 4 months before expiration to present and analyze data. Topics for negotiations include "items which are presented by mutual agreement of the parties."	Binding arbitration is the final step in dispute settlement
Quebec	No	Civil Service Act covers direct public employees, public agency employees, publicly subsidized employees and public interest employees. (Bill 46, 1971) provided for government participation on the	All government employees (except professional groups) eligible to bargain collectively and to organize in unions of their choice. Professionals may organize in single or multiprofessional unions as long as	Negotiations involving monetary issues are carried on between the government and a "Common Front" of unions. Negotiations are also carried on with separate groups to discuss issues peculiar to each group after a central	The Quebec government does not allow arbitration on the wage bill in the public sector. Employees in all public services are eligible to use strike action after the formula for delaying work stoppages has been

Figure 13.1 (Continued)

Jurisdiction	Does Private Sector Labor Relations Act Apply?	Applicable Act(s) and Coverage	Certification Rights	Bargaining Rights	Permissible Impasse Procedures
		management bargaining teams and province-wide negotiations for all employees negotiating in the health and education sectors)	they remain separate from nonprofessional employees	agreement is arrived at	adhered to. Technically strikes are not legal until an agreement has been reached by the parties (or by decision of the court) on the provision of essential services
Saskatchewan	Yes	Trade Union Act	—	—	—
Federal Government	No	Public Service Staff Relations Act (PSSRA) covers direct public employees covers a few public agency employees such as Atomic Energy, Economic Council of Canada, National Research Council, National Film Board	Administered by Public Service Staff Relations Board bargaining unit usually defined in terms of occupational categories and groups defined in PSSRA. PSSRB may include supervisory employees and professionals within bargaining unit	Matters precluded from bargaining by PSSRA include: appointments, transfers, and promotions layoffs and discharge superannuation, death benefit, accident compensation	Before giving notice to bargain, bargaining agent must choose whether a conciliation strike procedure or arbitration procedure will be used if an impasse develops. When employer receives notice to bargain, he is required to furnish PSSRB and bargaining agent with a list

Figure 13.1 (Continued)

Jurisdiction	Does Private Sector Labor Relations Act Apply?	Applicable Act(s) and Coverage	Certification Rights	Bargaining Rights	Permissible Impasse Procedures
	Yes	Canada Labor Code covers most public agency employees	---	---	of designated "essential" employees who cannot strike. PSSRB has final say in disputes over the definition of designated employees

Source: Phillips, G.E.   "A Comparative Analysis of Canadian Public Service Labour Relations Statutes". *Journal of Collective Negotiations in the Public Sector.* Vol. 5, No. 1, 1976.

IV   COLLECTIVE BARGAINING BY MUNICIPAL EMPLOYEES (13.4)

In most provinces, the right of municipal employees to organize and bargain collectively with municipal governments is governed by the same legislation which applies to the private sector. However, certain categories of municipal employees, such as police, firefighters and members of specified professional groups may be governed by special provincial statutes. As a rule this special legislation requires those employees involved to be organized in separate bargaining units and prohibits the withdrawal of services in the event of an impasse.

In the future it is expected that both federal and provincial public employees will receive the same legal rights as their counterparts in municipal government. According to Professor Crispo, one must recognize that:

". . . while collective bargaining in general is under attack, it is particularly suspect and vulnerable in the public service. This is to be expected, given the wave of strikes that have beset public services, previously almost uninterrupted through industrial disputes. Yet such disputes were themselves to be anticipated sooner or later, as public servants began to demand the same collective bargaining rights as employees in the private sector of economy. Indeed, it could be argued that there has been less strife than might have been expected in this period of experimentation, innovation, and almost trial-and-error in public service collective bargaining.

"To keep things in historical perspective, a possible comparison with current developments in government employee-employer relations is to be found in the state of bargaining in basic and secondary manufacturing shortly after World War II. The then relatively newly-formed industrial unions found themselves with new-found powers and rights, which they asserted in an unprecedented wave of industrial strife. Yet, after a short time, industrial relations settled down in these industries to the fairly stable form they have retained to this day. A similar settling and stabilizing pattern could soon begin to establish iteslf in the public service . . . " (13.5)

Summary

1.   Explanations of why differences exist between collective bargaining in the public and private sectors include the essentiality of public services, the diminished significance of the discipline of the balance sheet, government sovereignty and the "advantageous" employment conditions in the public service.

2.   Public service employees can be subclassified as direct public employees, public agency employees, publicly subsidized employees and public interest employees.

3.   Federal public employees are governed by a special statute, the Public Service Staff Relations Act. The PSSRA sets out specific procedures for certification of a bargaining agent, contract negotiations and contract administration. Strikes are permitted under the PSSRA, but there is a provision which enables the employer to designate certain "essential" employees who are not permitted to strike.

4.   The laws governing collective bargaining in Canada's ten provincial jurisdictions vary quite significantly. All jurisdictions have now granted public

employees the right to join an association and to negotiate a collective agreement. However, there are a variety of restrictions on the types of unions that can be certified, the topics that can be negotiated and the methods that can be used should an impasse develop in the negotiation process.

5.   Most municipal employees are covered by the same provincial legislation which applies in the private sector.

References

13.1 Dunlop, J.T. "The Social Utility of Collective Bargaining" in *Challenges to Collective Bargaining* edited by L. Ulman. Engelwood Cliffs, N.J., Prentice-Hall, Inc., 1967, p. 169.

13.2 The Institute of Public Administration of Canada. *Collective Bargaining in the Public Service,* 1972, pp. 45-55.

13.3 Phillips, G.E. "A Comparative Analysis of Canadian Public Service Labour Relations Statutes". *Journal of Collective Negotiations in the Public Sector.* Vol. 5, No. 1, 1976.

13.4 The Institute of Public Administration of Canada. *op. cit.,* pp. 1-10.

13.5 *Ibid.,* p. 105.

Suggested Readings for Further Study

Arthurs H. W. *Collective Bargaining By Public Employees In Canada: Five Models.* Ann Arbor, Institute of Labour and Industrial Relations, Wayne State University, 1971.

Herman, E. "The Canadian Approach To Grievance Adjudication In The Public Sector". *Journal of Collective Negotiations,* Vol. 3(1), Winter, 1974.

Institute of Public Administration of Canada. *Collective Bargaining In The Public Service.* March, 1973.

Kruger, A. *Bargaining In The Public Sector: Some Canadian Experiments.* London, England: International Industrial Relations Association, September, 1973.

Muir, J. "Canada's Experience With the Right of Public Employees to Strike". *Monthly Labour Review,* July, 1969.

Chapter 14

The Canadian
Professional Sector

I   THE MEANING OF PROFESSIONALISM

Attempting to find a precise definition of professionalism in the relevant literature can be an extremely frustrating experience. Almost anyone who wants to be called a professional and almost every occupation that wishes to lay claim to professional status can find some justification for doing so. One of the most useful definitions of a "professional worker" is that provided by Professor Goldenberg in her classic study on professional workers and collective bargaining. In this study, Professor Goldenberg uses a broad definition:

"based on criteria of educational standards and group organization in the following combinations (14.1):

1. Academic Specialization and Formal Organization.

Some professions, particularly the older ones, combine a high level of specialized academic training with organization into exclusive professional associations. By virtue of their licensing and disciplinary powers, granted by provincial legislation, such professional associations, in effect, constitute 'closed shops'. Doctors, dentists, lawyers, engineers, etc., belong in this category.

2. A Formal Professional Organization and Specialized Training but not Necessarily a University Degree.

Others are identifiable as separate groups, but without the exclusiveness or rigid academic requirements of the traditional professions. Their members require some specialized competence and training, but this may or may not include a university degree and membership in the governing body is not always a condition for the practise of the profession. Teachers and nurses, having fulfilled their respective licensing qualifications will be considered as professionals by this definition and are, in fact, already treated as professionals in much of the legislation governing their employment relationships.

3. Academic Specialization Without Corporate Organization.

With the proliferation of the social and physical sciences in recent years, a third category of professional personnel has emerged. This category covers all university graduates with specialized degrees who do not fit into either of the classifications defined above. In this way, we avoid excluding from the status of professional those persons who do not hold a licence or who practise in a profession or type of work for which no licensing body exists. By this definition, we may consider as professionals librarians, social workers, dietitions, etc., as well as any person with a minimum of a B.A. degree in some area of academic specialization. This covers a wide range of occupations such as economists, sociologists, psychologists, physicists, chemists, statisticians, many of which are represented in the 'multi-professional' civil service unions."

II   THE RELATIONSHIP BETWEEN PROFESSIONALS AND COLLECTIVE BARGAINING

Until recent times the number of professional associations was small and almost exclusively comprised of self–employed practioners, such as doctors or lawyers. Such individuals were granted special privileges of self-government because their clients were judged to be incapable of judging who is a qualified practioner and the quality of service that should be expected. To protect their clientele, associations of professionals were given three basic rights:

1. *Control of entry to the profession:* This was accomplished by developing a system of certification and specific requirements necessary for certification. In many cases, these regulations were backed up by government decrees.

2. *Control over professional behaviour:* Most professional associations have a code of ethics to which all members must adhere.

3. *Control over the provision of a service:* Professional associations usually specify the types of activities which their members have the exclusive right to perform or not perform.

Each of these rights was intended to regulate relations between professionals and their clients, or between professionals and other professionals. In recent years, certain dramatic changes have had a profound impact on the goals of both professional associations and professional employees. Some of these changes include:

1. *The increasing proportion of professionals who are "employed professionals" rather than private practitioners:* Professional associations normally have no power to impose their fee schedules or conditions of employment on the employers of their members unless such employers themselves are members of the professional association.

2. *Impersonal work relationships:* The growing involvement of the government as an employer and regulator of employment conditions of professionals, combined with the tendency of professionals to be just "another employee", one of a thousand engineers in a plant, or one of a thousand accountants in a large scale bureaucracy, has eroded the individual initiative and undermined the perceived "professional status" of many employees.

3. *Declining personal mobility:* The membership in new and existing professions has increased rapidly both in absolute numbers and in proportion to the labour force as a whole. This, combined with the increasing use of complex technology and subprofessionals, has meant that employment prospects and job security for professionals are no longer as reliable as they once were believed to be.

4. *A perceived deterioration in the economic status of professionals:* Many professionals believe that there has been a narrowing of the differential between the salaries of professionals and those of other workers.

Recent events have shown that although many professional associations have traditionally opposed "trade unionism", they are certainly not opposed to collective bargaining. In fact, some professional associations now deem it unprofessional *not* to take actions to improve the lot of its membership because failure to do so could endanger the availability of services to their clientele in the future.

Even those professional associations which sincerely opposed the use of collective bargaining tactics have been gradually forced to adopt some of the characteristics of unions to prevent traditional unions from organizing their membership. In many instances, professional associations had a number of features which helped them to ward off traditional trade unions:

1.   Salaried professionals felt it was more respectable to join professional associations.

2.   Salaried professionals feared that unions did not have the capacity to perform any of the functions unrelated to collective bargaining which professional associations perform (for example, education standards, entry standards, work standards and relations with other professionals).

3.   Professionals tended to be conservative, supporting a known association of peers rather than an unknown trade union.

III   TROUBLESOME ISSUES IN COLLECTIVE BARGAINING BY PROFESSIONALS

More than a decade ago, Professor Crispo identified the following areas of concern for future relationships between professionals and collective bargaining (14.2):
1.   The compatibility of professionalism and collective bargaining.
2.   The compatibility of the licencing function of professional bodies with collective bargaining functions.
3.   The determination of appropriate bargaining units for professionals.
4.   The development of appropriate methods of dispute settlement for professionals.
5.   The development of an appropriate legal framework within which professional employees should be allowed to bargain.

The first issue has been largely resolved by most professional associations in an affirmative way. As a general rule, the use of collective bargaining techniques by professional associations is "professional", but membership in traditional trade unions by professionals is "unprofessional".

The second issue, the licensing function of professional associations, remains a controversial topic. Some glaring abuses of this power can be found in Canada. At present, however, there seems to be a trend in some jurisdictions towards extending rather than limiting the licensing powers of professional associations. Some associations have experimented with non-professional clientele and governmental representatives on their executive boards, but these have been, for the most part, token gestures designed to promote public relations rather than the public interest.

The third issue, appropriate bargaining units, has been resolved in a variety of ways. As a rule, professional associations have not become directly involved in negotiations which pertain to professionals employed alongside other types of workers in government departments, government agencies and private companies. It is common to find such professionals in separate bargaining units, which are exclusively comprised of professional employees. Also, professionals designated as "managerial employees", or "employees having access to confidential information", have been excluded from collective bargaining altogether. This division in relation to the negotiation function does not appear to have had the profound effects on professional associations that some experts were predicting a decade ago.

Where professionals have become dependent upon funds from intermediary agencies, professional associations have normally taken a more active role in "consultative" and negotiating functions. A common approach that has been used involves province-wide negotiations on general issues, such as fee schedules, and separate local negotiations on issues peculiar to various segments of the association. Most professional associations have won the right to be consulted on a variety of "professional" issues and are now striving to augment their rights to negotiate such issues.

With respect to the fourth issue, professional associations have chosen a variety of procedures to handle bargaining impasses. These include:
1.   The use of licensing powers to prohibit professionals from seeking employment with blacklisted or censured agencies.
2.   Lobbying to gain political or public support on certain issues.
3.   Initiating work slowdowns and work-to-rule procedures.
4.   Engaging in "disguised strikes", such as study sessions and mass resignations.
5.   Engaging in undisguised legal and illegal work stoppages.
6.   Referring the unresolved issues to binding arbitration.

It has already been mentioned that many professional associations have not hesitated to use their licensing privileges to make it an "unprofessional act" for members to refuse to participate in impasse procedures chosen by the association. At the same time, most professional associations have taken it upon themselves to define the level of "essential services" that will be provided while impasse prcedures are being invoked. Generally, there is a significant divergence between the definition of "essential services" provided by the association and that which prevails in the minds of their members' clientele.

Finally, at least four kinds of general legal frameworks can be used to govern collective bargaining by professionals. These include (14.3):

1. A single act which covers all professionals in a particular jurisdiction : As yet no Canadian jurisdiction has opted for this approach.

2. A separate act for each profession: Examples of jurisdictions which do have special acts governing particular professions abound in Canada. Doctors, lawyers, nurses and teachers have all been given special consideration in a number of Canadian jurisdictions during the past decade.

3. The use of the Labour Relations Act which applies to the private sector: There is a tendency for professional associations to attempt to attain the complete range of bargaining rights possessed by unions in the private sector. Once an association has achieved these rights, there is usually nothing to justify the need for a separate act.

4. Reliance on civil laws: It is still possible to find in Canada isolated cases of professions which are excluded from private sector labour legislation and which are not covered under any special act. However, as these associations find it necessary to collectively promote the economic as well as the ethical interests of their members, it is likely that some specific set of applicable legal guidelines will gradually emerge.

Summary

1.   A useful definition of a "professional" can be derived on the basis of a particular group's specialized competence and/or formal organization.

2.   A professional association usually has the right to control "professional behaviour" and the provision of services.

3.   Professional associations have become more involved in collective bargaining for a number of reasons:
— more professionals are in the role of employees rather than self-employed individuals.
— even "self-employed" professionals have been more closely regulated by governmental and other "fee-paying" agencies.
— some trade unions were attempting to include professionals in their membership.

4.   Recent experience with collective bargaining by professionals leads to the following conclusions:
— collective bargaining and professionalism have been accepted as being compatible by the membership of professional associations.
— the compatibility of collective bargaining and the licensing functions of professional associations has been seriously questioned by the clientele which the profession serves.
— "appropriate bargaining units" for professionals are usually defined as separate bargaining units.

- professionals have not avoided the use of traditional trade union tactics where an impasse develops during collective negotiations.
- there is no single "appropriate" legal framework that has been applied to collective bargaining for all professionals.

References

14.1 Goldenberg, S. "Professional Workers and Collective Bargaining". A Study for the Task Force on Labour Relations. Ottawa, Queen's Printer, 1968, pp. 8-9.
14.2 Crispo, John H.G. *Collective Bargaining and the Professional Employer.* Toronto, University of Toronto, 1966, pp. 119-122.
14.3 *Ibid.* p. 122.

Suggested Readings for Further Study

Adell, B.L. and D.D. Carter. *Collective Bargaining For University Faculty In Canada.* Kingston, Industrial Relations Centre, Queen's University, 1972.
Bairstow, Frances. "White Collar Workers and Collective Bargaining" A Study for the Task Force on Labour Relations, Ottawa, 1968.
Crispo, J. *Collective Bargaining and the Professional Employer.* Toronto, Industrial Relations Centre, University of Toronto, 1966.
Goldenberg, S. B. "Professional Workers and Collective Bargaining". A Study of the Task Force on Labour Relations. Ottawa, 1968.
Labour Canada. *Collective Bargaining Legislation for Special Groups in Canada.* Ottawa, Canada Department of Labour, 1975.

Part E: Interaction Processes Which Complement Collective Bargaining

The central theme of this book is the practice of labour relations and collective bargaining in Canada. The successful negotiation and administration of a collective agreement often requires that the parties involved are knowledgeable about personnel policies, labour market analysis and labour standards legislation. In Chapter 15, the centre of interest is the definition of some basic concepts in personnel administration. Chapter 16 is concerned with describing selected topics of labour market analysis and presenting areas that are most often covered by labour standards legislation.

Chapter 15

Concepts From
Personnel Administration

I INTRODUCTORY TERMINOLOGY

The personnel function of a business organization is concerned with the development and maintenance of its human resources. As is the case in most fields of study, there are certain terms frequently used by those engaged in the practice of personnel administration.

1. Terms Used In Connection With the Work People Perform

a) Job: The term "job" refers to the contents of a particular task (*i.e.*, the duties, responsibilities and conditions attached to a particular work assignment). For example, two machinists who are performing similar duties and who require similar training, experience and personal characteristics would be said to hold the same kind of job.

b) Position: As previously noted, a job refers to a classification of work. The number of slots authorized for a particular classification are referred to as the number of positions. Each person performing a job occupies a position, but there may also be positions that are unoccupied at certain periods of time.

Thus, a firm may have five positions authorized for the job of typist, but may only have three people filling the job of typist.

It should be mentioned that there is also a tendency to use the term "position" to denote "high status" work. For instance, a personnnel director would be described as having a position, while his secretary would be said to have a job. Obviously, this is quite a different interpretation than that previously described.

c) Occupations and job families: These terms cover groupings of jobs with common characteristics. For example, clerical work may comprise a wide variety of jobs and the individual occupying any of these jobs could be said to hold the occupation of a clerk.

d) Job grades: At the other extreme, a particular job may be broken down into a series of grades. Thus, a firm may distinguish between a Clerk I, Clerk II, and so on.

e) Job design: This term refers to the process of deciding what the content of jobs should be. Job design may be the responsiblity of a wide variety of individuals, ranging from the workers themselves to professional industrial engineers. It is still quite common to find many decisions pertaining to job design residing with a worker's immediate supervisor.

f) Job assignment: Job assignment refers to the process by which individuals are placed in various job classifications.

2. Terms Used In Connection with Describing Jobs

a) Job analysis: Job analysis involves the process of gathering information about the jobs of an organization.

b) Job descriptions: Job descriptions are records of what each job consists of. Such descriptions usually contain information on the job title, the "average" duties of those occupying the job and the organizational aspects of the job (*i.e.*, the persons to whom the holder of the job must report).

c) Job specifications: Job specifications refer to the employee qualifications that are necessary to perform a given job. Once a job description has been prepared, it may then be possible to enumerate the personal, mental and physical attributes appropriate to a particular job. This information can be used during the hiring process and in evaluating the relative worth of jobs.

There is a certain amount of ambiguity in the personnel field concerning the use of the terms "job descriptions", "job specifications" and "employee specifications". In some contexts, the terms "job description" and "job specification" are used as synonyms that refer to statements describing the job itself, while the term "employee specifications" is used to refer to statements describing the kind of employee who should fill a given job.

II   JOB EVALUATION METHODS

Job descriptions and job specifications provide the data for assessing the "value" of a job relative to all other jobs in an organization (*i.e.*, job evaluation). Some of the most common methods of job evaluation include:

1. *The ranking method:* Under this method of job evaluation, jobs are ranked in order of importance in accordance with the judgments handed down by a committee. Next, the jobs are grouped into a reasonable number of classes and wage rates are established for each of the classes.

This method is simple and easy to establish. However, it is also extremely subjective and the rationale for the final ranks is often difficult to explain.

2. *The job classification method:* Under the job classification method, job classes or grades are established first. Once this has been done, specified individuals or committees read the job descriptions and place each job in one of the classes or grades. Each grade is given a minimum and maximum salary or wage for employees performing jobs categorized within that grade.

This method possesses the simplicity of the ranking method, but tends to be a more accurate system. However, there is still a great deal of subjectivity in the establishment of classes and the determination of the appropriate class for each job.

3. *The point system.* This system of a job evaluation is most widely used by large organizations. The following is a brief outline of the point system:

a) A listing of six to nine major characteristics common to all jobs being covered is prepared. These characteristics are referred to as "job factors" and often include such things as skill, effort, responsibility and job conditions. In some cases, these major factors may be broken down into a series of subfactors.

b) A certain number of "points" or a range of "points" is assigned to each factor. These "points" are assigned by a committee and determine the relative value of the chosen factors. As with the other systems described, a certain amount of subjectivity is involved in this process.

c) Job descriptions are used to assess the job factors contained in each job and the degree in which each factor is necessary for performing a specified job. Point totals are then assigned to each job, determining the relative value of each job.

d) In the final stage, the point values are converted into dollar units. Generally, a series of job classes is established, with each job class encompassing a range of point values as shown in Table 15.1

TABLE 15.1

Range of Point Values	Salary
100-139	500
140-179	550
180-219	600

A major disadvantage of the point system is its complexity. As a result, the system is difficult to implement and is frequently not understood by employees.

4. Factor comparison: The factor comparison system also starts out with an analysis of job descriptions. In this case, however, job descriptions are used to determine "key" jobs in a company which:
 a) cover the spectrum of low and high paid jobs;
 b) job analysts can assign an "acceptable" rate of pay;
 c) are clearly definable.
These key jobs are ranked on an overall basis and then on a factor by factor basis. Next, the basic pay for each job is allocated to each factor. For example:

Step 1 (Overall ranking)

Key Job No.	Overall Rank	Base Rate
Job 5	1	10.00
Job 10	2	8.00
Job 15	3	6.00

Step II (Factor by factor ranking)

Key Job No.	Overall Rank	Base Rate	Mental Req'ts		Physical Req'ts		Working Conditions	
			Rank	Rate	Rank	Rate	Rank	Rate
Job 5	1	10.00	1	4.00	1	3.00	2	3.00
Job 10	2	8.00	3	2.00	2	2.00	1	4.00
Job 15	3	8.00	2	3.00	3	1.00	3	2.00

After the key jobs have been selected, ranked and assigned base rates for each factor, every other job can be compared to these key jobs. The similarity between a job factor and the key job factor is noted and the job being evaluated is given the appropriate factor value. For instance, if Job 9 is deemed to have the following similarities to key jobs, it would be evaluated in this manner:

Factor	Similar To	Assigned Rate
Mental Requirements	1	4.00
Physical Requirements	2	2.00
Working Conditions	3	2.00
Total Base Rate		8.00

Once again, this is a complex system which employees may find very difficult to comprehend.

III   EMPLOYEE EVALUATION

Many salaried personnel are subjected to certain formal or informal evaluation processes as a basis for hiring and establishing salary scales. As increasing numbers of scientific, technical, and professional employees are unionized, it is becoming increasingly important for their representatives to understand the basic features of existing employee appraisal systems.

Some examples of employee evaluation techniques currently used in industry include:

1. Graphic rating scales: One of the most frequently used employee evaluation techniques is the graphic rating scale. A list of qualities to be rated, such as quality of work, quantity of work and relationships with co-workers is developed. In addition, different degrees of each characteristic are provided, ranging from outstanding to unsatisfactory. A certain number of points is assigned to each degree. The rater next makes a decision as to which of the degrees most accurately describes the employee being evaluated. Finally, a total point score is calculated.

2. Ranking method: This method involves rating employees of a given job against one another. As was the case with the graphic rating scale, a list of desirable traits is provided. Points are assigned to each employee on the basis of his ranking relative to other employees with respect to each trait. For instance, if five employees are being rated, the appraiser would rank each person from first to fifth for each trait. The individual ranked first for quality of work would receive five points, the individual ranked second would receive four points, and so on. The employee's scores in all categories are then totalled.

3. Forced choice method: This method uses an appraisal form which contains sets of four attributes. The appraiser is required to choose the attribute which is most characteristic of the employee and then the attribute least characteristic of the employee. The points attached to the various responses are unknown to the appraiser. After the form has been completed, another individual tabulates the final result. Although this method tends to eliminate bias, it is complex and not useful for employee counselling.

4. Critical incident method: The critical incident method requires the appraiser to keep a record of unusually good and bad impressions of each employee. This record is then analyzed and the collected impressions or incidents are ranked in order of frequency and importance. Numerical weights can then be assigned to the incidents and a score obtained.

Employee evaluation systems such as these are not without their weaknesses. In general, many formal evaluation systems become unacceptable to employees and useless to the employer because of the following problems:

1) The appraiser does not possess adequate knowledge of the employee being rated.

2) The appraiser does not understand the meaning that should be attached to the terminology appearing on the appraisal form.

3) The appraiser may be unduly influenced by recent events and isolated or abnormal conditions.

4) Those using the appraisal results fail to recognize the psychological and sociological repercussions of the system.

IV   WAGE PAYMENT PLANS

There are a significant variety of wage payment plans that an organization can adopt. The following are the main methods of wage payment that are currently used:

1. Daywork plans: These plans represent the simplest and most common methods of paying employees. They involve paying employees a fixed amount per hour, day, week, month or some other time period. Such plans are easy to compute and readily understood by employees. Also, employees are not required to meet a specified quantity standard.

2. *Measured daywork plans:* As with the daywork plan, employees working under measured daywork plans are paid a fixed amount per time period. In addition, each employee is required to produce a certain number of units during this time period. This standard number of units is formulated after a careful study of each job and is communicated to the employee. Employees who do not maintain the desired standard over a given time period *i.e.,* monthly or quarterly), may be subjected to a decreased level of compensation during the subsequent time period.

3. *Individual incentive plans:* Two of the best known types of individual incentive plans are:

a) Piecework plans: Piecework plans constitute the simplest type of incentive plans. Such plans pay an employee a fixed amount for each unit of production, and earnings vary with the level of output. The value prescribed for each unit of production is known as the piece rate and is generally set by time study techniques. A variation of this plan is to pay employees a bonus for any units produced in excess of a previously determined standard.

b) Timesaving plans: A more complex incentive system uses time as a measure of output. A standard time allowance is established for each task. If an employee completes the task in less than the standard time, he is given a bonus for the amount of time saved. The bonus payment is usually some fraction of the regular payment, thereby sharing any gains between both the employer and employee. For example, assume an employee whose rate of pay is $4.00 per hour takes 7 hours to complete a task which has been allotted a standard time of 8 hours. Assume also the bonus percentage is set at 75. The individual's earnings for this task would be:

$$(7 \times \$4.00) + (8 - 7) (\$4.00) (75\%)$$

$$= \$28.00 + \$3.00 = \$31.00$$

In addition, the individual would be able to start his next task during the eighth hour and would be receiving full pay for this work. Thus, the employee will earn $31.00 + $4.00 = $35.00 during the eight hour time period rather than 8 hours x $4.00 = $32.00 if he had not saved any time. The tasks completed will cost the employer $35 rather than the $36 (*i.e.,* $32 for Task 1 plus $4.00 for one hour of Task 2) outlay that would have been necessitated without a time saving plan.

4. *Group incentive plans:* In some companies, incentive payments are allocated to groups of employees and prorated among the group on an equal basis or in proportion to some factor such as wage rates, hours worked or total basic wages. Group plans are relatively easy to administer, but can be extremely demoralizing for employees who have no control over the individuals within their work group.

5. *Co-partnership plans:* Another group of plans includes the sharing of profits (usually above a certain basic profit level) and stock ownership with employees. Such plans are designed to encourage employees to strive for "acceptable" and even "exceptional" profit levels. Unfortunately, few co-partnership plans have provided significant benefits for the companies adopting them. For the most part employees are not readily able to see a direct connection between the extra efforts they exert now and the relevant rewards that may or

may not be forthcoming until some time in the future.

V.   EMPLOYEE TESTING

The use of psychological tests is a controversial matter in labour management relations. The validity of testing practices has come under scrutiny by labour unions and has been questioned through grievance and arbitration procedures on a number of occasions.

Psychological tests are used in industry as a means of measuring how well a person has done something or to predict how well that person will do something in the future. Although thousands of different types of tests have been developed, it is useful to group them under the following headings:

1.   Ability and skills tests

a) Intelligence tests: Intelligence tests are used to ascertain whether or not an individual possesses certain basic mental abilities deemed necessary to adequately perform a specified job. Such tests attempt to assess an individual's capability with respect to reason, comprehension, memory and numerical facility.

b) Aptitude tests: An "aptitude" refers to an inborn or potential ability to perform specified tasks. Aptitude tests or simulations are designed to measure whether or not an individual possesses a sufficiently high degree of a particular aptitude to adequately perform a job.

c) Achievement tests: These tests are used to assess individuals who are already experienced in a particular skill. Achievement tests may consist of oral or written questions and performance requirements.

2.   Interest tests

The tests for abilities and skills may not be reliable because individuals can possess varying degrees of interest towards particular types of work. Consequently, tests have been developed to measure job "interest". It is assumed, sometimes incorrectly, that an individual's motivation to perform well in a particular type of job can be inferred from the results of interest inventories. Because interest tests can be faked so easily, they often have a very limited value.

3.   Personality characteristics

Personality tests are conducted to provide information on such human traits as sociability, dominance and emotional stability, to name a few. However, the fact that it is possible to fake the results of most personality tests seriously beclouds their usefulness in an industrial setting.

Employment tests are used in a variety of personnel related functions such as, employee selection, career counselling and training and development. There are studies in each of these areas which confirm that certain tests have been beneficial to particular companies and individuals. Those tests that do prove useful generally meet the following criteria:

a) Appropriateness: The test must be designed to suit the applicable job and organization under consideration. Tests "borrowed" from other jobs and other organizations often prove to be invalid.

b) Reliability: Test results should be consistent when repeated over a period of time.

c) Validity: The test should actually measure what it sets out to measure.

d) Proper Administration and Interpretation: The tests must be administered and interpreted by competent individuals.

e) Cautious use: Test results should be treated as one of many sources of information about an individual. Care must be taken that other valid and reliable information is not excluded in the decision-making process.

f) Ethical acceptability: Tests should not constitute an unwarranted invasion of human privacy nor should they discriminate against individuals whose cultures differ from the majority of the population.

Summary

1. A distinction was made between the terms job, position and occupation.
2. Concepts that are frequently used in the process of describing jobs include job analysis, job descriptions and job specifications.
3. There are a variety of methods of *job* evaluation currently being used in industry.
4. Some of the *employee* evaluation techniques that have been developed include graphic rating scales, ranking methods, forced choice methods and critical incident methods.
5. Employees may be paid on the basis of daywork plans, incentive plans or some combination of these plans.
6. Psychological tests have been used in industry to obtain information on the ability, skills, interests and personality of employees.

Chapter 16

Labour Market Concepts
And
Labour Standards Legislation

I   LABOUR MARKET CONCEPTS

Many aspects of labour relations are influenced by labour market considerations. The purpose of this section is to provide the reader with an understanding of some important labour market concepts.

1.   Labour Force

The labour force refers to the number of persons assumed to be available for work at going wages at a given point in time. In Canada, the number of individuals in the labour force is derived in the following manner:

| Total Population |

less
Population 14 years of age and under
gives

| Working Age Population |

less
Institutional population (prison inmates, etc.)
less
Armed Forces personnel
gives

| Civilian Population = Potential Labour Force |

less
Persons going to school, keeping house, infirm, disabled, retired, or voluntarily idle
gives

| The Actual Labour Force |

which is composed of

| Employed Individuals |

and

| Unemployed Individuals |

2.   The Total Population

The size of the Canadian population is dependent upon the rates of natural increase, immigration and emigration. Natural increases in the Canadian population refer to the surplus of births over deaths. While birth rates have fluctuated over the years, advances in medical technology and improved accessibility to medical treatment have resulted in steadily declining death rates. Immigration also has had an impact on the size of the Canadian labour force. Over the years there have been influxes of immigrants into Canada. At the same time, large numbers of Canadians have emigrated south to the United States. The surplus of immigration over emigration is referred to as "net immigration".

3.   The Potential Labour Force and Participation Rates

The potential labour force historically represents between 65 and 70 percent of the total population and its size is influenced by such factors as legislation concerning eligibility for employment, the age distribution of the population and the size of the armed forces and institutional population. At no time, however, does the entire potential labour force actively participate in productive activity. The percentage of the potential labour force participating (the participation rate) has varied between 52 and 56 percent since the Second World War. Over the years, there have been noticeable shifts in participation rates for young people (14-19 years), old people (over 65 years), and females.

4.   Unemployment
Members of the labour force may also be classified as employed or unemployed. Individuals are employed if they:

a) do any work for pay or profit;

b) do any work which contributes to the running of a farm or business operated by a related member of the household; or

c) have jobs but do not work because of bad weather, illness, industrial disputes, etc.

Unemployed persons in Canada are defined as those who are:

a) without work and are looking for work;

b) without work and would be looking for work but are temporarily ill, on indefinite layoff, believe suitable work is not available in the community, or are waiting to be called back to a job from which they have been laid off for less than 30 days. The best known measure of Canadian unemployment is the average annual percentage of the labour force that is out of work across the nation.

Studies of the incidence of unemployment among regions, age groups, levels of education, industries and occupations have generated the following conclusions:

a) The highest rates of unemployment in Canada are found in the Maritime region while, the lowest rates are found in the Prairie region.

b) Workers in the 14-19 years of age group tend to experience higher rates of unemployment than older workers.

c) The incidence of unemployment is higher among less educated groups.

d) Primary industries have higher unemployment rates than trade and service industries.

e) Labourers and construction workers experience higher rates of unemployment than office, administrative and professional occupations.

The causes of unemployment are frequently categorized in the following manner:

a) Seasonal factors: As the name implies, some employment tends to be seasonal in nature because of temperature conditions, product availability and consumer preferences. Possible means of lessening the impact of seasonal factors include policies and technology to lessen the seasonality of certain industries.

b) Cyclical factors: This refers to a condition whereby individuals have employment capabilities that are desired by society, but the products and services they are capable of producing are not in demand at the moment. Eventually, expansion in overall economic activity will restore the demand for these products and services. The cures for cyclical unemployment are simply to wait until natural forces generate a movement towards a favourable part of the "cycle", or for some agency (usually the government) to stimulate demand and create more employment opportunities.

c) Geographic or cultural factors: In some instances, individuals may possess employment capabilities that are desired by society, but not at their present location. To offset this type of unemployment, policies to improve labour mobility are necessary.

d) Technological factors: Technological factors that give rise to unemployment problems include: a) the introduction of new equipment or production techniques to produce the same products or services, and b) the introduction of new products which require different equipment or production techniques. As a result, the skills of certain individuals become obsolete, forcing them either to adapt to technological changes or become unemployed. Experience in Canada has demonstrated that some members of the labour force are less versatile than others and cannot adapt without special assistance.

e) Frictional factors: Frictional factors refer to the delays which workers experience when moving between occupations or jobs. Although a job opportunity is available, an individual may be required to take an unwanted one or two month holiday before finding and assuming another occupation or job.

5.   Labour Mobility

The term "labour mobility" refers to movements of the labour force in response to changing labour market conditions. Labour economists usually distinguish three categories of labour mobility:

a) Geographic mobility: This represents movements by members of the labour force from one geographic area to another.

b) Industrial mobility: This denotes movements by members of the labour force among different employers or industries.

c) Occupational mobility: This refers to movements by members of the labour force to different jobs and occupational classifications.

These three categories are by no means mutually exclusive. In many cases, all three types of labour mobility occur at the same time.

Studies of factors influencing labour mobility have generated the following findings:

a) Age: Young workers tend to have a higher rate of mobility than older workers.

b) Family status: Family heads tend to be less mobile than single individuals.

c) Occupation and skill: The more specialized a worker's skill or occupation, the lower will be his rate of mobility.

d) Information: Individuals possessing inadequate and inaccurate information will tend to be less mobile than those with more perfect information.

e) Job benefits related to length of service: The more advantages an individual has accumulated as a result of length of service, the lower will be his rate of mobility.

6.   Labour Productivity

The term "productivity" is often confused with the term "production". Changes in production refer strictly to increases or decreases in total output. Changes in productivity refer to changes in output per unit of input and represent a measure of the efficiency with which factor inputs are combined. Increases in productivity (or efficiency) may result from:

- increased production with constant inputs (or inputs which increased proportionately less than output)

- constant production with decreased inputs
- decreased production where inputs used decreased proportionately
  more than output.

Economists are usually concerned with the relationships of output to labour, materials and machines (referred to as factor inputs) that are used to make the goods and services we consume. The ratio of total output to total factor input is referred to as total factor productivity. The ratio of total output to total labour input (usually measured in man-hours) used in its production is referred to as labour productivity. The ratio of total output to total capital input used in its production is referred to as capital productivity, and so on. It should be stressed that no method has been found to measure accurately the relative contributions of labour, capital and other factors to increases in output. Instead, labour productivity and capital productivity are simply *instruments* for measuring *changes* in overall efficiency.

Various factors of production can account for improvements in productivity or efficiency. Consequently, the problem arises as to how the increments in productivity should be distributed among the factors of production. If it can be assumed that a factor input's share of the total product fully reflects its contribution to production, the problem is resolved by giving each factor an increment that is proportionate to its increase in productivity.

For example, assume the following relationship exists:

Value Added	=	Wages + Interest + Profit		
$10 m	=	$4m	+ $3m	+ $3m
Percent of total: 100%	=	40%	30%	30%

Now assume a 10 percent increase in value added. If all factors are given increases proportionate to the increase in productivity, the end result will be:

Value Added	=	Wages + Interest + Profit		
11m		$4.4m+	$3.3m	+ $3.3m
Percent Increase: 10%	=	10%	10%	10%
Percent of Total: 100%	=	40%	30%	30%

7.   Wage Differentials

Canadian workers have distinctive characteristics and preferences which are reflected in wage differences among them. These wage differences can be classified into three categories:

a) Regional wage differentials: Some of the major factors which account for different wage levels in different regions include:
- the regional economic structure
- the capital-labour ratios
- the occupational structure of the labour force
- the degree of urbanization
- the degree of labour mobility (16.1).

b) Industrial wage differentials: Differences in average wages between different industries in the same region have been attributed to:
- the skill mixes of their labour forces
- the phase of development of related industries
- the dissimilarity in processes of production

- the extent to which industries draw their labour from common markets
- whether they have common labour organizations (16.2).

c) Occupational wage differentials: Differences in average wages among occupations can be accounted for by:
- demand and supply conditions
- barriers to entry in employment and occupations
- costs incurred in the acquisition of educational and skill qualifications
- monopoly practices by various organizations (16.3).

8.   The Time Dimension of Labour

The labour market is strongly influenced by trends in working hours, vacations and holidays. While the size of the Canadian labour force has been growing, the average employee has been gradually working shorter days, fewer days per week and fewer weeks per year. It is important, therefore, to carefully consider changing trends not only in the size of the labour force, but also in the number of man-hours worked.

9.   Labour Market Analysis

So far, we have examined a number of important labour market definitions and concepts. Labour market analysis, which goes beyond simple definitions, involves four types of activities:

a) Measurement, which emphasizes numbers and asks the questions, "how many?" and "how much?"

b) Description, which emphasizes reporting in a literary way how people behave in the labour market and the reasons for such behaviour.

c) Prediction, which emphasizes the use of data to forecast future developments.

d) Prescription, which emphasizes the choice of policies to be adopted (16.4).

II   LABOUR STANDARDS LEGISLATION

All Canadian jurisdictions have enacted a variety of laws and regulations to which employers must adhere. The most important types of laws are as follows:

1.   Minimum wages

All jurisdictions have laws specifying minimum wage rates for various types of employment and individuals. Such laws are intended to guarantee all employees who are covered a certain minimum standard of living. Also, many jursidictions specify that wages must be paid by cash or cheque and details must be provided concerning deductions. These types of regulations prevent unscrupulous employers from taking advantage of employees.

2.   Maximum hours of work

Most jurisdictions specify the maximum number of hours per day or week that an employer may demand from his employees. Employees who volunteer to work more than this maximum number of hours generally must be paid premium rates for such overtime. Procedures are usually available to allow employers to apply for permits to require overtime at regular pay. Employers must demonstrate that special conditions prevail which justify exemption from the normal regulations.

3.   Vacation pay and statutory holidays

Employers are normally obligated to give employees either a vacation period with pay or vacation pay. This vacation period varies with the length of an employee's service with a particular employer. In addition, some jurisdictions specify that employees must receive their regular pay on specified public holidays or be paid special overtime rates if they do work on such holidays.

4.   Minimum age

Each province and the federal government specifies a minimum age below which a person may not be employed.

5.   No discrimination

Most jurisdictions forbid any discrimination by employers and unions on the grounds of race, colour, nationality, or religion. There is also a growing tendency to prohibit discrimination for reasons of age and marital status. Specific statutes have been enacted to prohibit wage discrimination by reason of sex and to forbid dismissal solely because of pregnancy.

6.   Notice of termination

In many jurisdictions, an employer is required to give written notice of termination of employment. Also, certain minimum periods of notification are required, depending on how long an employee has served a specific employer. If an employer wishes the employee to leave immediately, he usually will be required to pay the employee his regular wage for the notification period. This provision is designed to enable the employee to search for alternative employment while still on a regular income.

7.   Health, safety and comfort conditions

Every jurisdiction has some type of law designed to protect the health and safety of employees. The primary weaknesses of such legislation are related to the limited coverage and inconsistent enforcement of these regulations. The failure of some statutes to cover certain groups (such as farmworkers), and the tendency for governments to provide limited financial resources to enforce the statutes have been a persistent source of criticism in recent years.

Summary

1.   Labour market analysis consists of measurement, description, prediction and prescription with respect to trends in such areas as:
- population
- the labour force
- participation rates
- unemployment
- labour mobility
- labour productivity
- wage differentials
- man-hours worked per day, week, month, or year.

2. Canadian labour standards legislation usually regulates:
   - minimum wages
   - maximum hours of work
   - vacation pay and statutory holidays
   - minimum working age
   - discrimination by employers and unions
   - health, safety and comfort conditions.

References

16.1 Peitchinis, S.G. *Canadian Labour Economics.* Toronto, McGraw-Hill Company of Canada Limited 1970, p. 369.

16.2 *Ibid.,* p. 372.

16.3 *Ibid.,* p. 393.

16.4 Lampman, R.J. "New Facts and Interpretations of Labour Market Analysis". *Industrial and Labour Relations Review,* January 1957, pp. 297-311.

Part F: An Experiential Approach To Labour Relations

This part of the book contains a chapter with a number of assignments that are designed to complement the preceding descriptive material. Section I describes the Yourtown Public Library System (YPLS) which is used as the focal point for all assignments. Section II presents a brief historical overview of labour relations within the Yourtown Public Library System. This is followed by an assignment of the composition of the bargaining unit in Section III. Section IV contains a summary of the events that led up to the signing of the first collective agreement by the YPLS Board and its professional librarians. In Section V, a format for the negotiation simulation is provided which integrates the material on collective bargaining techniques and issues with the material on the YPLS. The final section provides an assignment on grievance arbitration.

Chapter 17

The Yourtown
Public Library System

I   THE INSTITUTION

The Yourtown Public Library System (YPLS) provides free service to all individuals and groups in the community. It accepts as its basic objectives the provision and servicing of expertly selected materials which aid the individual in the pursuit of education, information, or research, and in the creative use of leisure time. Since financial limitations generally prevent equal emphasis on all aspects of these objectives, the library recognizes that its major concerns must be positive contributions toward the development of the individual as a citizen and the removal of ignorance, intolerance and indifference.

Educational service to adults is a primary function, and the library pursues an active program of stimulation, leadership and cooperation with other agencies in encouraging the reading of socially significant materials. It accepts also its responsibility for the direct communication of ideas (*e.g.,* through organization of discussion groups, institutes, film forums and the like), seeking thereby to direct the individual toward a continuous learning process through use of books and related materials. In meeting its objective of providing recreational materials, it encourages such use of leisure time as will promote personal development and social well-being and tends increasingly to leave to commercial agencies the provision of trivial materials.

The library, recognizing its responsibility to develop adult citizens for whom the use of books and other media of communication is a necessary and natural part of intelligent living, provides special service for young people. It seeks to direct and stimulate young readers by making available expertly selected collections and skilled individual and group guidance.

In provision of special services for children, the library strives to guide the child toward a love of reading and an awareness of books as a means of satisfying his mental, emotional and activity interest. To integrate this program the library works closely with parents, schools and other educational agencies as well as with the children themselves.

Organization and Administration

The Yourtown Public Library System was established in 1940 and was incorporated under the laws of your province. The YPLS is governed by a board of trustees consisting of 9 members, who are appointed by the City Council for a term of 3 years, 3 members being appointed annually. The trustees serve without remuneration of any kind.

Legal responsibility is vested in the board, which is the policy-forming body of the institution. As stated in its by-laws, the board's responsibilities include selection and appointment of the chief librarian; promotion of library interests; securing of funds adequate for a progressive, expanding program; and control of library funds, property and equipment. Subject to existing statutes and ordinances, it has the power to determine the rules and regulations governing library service and personnel.

Regular meetings of the board are held every second month.

An organization staffing diagram for the Yourtown Library System appears in Appendix 17.1. There are three aspects of this diagram that require further explanation.

1.   The Chief Librarian

The chief librarian is the administrative officer of the institution. He acts in the advisory capacity of a professional expert to the board; recommends programmes, policies and changes; prepares agenda for and attends all board meetings; acts as secretary of the board; and has the right to speak on all matters under discussion. He is not a member of the board and has, therefore, no vote on matters under consideration. His duty, broadly speaking, is to carry out the policies and decisions of the board as they affect both clientele and employees. He is responsible for preparation of the annual request for funds, which is based on estimates submitted by department heads, and for the expenditure of funds granted. He has full responsibility for determining internal policies and procedures; for selection of books and other materials, and for the complete discharge of all duties imposed upon him by law or by regulations of the board of trustees.

The chief librarian is in charge of library personnel and is responsible for the formulation and administration of personnel policies, including assignment of duties, service standards and staff development, and for creating an environment conducive to maintaining high staff morale. He appoints new members of the staff, makes promotions and transfers, and approves salary increments in conformity with the classification and pay plan. He has the authority to dismiss staff members, subject to procedures established for dismissal.

2.   Grouping of Positions

A number of positions in the library are grouped in classes which are equivalent in the following respects: kind, complexity and difficulty of duties; responsibility involved; and the qualifications required, including education, technical training and experience.

i) Professional librarians: Professional positions require for their adequate performance: (1) an understanding of library objectives, functions, procedures and techniques; (2) a familiarity with principles of bibliographical organization and library administration (including the interrelation of library departments); (3) acquaintance with the contents and use of basic reference tools; and (4) an understanding of books and readers, and the means by which they are brought into effective relationship. These positions normally require persons to have a knowledge of the basic principles of librarianship as taught in an accredited library school at the degree level.

ii) Library technicians: These positions normally require persons to have a diploma in studies related to librarianship.

iii) Library assistants: These positions do not require prior academic training in librarianship.

3.   The Position Classification of Professional Librarians

The YPLS has five grades of librarians with the following "average" profile applicable to each grade:

Librarian Grade	Years of Experience
I	0 - 5
II	3 - 10
III	6 - 15
IV	9 - 20
V	12 or more

Funding of the YPLS

The YPLS is supported mainly by a grant from the municipal government. The appropriate financial statements, which are made public each year by YPLS Board, are shown in Appendix 17.2.

II   HISTORY OF LABOUR RELATIONS IN THE
YOURTOWN PUBLIC LIBRARY SYSTEM

Ten years ago the non-professional staff in the library system decided to unionize because of:

- low wages
- lack of job security
- inconsistent treatment of staff.

Since that time the wages of the non-professional staff have become competitive in the area, layoffs can only be accomplished through attrition, and management has been required to follow the rules and procedures negotiated in the collective agreement.

Two years ago the Board decided it was time to "hold the line" on the salary component of the budget. The members of the Board agreed that this objective was to be accomplished by:

(a) laying off two professional librarians;

(b) freezing the salaries of the remaining professional librarians for one year.

The Chief Librarian agreed that this course of action was necessary and informed the professional staff of the decision.

The professional librarians were extremely concerned about this announcement. They immediately organized an "information" meeting and invited the Chief Librarian to discuss the matter further. The Chief Librarian refused to attend, stating that this was an irreversible decision. Within a few days he had sent out the termination notices and letters indicating that salaries would be frozen for one year.

The professional librarians held a secret meeting and voted to contact the local organizer for the Canadian Union of Public Librarians (CUPL) to discuss the possibility of unionization.

Three months later, CUPL and its newly formed Local 100 sought to be certified as the exclusive bargaining agent for all professional librarians employed in the system. However, a disagreement arose over the union's decision to include five individuals in the bargaining unit:

Mr. A.   One - District Librarian

Mrs. B.   Two - District Librarian

Miss C.   Three - Branch Librarian

Mrs. D. Four - Stock Editor

Miss E. Five - Children's Coordinator

It took nearly six months of legal wrangling for the matter to be resolved and for CUPL Local 100 to be granted its certification.

III   ASSIGNMENT ON CERTIFICATION

The testimony presented to the Labour Relations Board concerning the appropriate bargaining unit for CUPL Local 100 was long and complex. The applicant (CUPL) contended that five persons:

Mr. A. One - District Librarian

Mrs. B. Two - District Librarian

Miss C. Three - Branch Librarian

Mrs. D. Four - Stock Editor

Miss E. Five - Children's Coordinator

should be included in the bargaining unit, while the respondent (the Yourtown Public Library Board) argued that all five persons should be excluded.

The following is a summary of the facts presented in the Labour Relations Board's decision on the matter.

1.   The respondent claims that these persons exercise managerial functions or are employed in a confidential capacity in matters relating to labour relations

within the meaning of The Labour Relations Act. The applicant argues for the inclusion of these five persons in the bargaining unit on the grounds that they neither exercise managerial functions nor are employed in a confidential capacity in matters relating to labour relations.

2.   The respondent's three locations are on South Street, Central Street and North Street in the City of Yourtown. Mr. One is the district librarian at South Street. Mrs. Two is the district librarian at North Street. Miss Three is the branch librarian at the library on Central Street, which is by far the smallest of the three libraries.

3.   At the second hearing counsel for the respondent conceded that there were no precise lines of demarcation of authority between the five persons referred to herein and the persons they supervise. Thus, much of the evidence in the Report of the Examiner is conjectural in nature. Answers in reply to questions are subsequently modified by further probings which reveal that a specific authority has never been exercised and that the basis for its claim is uncertain. In addition, the respondent apparently did not reduce to writing the duties of the persons in dispute. Such persons orally received the delineation of their authority from the chief librarian. Against this background the Board weighs the duties and responsibilities of these five persons.

4.   Mr. One is directly in charge of five professional librarians, three library technicians and twelve library assistants. His basic function is to see that the library on South Street is efficiently run and that the respondent's decisions and instructions are executed. In addition, he is responsible for hiring temporary staff during the summer. At the end of a probationary period he is required to submit a written report which determines whether or not a person is taken on permanent staff. Mr. One is responsible for the assignment of work to professional librarians and non-professional staff. There is some doubt about the authority of Mr. One to hire professional staff. After considering the evidence surrounding the hiring of Miss Smith, we are satisfied that he has the authority to hire professional librarians and has exercised this authority. He attends monthly post-board meetings (*i.e.,* those meetings which are held after the respondent's stewards hold their periodic meetings) with the Chief Librarian and the other four persons under consideration where the proceedings of board meetings and matters of concern in running the libraries are discussed.

5.   Mrs. Two has three professional librarians working for her. She is responsible for directing their work and for the administration of the library on North Street. She has hired one temporary library assistant and one Sunday part-time staff. The temporary assistant was interviewed by Mrs. Two and was hired by her without consulting anyone. In addition, she had effectively recommended a promotion for a professional librarian and schedules the vacations for the three professional librarians who work for her. She also has the authority to grant time off with pay and has exercised this authority. Mrs. Two has the authority to reschedule work and has also exercised this authority. In addition to the three professional librarians she has a support staff of fourteen. If a vacancy occurs among the support staff, Mrs. Two decides if it is to be filled and posts notice of it. While Mrs. Jones, a ground floor supervisor at North Street, may recommend a course of action, Mrs. Two has the ultimate responsibility on any course of action affecting this library.

6.   Miss Three is the branch librarian at Central Street and her immediate supervisor is Mr. One. She has two full-time and one part-time library assistants and about six pages who report to her. Miss Three has never made a written or oral report on any of the employees and a technical or staff problem would be checked with Mr. One. In contrast to the other four persons referred to herein she has attended only two post-board meetings. She did not select the summer

student in 1973. However, Miss Three is the only person at Central Street who is responsible for ensuring that the work is done properly and she has the authority to reschedule work. While she may initiate her own programme, Miss Three generally follows the programme laid down by the library at South Street in the selection of new books. The Chief Librarian has a different perception of the duties and responsibilities of Miss Three and, according to his evidence, she has the direct responsibility for disciplining, instructing, interviewing, overtime, final decisions and hiring of the non-professionals. Moreover, he states in his evidence that she has hired pages. On the other hand, Miss Three states that in her present position she "has had no occasion to hire, fire discipline, suspend, recommend a salary increase, promote, or demote . . .". On this conflict in the evidence we accept the evidence of Miss Three in preference to that of the Chief Librarian.

7.   Mrs. Four is the stock editor. A clerk, a clerk-typist, a part-time clerk-typist and a professional librarian (cataloguer) report to her. A sub-professional, a clerk-typist and a part-time processor report to the cataloguer. Indirectly the cataloguing staff report to Mrs. Four. The positions of clerk and clerk-typist were filled through her actions. She contacted Canada Manpower and was supplied with three clerks and five or six typists. She interviewed the prospects and hired after a brief discussion with the Chief Librarian. She made the decision to hire and the Chief Librarian upheld her recommendation. It is her responsibility to reprimand or discipline her staff and she keeps a record of all sicknesses. Mrs. Four has attended post-board meetings and prepared a probationary report on the cataloguer. She does not have the power to suspend an employee, but could recommend suspension of an employee.

8.   Mrs. Four's duties consist chiefly of book selection, stock records and coordination. She is able to authorize overtime and, in addition, she oversees the spending of the budget. She receives the orders from the three librarians and, in the event of a difference of opinion, she has the power to overrule the order in question. There is scant evidence that Mrs. Four actually exercises any appreciable amount of supervisory powers. However, she is able to exercise considerable discretion and independent judgment in her responsibility for the implementation of the respondent's book buying policies. The sum of money involved for the purchase of adult books alone is $97,000.00 annually.

9.   Miss Five is the children's coordinator. The Chief Librarian is her immediate supervisor. No staff report to her. She gives neither instructions nor directions to the three children's librarians, but makes suggestions that they do not have to follow. She has done a six month's probation report on Miss Three and on one of the children's librarians and she hired two of the children's librarians after consulting the Chief Librarian. She spends only a small percentage of her time on supervision and, although her acts of hiring personnel are subject to consultation with the Chief Librarian, Miss Five makes the final judgment in hiring professional and non-professional staff.

10.   Miss Five is ultimately responsible for book purchases in the children's department, for interpreting the respondent's policy for the children's department and for the overall budget requirements for the children's department.

ASSIGNMENT

1.   Discuss what you consider to be the most significant *criteria* for determining whether or not individuals should be excluded from a bargaining unit because they:

    (a) exercise managerial functions;

    (b) are employed in a confidential capacity in matters relating to labour relations.

2.   Assume that you are a member of the Labour Relations Board hearing this case. Prepare a report stating your decision with respect to the inclusion or exclusion from the bargaining unit of each of the five individuals and your logic for each decision.

IV   THE FIRST COLLECTIVE AGREEMENT OF
CUPL LOCAL 100

The negotiations for the first contract took place in a tense atmosphere. The Board was represented by the Chief Librarian, three members of the Board and a local lawyer experienced in labour negotiations. The union was represented by the local CUPL staff representative and four officers of the local (all of whom were professional librarians).

The Board Negotiating Committee presented an initial offer consisting of two items:

1.   No professional librarians will have their salary cut by more than ten percent.

2.   No more than five professional librarians will be laid off during the next twelve months.

The union representatives were extremely angered by this offer and stormed out of the meeting.

At the next meeting, the union provided the Board with an 80 page document which outlined the union's demands. The Board offered to carefully study these demands — provided the union was willing to wait six months for a reply! Once again the union stormed out of the meeting.

Despite the underlying hostility that had prevailed since the certification hearings, the two sides did eventually get down to serious bargaining and negotiated the clauses and conditions which appear in the next section.

The membership of the local voted to accept the agreement — six in favour, four against. However, the local CUPL staff representative was worried about the rumours that another union would be approached if the next agreement was not substantially better.

A special meeting was called and the membership were asked to summarize what they felt were the most serious shortcomings of the current agreement. A number of items were mentioned:

1.   Clause 3.02 — Should be deleted.
2.   Clause 4.01 — Need for a union shop.
3.   Clause 5.01 — Biased too much in favour of Board.
4.   Clause 5.02 — Should be replaced by a clause on Technological Change that prohibits layoffs in view of the recent rumours about reorganizing the library system.
5.   Clause 6.01 — Every employee in the bargaining unit should have to pay dues.
6.   Clause 10.01 — Salaries inadequate.
7.   Clause 11.01 — The work week should be 35 hours or less.
8.   Clause 12.01 — Should be double time and a half.
9.   Clause 13.01 — Should receive a holiday on the day before Christmas.
10.   Clause 17.01 — Employer should pay 100% of benefits and there should be a pension and dental plan.

The union officials assured their membership that next year's agreement would contain improvements in all these clauses and many new provisions. The membership was satisfied with the outcome of the meeting and gave their current executive a unanimous vote of confidence.

The members of the Board also approved the agreement. However, three new members of the Board were disturbed to find that professional librarians belonged to a union and indicated that they would find it difficult to support any further encroachments on the rights of management in the Yourtown Public Library System. A motion was put before the Board to investigate the feasibility of establishing a new administrative system which would minimize the need for professional librarians. The motion was passed unanimously.

V   ASSIGNMENTS ON CONTRACT NEGOTIATIONS

1.   INTRODUCTION

This assignment is designed to simulate a real-life bargaining experience. You will be assigned to either a Library Board or Union Team and will be required to negotiate with your opponents in an effort to arrive at a collective agreement between the Professional Librarians and the Yourtown Public Library System.

All participants must take their roles seriously and abide by the relevant ground rules if they wish to derive the maximum benefits from the simulation. Those that do so will find themselves in a stimulating learning environment which provides both the frustration and satisfaction of real-life negotiations without endangering the economic position of their company or their union.

2.   GROUND RULES

1.   There must be no collusion between any negotiating committees.
2.   All proposals and background information used must be consistent with the information in this book on the Yourtown Public Library System.
3.   You must give your opponents a fair hearing and permit them to develop their position.
4.   Bargaining sessions must be conducted at the times and of the duration set out by your instructor. A suggested time sequence is provided in this book.
5.   Participants must adhere to the contract deadline established by their instructor.
6.   The agreement is to be for a period of one year.

3.   SUGGESTED TIME SEQUENCE FOR CONTRACT NEGOTIATIONS

Time

(1 hours)   Meeting 1: Getting Acquainted
    1.   Meet members of negotiating committee.
    2.   Clarify ground rules.
    3.   Choose committee chairman.

(2 hours)   Meeting 2: Division of Labour
    1.   Discuss institutional aspects of the YPLS.
    2.   Divide up work of gathering information useful to development of proposals and positions.
    3.   Gather information.

(2 hours)   Meeting 3: Start Strategy Report

1.   Discuss opposition and anticipate the nature of their actions and reactions.
2.   Develop strategy report:
- what your initial position will be
- what your "strike" position should be
- what package are you realistically hoping to end up with?
- special tactics to be used.

(1 hour)   Meeting 4: Cost   Your Proposals and Complete Strategy Report
1.   Provide instructor with a completed copy of strategy report.

(1 hour)   Meeting 5: Opening Bargaining Session
1.   Presentation of initial proposals to opponents with verbal clarification.

(1-2 hours)   Meeting 6: Strategy Caucus
1.   Committees meet separately to analyze proposals of their opponents
- strengths
- weaknesses
- priorities.
2.   Revise strategies.
3.   Gather additional information.

(4-6 hours)   Meeting 7-10: Bargaining Sessions
1.   Negotiate proposals.
2.   Call caucus if Committee is split on an issue or caught by surprise.

(1 hour)   Meeting 11: Initial The Final Positions
1.   If agreement is reached, *each* clause of the contract must be initialed by the Chairmen of both committees. The Agreement is then turned over to the instructor.
2.   If agreement is *not* reached, each clause of the *final* position of each party must be initialed by the Chairmen of both committees. The final positions are then turned over to the instructor.

(1 hour)   Meeting 12: Evaluation Session
1.   Discuss new contract or final positions.
2.   Discuss strategies employed.
3.   What would you do differently if you could start from the beginning again?
4.   Has the simulation been of any value to the participants?

IV   THE CURRENT AGREEMENT

THIS AGREEMENT made and entered into this _____ day of _____ , 19 _____ .

BETWEEN:

THE YOURTOWN PUBLIC LIBRARY BOARD
hereinafter referred to as the "Employer"

OF THE FIRST PART

- and -

THE CANADIAN UNION OF PUBLIC LIBRARIANS AND
ITS LOCAL 100

hereinafter referred to as the "Union"

OF THE SECOND PART

ARTICLE 1.00 – PURPOSE
The purpose of this agreement is to maintain a harmonious relationship between the Employer and its employees; to provide an amicable method of fairly and peacefully adjusting any disputes which may arise between the Employer and its employees.

ARTICLE 2.00 – RECOGNITION
The Employer recognizes the Canadian Union of Public Librarians and its Local 100 as the sole and exclusive collective bargaining agent for professional librarians employed by the Yourtown Public Library Board in the City of Yourtown, save and except, Chief Librarian, Secretary to the Chief Librarian, District Librarians, Stock Editor, Children's Coordinator, and persons regularly employed for not more than twenty-four (24) hours per week.

ARTICLE 3.00 – DEFINITIONS
3.01 An employee is defined in this agreement as a person holding a degree from an accredited library school or one whose training in another country is recognized by the Canadian Library Association to be equivalent to such a degree.
3.02 The Board reserves the right to hire persons ineligible to join the Union for positions in which a clear and specific type of skill or training is of more value than general librarianship.

ARTICLE 4.00 – RELATIONSHIP
4.01 The parties hereto mutually agree that any employee of the Employer covered by this agreement may become a member of the Union if he wishes to do so and may refrain from becoming a member of the Union if he so desires.
4.02 The Employer and the Union agree that there will be no intimidation, discrimination, interference, restraint, or coercion exercised or practised by either of them or by any of their representatives or members because of an employee's membership or non-membership in the Union or because of his activity or lack of activity in the Union.

4.03   It is agreed that the Union and the employees will not engage in Union activities during working hours or hold meetings at any time on the premises of the Employer without the permission of management.

ARTICLE 5.00 — MANAGEMENT'S RIGHTS

5.01   The management of the library and the direction of the working forces, including the right to direct, plan and control library operations, and to schedule working hours, and the right to hire, promote, demote, transfer, suspend or discharge employees for cause, or to release employees because of lack of work or for other legitimate reasons, or the right to introduce new and improved methods or facilities and to manage the library in a traditional manner is vested exclusively in the Yourtown Public Library Board subject to the express provisions of this agreement.

5.02   The Board reserves the right to lay off employees because of lack of work and for other legitimate reasons.

ARTICLE 6.00 — UNION CHECK-OFF

6.01   The Employer agrees to deduct union dues from the pay of all employees who are members of the Union covered by this agreement and remit same monthly to the financial secretary of the Union.

ARTICLE 7.00 — GRIEVANCE PROCEDURE

7.01   The parties to this agreement are agreed that it is of the utmost importance to adjust complaints and grievances concerning the interpretation or alleged violation of the agreement as quickly as possible.

7.02   No grievance shall be considered where the circumstances giving rise to it occurred or originated more than three (3) full working days before the filling of the grievance.

7.03   Grievances properly arising out of this agreement shall be adjusted and settled as follows:

Step No. 1
The grieved employee shall present his grievance orally or in writing to his Supervisor. He shall have the assistance of a Union representative if he so desires. The Supervisor shall give his decision within one (1) working day following the presentation of the grievance to him. If the Supervisor's decision is not satisfactory to the employee concerned, then the grievance may be presented as follows:

Step No. 2
Within two (2) working days after the decision is given at Step 1, the grieved employee may, with or without the Union representative, present the grievance to the District Librarian or designated official, who shall consider it in the presence of the person or persons presenting same and the Supervisor, and render his decision in writing within two (2) working days following the presentation of the grievance to him. If settlement satisfactory to the employee concerned is not reached, then the grievance may be presented as follows:

Step No. 3
Within two (2) working days after the decision is given under Step No. 2, the grieved employee, accompanied by his Union representative, shall meet with the Chief Librarian or designate and such persons as management may desire, to consider the grievance. At this stage they may be accompanied by a full-time representative of the Union if his presence is requested by either party. The

Chief Librarian will render his decision in writing within five (5) working days following such meeting.

Step No. 4
If the final settlement of the grievance is not reached at Step No. 3 then the grievance may be remitted in writing by either party within five (5) days to the appropriate committee of the Board.

If final settlement of the grievance is not reached at Step No. 4 and if a grievance is one which concerns the interpretation or alleged violation of the agreement, then the grievance may be referred in writing by either party to a Board of Arbitration as provided for in Article 8.0 below at any time within ten (10) calendar days after the decision is given under Step No. 4 and if no such written request for arbitration is received within the time limit, then it shall be deemed to have been abandoned.

ARTICLE 8.00 — ARBITRATION
8.01 A Board of Arbitration shall be duly constituted as provided by the Provincial Labour Relations Act.

Each of the parties hereto shall bear the expenses of the Arbitrator appointed by it and the parties hereto shall bear equally the expense of the Chairman of the Board of Aribtration.
8.02 The Board of Arbitration so appointed has no jurisdiction to alter, amend, set aside, add to or delete from any of the provisions herein contained or to render any decision which is inconsistent with the provisions of this Agreement.

ARTICLE 9.00 — NO STRIKES, NO LOCK-OUTS
9.01 In view of the orderly procedures established by this Agreement for the settling of disputes and the handling of grievances, the Union agrees that, during the life of this Agreement, there will be no strike, picketing, slowdown or stoppage of work, either complete or partial and the Employer agrees that there will be no lock-out.
9.02 The Employer shall have the right to discharge or otherwise discipline employees who take part in or instigate any strike, picketing, stoppage or slowdown, but a claim of unjust discharge or discipline may be the subject of a grievance if dealt with as provided for in Article 7.00 above.
9.03 However an employee covered by this agreement shall have the right to refuse to cross a picket line arising out of labour disputes involving The Yourtown Library Board. Failure to cross such a picket line by a member of this Union shall not be considered a violation of this agreement, nor shall it be grounds for disciplinary action. However, an employee who chooses not to cross the picket line shall not be paid for such time missed.

ARTICLE 10.00 — SALARIES
10.01 The schedule headed "Salaries and Classifications" is hereby made part of this Agreement:

Salaries

Classification	Years of Experience				
	1	2	3	4	5
Librarian I	10,000	10,500	11,000	11,500	12,000
II	12,000	12,500	13,000	13,500	14,000
III	14,000	14,500	15,000	15,500	16,000

ARTICLE 11.00 – HOURS OF WORK
11.01 The normal hours of work shall be forty (40) hours per week for all employees.

ARTICLE 12.00 – OVERTIME
12.01 All work performed before and after regular weekly hours and all work performed on the seventh day and holidays shall be paid for at the rate of time and one-half or time off in lieu thereof.

ARTICLE 13.00 – PAID HOLIDAYS
13.01 The Board agrees to recognize the following as paid holidays: New Year's Day, Good Friday, Easter Monday, Victoria Day, Dominion Day, Civic Holiday, Labour Day, Thanksgiving Day, Rememberance Day, Christmas Day, and Boxing Day.
13.02 Whenever any of the above holidays falls on a Sunday, the next day following shall be, in lieu thereof, a holiday, and the provisions of this section shall apply thereto.

ARTICLE 14.00 – VACATIONS WITH PAY
14.01 An employee shall receive an annual vacation with pay in accordance with his years of employment as follows:
Less than one year - 1 2/3 working days for each month;
In subsequent years - 4 weeks.
The vacation year shall be the calendar year.

14.02 An employee terminating his employment at any time in his vacation year before he has had his vacation shall be entitled to a proportionate payment of salary in lieu of such vacation.
14.03 Employees will take their vacations in the calendar year in which they are earned.
14.04 When a recognized holiday falls during an employee's vacation, he shall be entitled to an additional day off with pay.

ARTICLE 15.00 – LEAVE OF ABSENCE
15.01 Leave of absence with or without pay may be granted at the discretion of the Chief Librarian.

ARTICLE 16.00 – SICK LEAVE WITH PAY
16.01 Employees shall be entitled to nine (9) days per calendar year for casual sick leave which shall be non-accumulative. Employees shall be given credit for their sick leave on January 1 of each year. If employees leave before the end of the year, they shall be eligible for such sick leave on a pro-rated basis. If employees have taken more sick leave than they were eligible for, such excesses shall be deducted from their last cheques from the Board.
16.02 New employees shall be eligible for casual sick leave after their third month of employment. The number of days for which they will be credited shall be pro-rated to the end of the year starting with the fourth month of their employment.

ARTICLE 17.00 – EMPLOYEE BENEFITS
17.01 The employer agrees to contribute eighty (80) per cent of the billed premiums covering the benefits under the Provincial Health Insurance Plan, Semi-Private Ward Accomodations Supplement and Blue Cross Extended Health Care benefits on the basis of 10-20 percent deductible.

17.02 The provisions of the foregoing plan shall not apply to an employee when he resigns, is laid off, discharged or is on an extended leave of absence.

ARTICLE 18.00 – ROLE OF SENIORITY IN PROMOTIONS AND TRANSFERS

18.01 When any vacancy occurs within the bargaining unit, it shall be filled on the basis of seniority, provided the senior employee is reasonably qualified to perform the duties of that position. Notice of such vacancy shall be posted on the bulletin board at least three working days before the vacancy is filled. Employees shall have the right to bid for the job within that period of time.
18.02 The successful applicant shall be placed on trial for a period of three months. Conditional on satisfactory service, the employee shall be declared permanent after the period of three months. In the event the successful applicant proves unsatisfactory in the position during the trial period, or if the employee is unable to perform the duties of the new job classification, he shall be returned to his former position, wage or salary rate and without loss of seniority. Any other employee promoted or transferred because of the re-arrangement of positions shall also be returned to his former position.

ARTICLE 19.00 – PLURAL OR FEMININE TERMS MAY APPLY

19.01 Wherever the singular or masculine is used in this Agreement it shall be considered as if the plural or feminine has been used where the context of the party or the parties hereto so requires.

ARTICLE 20.00 – TERMINATION

20.01 This Agreement shall remain in force for a period of one year and shall continue in force from year to year thereafter unless in any year not more than ninety (90) days and not less than thirty (30) days before the date of its termination either party shall furnish the other with notice of termination of or proposed revision of this Agreement.

IN WITNESS WHEREOF the party of the first part and the party of the second part have caused their proper Officers to affix their signatures the day and year first above written.

FOR THE YOURTOWN PUBLIC
LIBRARY BOARD

FOR THE CANADIAN UNION OF
PUBLIC LIBRARIANS AND ITS
LOCAL 100

. . . .

. . . .

. . . .

. . . .

5.   NEGOTIABLE ITEMS

In real-life situations many months of work go into developing well documented and carefully worded proposals. To compress this simulation into a reasonable time frame, it is necessary to designate only a reasonable number of issues as "negotiable". In addition, these negotiable issues are further subdivided into three other categories: issues that can be retained as they stand or be deleted; issues that can be negotiated using only the optional clauses supplied; and issues that can be bargained in detail.

All clauses mentioned refer to the collective agreement which appears in Part 4 of this section.

A.   Issues that Should Be Either Retained As They Stand Or Deleted
NOTE: The negotiating committees have the option of leaving the following clauses as they appear in the current agreement *or* deleting the following clauses from the agreement. Do *not* change the wording of these clauses.

1. Clause 3.02
2. Clause 4.02
3. Clause 4.03
4. Clause 5.02
5. Clause 6.01
6. Clause 9.03

B.   Issues That Should Be Bargained Using Only The Optional Clauses Supplied
NOTE: Choose *one* of the options given for each issue.
Do *not* make any changes in the wording of these clauses.

1. Clause 4.01 - Relationship

   Option 1: Clause 4.01 as it now stands.

   Option 2: The parties hereto mutually agree that all employers who are, or who become members of the Union, must remain dues paying members for the duration of this agreement as a condition of continued employment.

   Option 3: The parties hereto mutually agree that all present employees of the Employer, falling within the scope of the bargaining unit, as a condition of continued employment shall become and remain members in good standing in the Union according to the Constitution and By-laws of the Union. All new employees falling within the scope of the bargaining unit, shall, as a condition of continued employment, become and remain members in good standing in the Union within thirty (30) working days of employment.

   Option 4: The parties hereto mutually agree that for jobs in the bargaining unit the Employer will hire only employees who are members of the Union.

2. Clause 5.01 - Management Rights

   Option 1: Leave Clause 5.01 as it now stands.

   Option 2: The Union recognizes the rights of the Board to operate and manage its business and affairs in all respects and to hire, promote, demote, transfer, suspend and otherwise discipline and/or discharge an employee for sufficient cause subject to the Grievance Procedure and Arbitration Procedure.

Option 3: The right to manage the Library System resides with the Library Board except those items dealt with in the terms of this agreement.

Option 4: The Library Board has the right to manage the Library System in a manner that is consistent with the terms and intent of the clauses negotiated in this agreement.

3. A New Clause on Technological Change

Option 1: Three months before the introduction of any technological or other change, or new methods of operation which affects the rights of employees, conditions of employment, wage rates or work loads, the Employer shall notify the Union of the proposed change.

Option 2: Three months before the introduction of any technological or other change, or new methods of operation which affects the rights of employees, conditions of employment, wage rates or work loads, the Employer shall notify the Union of the proposed change. Any such change shall be made only after the Union and the Employer have reached agreement on such change through collective bargaining.

Option 3: Three months before the introduction of any technological or other change, or new methods of operation which affects the rights of employees, conditions of employment, wage rates or work loads, the Employer shall notify the Union of the proposed change. Any such change shall be made only after the Union and the Employer have reached agreement on such change through collective bargaining.

If the Employer and the Union fail to agree on the results of the change, the matter shall be referred to the Grievance Procedure of this Agreement.

Option 4: Three months before the introduction of any technological or other change, or new methods of operation which affects the rights of employees, conditions of employment, wage rates or work loads, the Employer shall notify the Union of the proposed change. Any such change shall be made only after the Union and the Employer have reached agreement on such change through collective bargaining.

If the Employer and the Union fail to agree on the results of the change, the matter shall be referred to the Grievance Procedure of this Agreement. No regular employee shall be dismissed by the Employer because of mechanization, technological or other changes.

Option 5: Three months before the introduction of any technological or other change, or new methods of operation which affects the rights of employees, conditions of employment, wage rates or work loads, the Employer shall notify the Union of the proposed change.

Any such change shall be made only after the Union and the Employer have reached agreement on such change through collective bargaining.

If the Employer and the Union fail to agree on the results of the change, the matter shall be referred to the Grievance Procedure of this Agreement.

No regular employee shall be dismissed by the Employer because of mechanization, technological or other changes.

An employee who is displaced from his job by virtue of technological change or improvements will be given the opportunity to fill other vacancies according to seniority.

Option 6: No regular employee shall be dismissed by the Employer because of mechanization, technological or organizational changes. An employee who is displaced by such change, will be offered employment elsewhere by the Employer in the same classification and at the same salary. If the employee refuses such transfer, he shall then be subject to the lay-off procedure.

C.   Issues That Should be Bargained In Detail

NOTE: The following clauses should be carefully negotiated and all different proposals should be costed. Both parties are free to add, delete, or alter the wording of the existing clauses and to add new clauses or subclauses.

1. Article 10.00 - Salaries (The parties may wish to negotiate the addition of a Cost-of-Living Allowance Clause)

2. Article 11.00 - Normal Hours (The parties may wish to negotiate lunch and coffee breaks)

3. Article 12.00 - Overtime

4. Article 13.00 - Paid Holidays

5. Article 14.00 - Vacations with Pay

6. Article 15.00 - Leave of Absence

7. Article 16.00 - Sick Leave

8. Article 17.00 - Employee Benefits

6.   COSTING PROCEDURES

Cost calculations are always difficult and confusing in any round of negotiations. In fact, it is common for the opponents to spend more time arguing over the costing assumptions and techniques than over the contents of the agreement. The following assumptions may be used for the purpose of cost calculations. Other assumptions will require the mutual agreement of both the Board and the Union.

A.   SCHEDULE OF INDIVIDUAL SALARIES IN THE BARGAINING UNIT

INDIVIDUAL	CURRENT SALARY
1	10,000
2	12,500
3	15,500
4	11,000
5	15,500
6	13,000
7	11,500
8	13,500
9	14,500
10	13,000
TOTAL	$130,000

B.   OVERTIME
The average amount of overtime worked by each employee is 5 hours per month.

C.   EMPLOYEE BENEFITS
Present Employee Benefits (as defined in the agreement) cost the employer an average of $60 per month per employee.

Three costing schedules have been designed to encourage consistency in the costing method used by participants. However, participants should be aware that the costing method used in these schedules is by no means universally accepted by either management or unions. Illustration I shows the results that are obtained by using these schedules to cost the current agreement. Illustration 2 shows the costs that would be obtained if the following alterations were made in the contract. Please note that these alterations have been chosen to demonstrate a costing procedure and are *not* intended to provide realistic guidelines for bargaining.
1.   Article 10.00 - Salaries
Assume the total salary figure is to increase to $200,000
2.   Article 11.00 - Hours of Work
a) Assume the normal work week is reduced to thirty hours for all members of the bargaining unit.
b) Assume members of the bargaining unit are also given a one hour paid lunch break
3.   Article 12.00 - Overtime
Assume overtime rates are increased to triple time overtime

A comparison of the results of the two contracts shows that these changes amount to a percentage increase of approximately 230 percent.

Illustration 1
SCHEDULE 1
Computation of Basic Straight Time Average Hourly Rate For

ITEM	COMPUTATION METHOD	AMOUNT
1. Number of employees in group		10
2. Standard Hours Per Day		8
3. Standard Hours Per Week		40
4. Total normal paid hours during the year	Standard Weekly Hours x 52 x Total number of employees (40 x 52 x 10)	20,800
5. Total normal paid salaries during the year	Sum of Salaries	130,000
6. Basic Straight Time Average Hourly Rate	Total Normal Paid Salaries ÷ Total Normal Paid Hours (130,000 ÷ 20,800)	$ 6.25

Illustration 1 (continued)
SCHEDULE 2
Computation of Benefit Average Hourly Rate For

ITEM	COMPUTATION METHOD	AMOUNT
1. Pay for Time Not Worked		
1.1 Paid Holidays	Number of Days x Standard Hours Per Day x Number of Employees x Basic Straight Time Average Hourly Rate (11 x 8 x 10 x 6.25)	$ 5,500
1.2 Vacation With Pay	Number of Days x Standard Hours Per Day x Number of Employees x Basic Straight Time Average Hourly Rate (20 x 8 x 10 x 6.25)	$10,000
1.3 Paid Rest Breaks	260 x (Number of Minutes Per Day ÷ 60) x Number of Employees x Basic Straight Time Average Hourly Rate 260 x (60 ÷ 60) x 60 x 6.25	$16,250
2. Premium Pay	(Total Hours of Overtime Per Year) x (Premium Rate − Basic Straight Time Average Hourly Rate) (600) x (9.38 - 6.25)	$ 1,878
3. Employer Paid Benefits (Health Insurance, Pensions etc.)		$ 7,200
4. Total Cost of Benefits	Sum of Items 1, 2, and 3	$24,578
5. Benefit Average Hourly Rate	Total Cost of Benefits − Total Normal Paid Hours (24,578 ÷ 20,800)	$ 1.18

Illustration 1 (continued)
SCHEDULE 3
Computation of Total Hourly Compensation Rate For

ITEM	COMPUTATION METHOD	AMOUNT
1. Projected Hourly Cost-of-Living Allowance Rate	Use Annual Rate of Increase In Appropriate Index for Previous 12 Months	—
2. Total Hourly Compensation Rate	Basic Straight Time Average Hourly Rate + Benefit Average Hourly Rate + Projected Hourly Cost of Living Allowance Rate (6.25 + 1.18 + 0)	7.43

Illustration 2
SCHEDULE 1
Computation of Basic Straight Time Average Hourly Rate For

ITEM	COMPUTATION METHOD	AMOUNT
1. Number of employees in group		10
2. Standard Hours Per Day		6
3. Standard Hours Per Week		30
4. Total normal paid hours during the year	Standard Weekly Hours x 52 x Total number of employees (30 x 52 x 10)	15,600
5. Total normal paid salaries during the year	Sum of Salaries	200,000
6. Basic Straight Time Average Hourly Rate	Total Normal Paid Salaries ÷ Total Normal Paid Hours (200,000 ÷ 15,600)	12.82

Illustration 2 (continued)
SCHEDULE 2
Computation of Benefit Average Hourly Rate For

ITEM	COMPUTATION METHOD	AMOUNT
1. Pay for Time Not Worked		
1.1 Paid Holidays	Number of Days x Standard Hours Per Day x Number of Employees x Basic Straight Time Average Hourly Rate (11 x 6 x 10 x 12.82)	$ 8,461.20
1.2 Vacation With Pay	Number of Days x Standard Hours Per Day x Number of Employees x Basic Straight Time Average Hourly Rate (20 x 6 x 10 x 12.82)	$15,384
1.3 Paid Rest Breaks	260 x (Number of Minutes Per Day ÷ 60) x Number of Employees x Basic Straight Time Average Hourly Rate 260 x (60 ÷ 60) x 10 x 12.82	$33,332
2. Premium Pay	(Total Hours of Overtime Per Year) x (Premium Rate - Basic Straight Time Average Hourly Rate) (600) x (38.46 - 12.82)	$15,384
3. Employer Paid Benefits (Health Insurance, Pensions, etc.)		$ 7,200
4. Total Cost of Benefits	Sum of Items 1, 2, and 3	$79,761.20
5. Benefit Average Hourly Rate	Total Cost of Benefits − Total Normal Paid Hours (79,761 ÷ 15,600)	$ 5.11

Illustration 2 (continued)
SCHEDULE 3
Computation of Total Hourly Compensation Rate For

ITEM	COMPUTATION METHOD	AMOUNT
1. Projected Hourly Cost of Living Allowance Rate	Use Annual Rate of Increase In Appropriate Index for Previous 12 Months	—
2. Total Hourly Compensation Rate	Basic Straight Time Average Hourly Rate + Benefit Average Hourly Rate + Projected Hourly Cost-of-Living Allowance Rate (12.82 + 5.11 + —)	$17.93

7.   **FINAL REPORTING FORMS**

Board Team Number ( )   **FINAL REPORT**   Agreement ( )

OR   **COLLECTIVE BARGAINING**   OR

Union Team Number ( )   **SIMULATION**   Strike ( )

A. **ISSUES RETAINED OR DELETED**

Clause Number	Place An 'X' In The Appropriate Box		Initials	
	Retained	Deleted	Board	Union
3.02				
4.02				
4.03				
5.02				
6.01				
9.03				

B. **ISSUES THAT REQUIRE SELECTION OF OPTIONAL CLAUSES**

Clause Number	Place An 'X' In The Appropriate Box Showing Option Number Selected						Initials	
	1.	2.	3.	4.	5.	6.	Board	Union
4.01-Relationship								
5.01-Management Rights								
New-Technological Change								

C. ISSUES THAT SHOULD BE BARGAINED IN DETAIL
(Note: All Changes Should Be Costed on Appropriate Costing Form)

Article Number	'X' If no change	New Wording	Initials Board	Initials Union
10.0				
11.0				
12.00				
13.00				
14.00				
15.00				
16.00				
17.00				

Strategy Report
SCHEDULE 1
Computation of Basic Straight Time Average Hourly Rate For

ITEM	COMPUTATION METHOD	AMOUNT
1. Number of employees in group 2. Standard Hours Per Day 3. Standard Hours Per Week 4. Total normal paid hours during the year	Standard Weekly Hours x 52 x Total number of employees (x 52 x)	
5. Total normal paid salaries during the year	Sum of Salaries	
6. Basic Straight Time Average Hourly Rate	Total Normal Paid Salaries ÷ Total Normal Paid Hours (÷)	

Strategy Report
SCHEDULE 3
Computation of Total Hourly Compensation Rate For

ITEM	COMPUTATION METHOD	AMOUNT
1. Projected Hourly Cost-of-Living Allowance Rate	Use Annual Rate of Increase In Appropriate Index for Previous 12 Months	
2. Total Hourly Compensation Rate	Basic Straight Time Average Hourly Rate + Benefit Average Hourly Rate + Projected Hourly Cost-of-Living Allowance Rate (+ +)	

Strategy Report
SCHEDULE 2
Computation of Benefit Average Hourly Rate For

ITEM	COMPUTATION METHOD	AMOUNT
1. Pay for Time Not Worked		
1.1 Paid Holidays	Number of Days x Standard Hours Per Day x Number of Employees x Basic Straight Time Average Hourly Rate (x x x)	
1.2 Vacation With Pay	Number of Days x Standard Hours Per Day x Number of Employees x Basic Straight Time Average Hourly Rate (x x x)	
1.3 Paid Rest Breaks	260 x (Number of Minutes Per Day ÷ 60) x Number of Employees x Basic Straight Time Average Hourly Rate 260 x (÷ 60) x x)	
2. Premium Pay	(Total Hours of Overtime Per Year) x (Premium Rate − Basic Straight Time Average Hourly Rate) ( ) x (-)	
3. Employer Paid Benefits (Health Insurance, Pensions, etc.)		
4. Total Cost of Benefits	Sum of Items 1, 2, and 3	
5. Benefit Average Hourly Rate	Total Cost of Benefits − Total Normal Paid Hours (÷)	

Final Report
SCHEDULE 1
Computation of Basic Straight Time Average Hourly Rate For

ITEM	COMPUTATION METHOD	AMOUNT
1. Number of employees in group 2. Standard Hours Per Day 3. Standard Hours Per Week 4. Total normal paid hours during the year	Standard Weekly Hours x 52 x Total number of employees (x 52 x)	
5. Total normal paid salaries during the year	Sum of Salaries	
6. Basic Straight Time Average Hourly Rate	Total Normal paid Salaries ÷ Total Normal Paid Hours (÷)	

Final Report
SCHEDULE 3
Computation of Total Hourly — Compensation Rate For

ITEM	COMPUTATION METHOD	AMOUNT
1. Projected Hourly Cost-of-Cost-of-Living Allowance	Use Annual Rate of Increase In Appropriate Index for Previous 12 Months	
2. Total Hourly Compensation Rate	Basic Straight Time Average Hourly Rate + Benefit Average Hourly Rate + Projected Hourly Cost of Living Allowance Rate (+ +)	

Final Report
SCHEDULE 2
Computation of Total Hourly Compensation Rate For

ITEM	COMPUTATION METHOD	AMOUNT
1. Pay for Time Not Worked		
1.1 Paid Holidays	Number of Days x Standard Hours Per Day x Number of Employees x Basic Straight Time Average Hourly Rate (x x x)	
1.2 Vacation With Pay	Number of Days x Standard Hours Per Day x Number of Employees x Basic Straight Time Average Hourly Rate (x x x)	
1.3 Paid Rest Breaks	260 x (Number of Minutes Per Day ÷ 60) x Number of Employees x Basic Straight Time Average Hourly Rate 260 x (÷ 60) x x)	
2. Premium Pay	(Total Hours of Overtime Per Year) x (Premium Rate – Basic Straight Time Average Hourly Rate) ( ) x (-)	
3. Employer Paid Benefits (Health Insurance, Pensions, etc.)		
4. Total Cost of Benefits	Sum of Items 1, 2, and 3	
5. Benefit Average Hourly Rate	Total Cost of Benefits – Total Normal Paid Hours (÷)	

8. FINAL OFFER SELECTION

If time permits, it is a useful exercise for those parties that did not reach an agreement to prepare a report showing their final position on the negotiable issues and the background information which supports this position. These reports should be turned over to "selection officers" (chosen from the parties that did reach agreement) who must select one of the "final offers" in total and prepare a report which provides the logic for the decision rendered.

SECTION 6

ASSIGNMENT ON GRIEVANCE ARBITRATION

A collective agreement has to be a flexible document open to interpretation. The mechanism which provides this flexibility is known as a grievance procedure.

A grievance procedure specifies a series of actions or negotiations that must be followed if any dispute arises out of the interpretation or application of a collective agreement. Normally, a grievance procedure will contain a clause that obliges the parties to refer any unresolved disputes to arbitration and to accept the decision of the arbitrator as final and binding.

What follows is an outline of the relevant facts associated with a grievance in the Yourtown Public Library System.

YOURTOWN PUBLIC LIBRARY SYSTEM
GRIEVANCE

Background

This grievance arose after a senior employee was by-passed for promotion in favour of a junior employee. As the senior employee had occasionally performed the job before and felt she had the required skill she believed her contractual rights were violated.

The Chief Librarian admits there is no question of the senior employee's ability to perform the job. Because of a chronic illness at home, and other less excusable reasons, the grievant has an excessive absenteeism and lateness record. The Chief Librarian is not disposed to discipline the grievant for this reason, but maintains that the job in question is such that both the Library and other employees would suffer because of irregular attendance at work.

After processing the case through the grievance procedure, it was referred to arbitration by the union through a demand which read:

"The union claims that the employer violated the collective bargaining agreement by not promoting Mrs. Able to the position of Reference Librarian at the South Street Library. The union demands that Mrs. Able be immediately promoted to this job.

The company in a letter to the union denying the contract violation states: ". . . Mrs. Able's attendance record is such as to disqualify her for any job, such as Reference Librarian where substantial inconvenience can be caused the Library and its employees because of irregular attendance".

Exhibits
1. A copy of the collective bargaining agreement is introduced as a joint exhibit. The promotion clause (18.01) reads:
"When any vacancy occurs within the bargaining unit, it shall be filled on the basis of seniority, provided the senior employee is reasonably qualified to perform the duties of that position. Notice of such vacancy •shall be posted on the bulletin board at least three working days before the vacancy is filled. Employees shall have the right to bid for the job within that period of time."

2. Mrs. Able's personnel record which notes 30 days absence and 45 days of lateness of more than 15 minutes within the past year.

Opening Statements by the parties:
Union   — The grievant, Mrs. Able was refused a promotion to Reference Librarian. A less senior person got the job at a higher rate of pay.
       The union maintains that because the grievant "can do the job and has done it," she is "reasonably qualified" and should be promoted.
Library — The Library gave the job to a less senior person because of Mrs. Able's bad attendance record. The Library does not question Mrs. Able's ability. The problem is "that she's not there often enough to do it".

Testimony:
Testimony by the grievant establishes that:
1.   She has been assigned the job of Reference Librarian "on occasions" without any complaints about her work.

On cross-examination she concedes that:
1.   She has been told by her supervisor to "watch her lateness and absences".
2.   The illness of her son which causes her lateness and absence will continue for a long time.

The union president testifies that:
1.   Mrs. Able is a good worker and has never been disciplined.
2.   The Library has given Mrs. Able oral warnings about her attendance.

On cross-examination the union president stated that:
1.   It is better for the employees and the Library if the Reference Librarian attends work consistently.

Testimony of the Chief Librarian establishes that:
1.   He had discussed Mrs. Able's absence and lateness record with both Mrs. Able and the union president.
2.   The company is sympathetic with Mrs. Able's home problem and does not want to discipline her because of absenteeism.
3.   It would be costly to replace Mrs. Able with another Librarian as the Reference Librarian when Mrs. Able didn't show up.
4.   The term "reasonably qualified" in the promotion clause, besides meaning skill and efficiency, allows the Library to take a person's lateness and absence record into consideration when a promotion is made.

Summary statements by the parties:

Union   — Promotions are a matter of right, not privilege. The proper action by the Chief Librarian, because of Mrs. Able's record, should have been disciplinary in nature. The parties never intended the promotion clause to be applied as in the present case.

Library — Discipline is not involved in this case. The term "reasonably qualified" in the promotion clause means more than skill and ability. It includes reliability and regular attendance at work. To give Mrs. Able the job would be a "travesty" because her fellow workers would be inconvenienced and the Library might be required to pay overtime to her replacement.

Required:

A.   GRIEVANCE PROCEDURE

1. Outline the strengths and weaknesses of the grievance and arbitration procedures contained in Article 7.00 and Article 8.00 of the YPLS Collective Agreement.

2. Would you say that the grievance and arbitration procedures in Article 7.00 and Article 8.00 of the YPLS Collective Agreement favour management or the union? Explain.

3. Assume you have been hired as a consultant by the union to suggest an alternative grievance and arbitration procedure that is more beneficial to the union. Prepare an appropriate consulting report.

4. Assume you have been hired as a consultant by the Board to suggest an alternative grievance and arbitration procedure that is more beneficial to management. Prepare an appropriate consulting report.

B.   GRIEVANCE ARBITRATION

Assume you have been requested to serve as arbitrator for the Yourtown Public Library System grievance.

1.   What additional information would you request before rendering your decision?

2.   Prepare an arbitration award using only the information that is provided in this book.

3.   How could clause 18.01 be revised to avoid a similar type of grievance in the future?

APPENDIX A

YOURTOWN PUBLIC LIBRARY SYSTEM
Staffing Diagrams
indicating major areas of responsibility; not job descriptions.

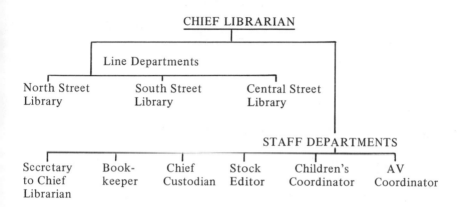

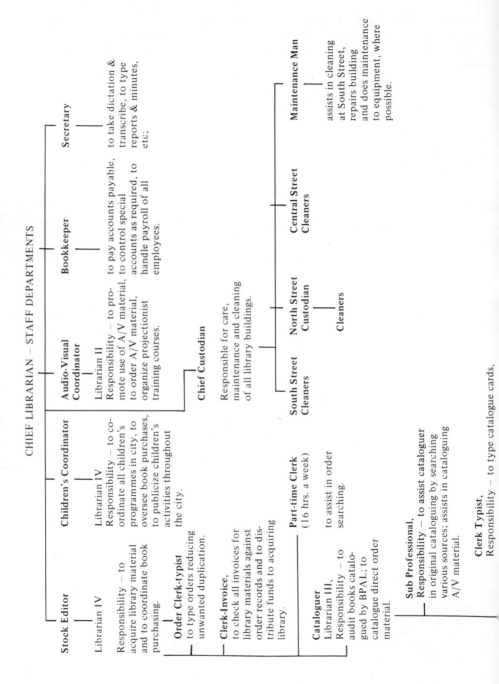

CHIEF LIBRARIAN – STAFF DEPARTMENTS

Stock Editor

Librarian IV

Responsibility – to acquire library material and to coordinate book purchasing.

Order Clerk-typist
to type orders reducing unwanted duplication.

Clerk-Invoice,
to check all invoices for library materials against order records and to distribute funds to acquiring library.

Part-time Clerk
(16 hrs. a week)
to assist in order searching.

Cataloguer
Librarian III,
Responsibility – to audit books catalogued by BPAL; to catalogue direct order material.

Sub Professional,
Responsibility – to assist cataloguer in original cataloguing by searching various sources; assists in cataloguing A/V material.

Clerk Typist,
Responsibility – to type catalogue cards,

Children's Coordinator

Librarian IV
Responsibility – to coordinate all children's programmes in city, to oversee book purchases, to publicize children's activities throughout the city.

Audio-Visual Coordinator

Librarian II
Responsibility – to promote use of A/V material, to order A/V material, organize projectionist training courses.

Chief Custodian

Responsible for care, maintenance and cleaning of all library buildings.

South Street Cleaners

North Street Custodian

Cleaners

Central Street Cleaners

Bookkeeper

to pay accounts payable, to control special accounts as required, to handle payroll of all employees.

Secretary

to take dictation & transcribe, to type reports & minutes, etc;

Maintenance Man

assists in cleaning at South Street, repairs building and does maintenance to equipment, where possible.

LINE DEPARTMENTS

CHIEF LIBRARIAN

North Street   South Street

— **District Librarian**
Librarian V

Responsibility: to
administer library on
day-to-day basis.

— **Librarian III**

Responsibility:
1. to run children's programmes,
   to recommend purchase of
   children's books;
2. assist District Librarian
   in operation of library;
   in charge during Librarian's
   absence.

— Library Technician
Children's programmes;
Working with children.

— Library Assistant
Working with children;
Charging books in and out;
creating art displays.

— Library Assistants
Working with children
Charging books in and out;
Overdues.

Adult Services Librarian
Librarian II
Responsibilities – 1.　working with public in
　　　　　　　　　　the library;
　　　　　　　　2.　providing service to shut-ins;
　　　　　　　　3.　working with groups to provide
　　　　　　　　　　collections of books or talks.

– Circulation Technician
Responsible to Adult Services'
Librarian for efficient operation
of circulation desk;
timetabling staff;
assisting in questions;
helping public;
in charge of local supplies.

– Sub-professional
Cash duties; assists at catalogue;
assists at information desk;
selects Language Books.

CIRCULATION TECHNICIAN

– Library Assistant

desk duties – assisting on
information desk; catalogue
maintenance.

– Library Assistant
desk duties; petty cash;
typing for Librarian; withdrawals of material.

– Library Assistant
Desk duties; assists with
A/V; overdue billing.

– Library Assistant
Desk duties; order checking;
filing in catalogue.

—— Library Assistant
Desk duties; checking in
periodicals; learning catalogue
maintenance.

Reference Librarian

Librarian II —
    Responsible for Reference
    Department; ordering material;
    answering questions; improving
    methods.

— Reference Technician
assists in Reference Department
answers questions; responsible
for Vertical File and local
clippings.

Audio Visual Technician

Responsible for A/V equipment;
bookings from library;
assisting in running programmes;
filing in A/V catalogue.

Part-time Librarian

(10 hours a week)
Responsible for overseeing
catalogue; assisting in
Reference.

CHIEF LIBRARIAN

South Street   North Street

District Librarian,

Librarian V:
Responsible for admin-
istration of library
on day-to-day basis.

— Reference Librarian

Librarian III
1. Responsible for Reference
   Department; selection of
   materials etc.

2. Assist District Librarian
   in running library; in
   charge during Librarian's
   absence.

Librarian — Reference Department

Librarian I
assists in Reference Department;
answers questions; responsible
for service to business.

Reference Technician

assists in Reference Department;
responsible for Periodicals;
works on Vertical File.

Library Assistant

assists in Reference Department;
controls incoming Government
Documents; assists on Vertical File.

Library Assistant

In charge of Inter Library Loans;
salary paid by Regional. This
library provides reference resources
for District.

Adult Services Librarian

Librarian I
1. Responsible for working with people
   coming into library;
2. works with shut-ins and groups;
3. assists in providing programmes
   at Central Street.

Circulation Technician

responsible to Adult Services'
Librarian for efficient operation
of circulation desk and
staffing; in charge of catalogue
maintenance.

Library Assistant

desk duties; typing;
processing books for Group
Services.

Library Assistant

desk duties; assists in film
room; works on withdrawals.

Library Assistant

desk duties; reserves &
organizes new books for
shelves.

Library Assistant

desk duties; filmroom;
assists on withdrawals.

Library Assistant

desk duties; (now working on
Systems Supplies).

Library Assistant

desk duties; overdues.

Children's Librarian

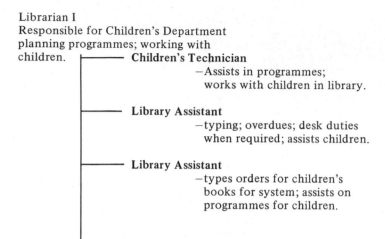

Librarian I
Responsible for Children's Department
planning programmes; working with
children.

— **Children's Technician**
    —Assists in programmes;
    works with children in library.

— **Library Assistant**
    —typing; overdues; desk duties
    when required; assists children.

— **Library Assistant**
    —types orders for children's
    books for system; assists on
    programmes for children.

CENTRAL STREET LIBRARY

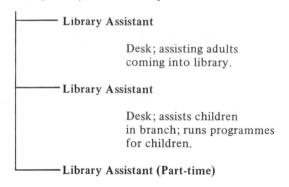

— in charge
Librarian II
Responsible for overall
administration of Branch;
children and adult programmes;
involving library in community.

— **Library Assistant**

Desk; assisting adults
coming into library.

— **Library Assistant**

Desk; assists children
in branch; runs programmes
for children.

— **Library Assistant (Part-time)**

Desk; overdues.

APPENDIX B

YOURTOWN PUBLIC LIBRARY BOARD
FINANCIAL STATEMENTS
YEAR ENDED LAST DECEMBER 31

Auditors' Report
Balance Sheet
Statements of Capital Fund Operations
Statement of Revenue and Expenditure
Notes to Financial Statements
Schedules of Expenditures

AUDITORS' REPORT

To The Chairman and Members,
Yourtown Public Library Board.

We have examined the balance sheet of the Yourtown Public Library
Board as at last December 31 and the statements of revenue and expenditure
and of capital fund operations for the year then ended. Our examination
included a general review of the accounting procedures and such tests of
accounting records and other supporting evidence as we considered necessary in
the circumstances.

In our opinion, these financial statements present fairly the financial
position of the Board as at last December 31 and the results of its operations for
the year then ended, in accordance with accounting principles generally
accepted for municipalities on a basis consistent with that of the preceding year.

Yourtown, Yourprovince   Chartered Accountants.

YOURTOWN PUBLIC LIBRARY BOARD

BALANCE SHEET – Last December 31
(with comparative figures at December 31 of Previous Years)

ASSETS	Last Year's	Previous Year's
REVENUE FUND		
Cash	$ 10,298	$ 94,083
Accounts receivable	115	647
Due from capital fund	13,778	
	24,191	94,730
CAPITAL FUND		
Cash	4,063	57,195
Due from City of Yourtown (note 1)	13,851	
Retail sales tax recoverable		2,891
Capital expenditures in excess of City advances on future debenture issue		61,113
	17,914	121,199
RESERVE FUND FOR ACCUMULATED SICK LEAVE		
Cash	1,592	405
Investment – trust company certificate 7½% maturing May 6, 2 years from now		5,345
	1,592	5,750
	$ 43,697	$221,679

LIABILITIES		
REVENUE FUND		
Current liabilities		
Accounts payable	$ 33,342	$ 46,516
CAPITAL FUND		
Due to revenue fund	13,778	
Accounts payable		59,379
Holdback on construction contract	2,500	61,820
Unexpended capital funds (note 1)	1,636	
	17,914	121,199
RESERVE FUND FOR ACCUMULATED SICK LEAVE		
Balance in fund	1,592	5,750

SURPLUS

REVENUE FUND SURPLUS (DEFICIT) FOR THE YEAR	(9,151)	48,214
	$ 43,697	$221,679

YOURTOWN PUBLIC LIBRARY BOARD
STATEMENT OF CAPITAL FUND OPERATIONS
YEAR ENDED LAST DECEMBER 31
(with comparative figures for previous year)

	Last Year	Previous Year
UNEXPENDED CAPITAL FINANCING (UNFINANCED CAPITAL OUTLAY)	$(61,113)	$ 13,476
CAPITAL FINANCING		
City of Yourtown (note 1)	138,851	375,000
Interest earned	387	2,319
Sales tax refund		10,509
Transfer from Revenue Fund	21,249	22,500
Other	156	
	160,643	410,328
CAPITAL EXPENDITURES		
Property purchase		1,257
Architect's fees	3,363	30,068
Contractor	93,685	412,136
Other construction costs	208	4,922
Furniture and equipment	638	36,534
	97,894	484,917
UNEXPENDED CAPITAL FINANCING (UNFINANCED CAPITAL OUTLAY) (note 1)	$ 1,636	$(61,113)

YOURTOWN PUBLIC LIBRARY BOARD
REVENUE FUND
STATEMENT OF REVENUE AND EXPENDITURE
YEAR ENDED LAST DECEMBER 31
(with comparative figures for previous year)

REVENUE	Last Year's Budget	Last Year's Actual	Previous Year's Actual
City of Yourtown Grant			
Operating costs	$ 721,496	$ 721,496	$ 627,273
Debenture charges	65,582	65,582	21,885
Yourprovince Grant	159,420	158,931	143,420
Regional Library			
System grant	18,000	18,000	18,000
Charges for lost books	1,000	1,053	1,576
Photo-copying charges	6,000	8,558	6,697
Projector rentals	1,200	1,251	1,217
Donations	50	131	92
Bank interest	1,200	2,895	453
Other revenue	20	1,804	884
	973,968	979,701	821,497
Surplus from prior year	30,542	48,214	16,192
	$1,004,510	$1,027,915	$ 837,689
EXPENDITURE (schedules attached)			
Salaries	$ 616,815	$ 621,468	$ 514,275
Library services	172,493	184,220	160,076
Building and equipment expenses	40,094	42,029	29,768
Capital expenditures	68,540	78,549	32,929
Administrative and general expenses	40,986	45,218	30,542
Charges on long term liabilities issued by the City of Yourtown			
Principal	23,000	23,000	19,000
Interest	42,582	42,582	2,885
	1,004,510	1,037,066	789,475
Surplus (Deficit) for the year		(9,151)	48,214
	$1,004,510	$1,027,915	$ 837,689

YOURTOWN PUBLIC LIBRARY BOARD
NOTES TO FINANCIAL STATEMENTS
YEAR ENDED LAST DECEMBER 31

1. CONTINGENCIES
    Construction on the addition to the North Street Library building
was completed during the past year at an approximate total cost of $670,000.
This project was financed by a City of Yourtown debenture issue of $600,000,
expected government grants and sales tax refunds of approximately $24,000, and
the balance from revenue refunds. Of the amount of $138,851 shown as capital
financing from the City of Yourtown, $125,000 is the balance of debenture
funds and $13,851 is the subsidy applied for from the provincial government
winter capital projects fund. This subsidy has not yet been received and is being
temporarily financed by the Library revenue fund. As provincial authorities
have indicated that this subsidy may not be paid, unexpended capital funds may
be overstated. Should this subsidy not be received, the resultant over-
expenditure on this project of approximately $12,200 must be obtained from
the revenue fund.

2. LIABILITY FOR VESTED SICK LEAVE BENEFITS
    Under the sick leave benefit plan of former years, certain employees
become entitled to a cash payment on termination of employment.
    The liability of last December 31, for the above payments amounted to
$4,616 of which an amount of $1,592 has been provided in a reserve fund
toward meeting this obligation. The balance of the liability, to the extent that it
is not earned as interest by the fund, will be provided from revenue funds as
required.
    The transactions in the reserve fund for accumulated sick leave for the
year were as follows:

	Last Year	Previous Year
Balance at end of prior year	$5,750	$5,345
Interest earned — net	70	405
	$5,820	$5,750
Payment of vested sick leave benefits	4,228	
Balance at end of year	$1,592	$5,750

3. LONG-TERM LIABILITIES
    The City of Yourtown debenture liability for library progress,
which is not included in the attached balance sheet, amounted to $610,000 at
December 31, as follows:

By-law No. 86/56	5½% December 1, Two Years From Now	$ 23,000
By-law No. 249/73	7¾% December 15, Fifteen Years From Now	587,000
		$610,000

YOURTOWN PUBLIC LIBRARY BOARD
NOTES TO FINANCIAL STATEMENTS
YEAR ENDED LAST DECEMBER 31

4.   CONTRACTUAL OBLIGATIONS

Contracts of approximately $29,153 for the provision of an airconditioning system at the Central Street Library building were let last year. Expenditures of $17,100 had been incurred on this project to December 31, and they are included in the attached statements. The balance of the cost of the project will be included in next year's expenditures.

YOURTOWN PUBLIC LIBRARY BOARD
REVENUE FUND
SCHEDULES OF EXPENDITURES
YEAR ENDED LAST DECEMBER 31

	Last Year's Budget	Last Year's Actual	Previous Year's Actual
SALARIES			
Librarians and assistants	$533,867	$529,759	$432,145
Custodial	39,610	39,288	42,711
Fringe benefits	43,338	52,421	39,419
	$616,815	$621,468	$514,275
LIBRARY SERVICES			
Books	$117,000	$118,946	$109,912
Book processing	18,523	28,545	16,694
Periodicals	11,000	9,074	11,149
Audio-visual	14,470	11,929	9,759
Microfilms and recordak	2,700	1,956	2,141
Reproducing service expenses	6,000	10,815	7,965
Extension services	2,800	2,955	2,456
	$172,493	$184,220	$160,076
BUILDING AND EQUIPMENT EXPENSES			
Repairs and maintenance	$ 7,556	$ 6,831	$ 6,943
Fuel	4,200	4,885	2,437
Utilities and telex	19,420	22,264	13,286
Insurance and taxes	4,918	4,490	4,168
Custodial supplies and expenses	4,000	3,559	2,934
	$ 40,094	$ 42,029	$ 29,768
CAPITAL EXPENDITURES			
Furniture, furnishings and equipment	$ 15,140	$ 13,645	$ 6,594
Air conditioning equipment (note 2)	30,900	43,655	3,835
Transfer to Capital Fund	22,500	21,249	22,500
	$ 68,540	$ 78,549	$ 32,929
ADMINISTRATIVE AND GENERAL EXPENSES			
Office and library supplies and expenses	$ 17,000	$ 16,704	$ 10,907
Conventions, conferences and memberships	7,708	7,177	6,729
Travel and truck expenses	1,000	898	897
Express, cartage and postage	6,500	6,793	6,169
Advertising	3,000	3,716	2,561
Consultants' fees	1,000	5,506	
Other general expenses	4,778	4,424	3,279
	$ 40,986	$ 45,218	$ 30,542

Other Relevant Data

1.   Population Covered by YPLS: 100,000 people
2.   Square Feet of Floor Area: 60,000 square feet
3.   Circulation: 600,000 books per year

Comparative Data

City	Total Expenditure/ Circulation	Circulation/ Square Foot	Circulation/ Professional	Circulation/ Staff	Professionals/ Total Staff
A	1.1	20	100,000	20,000	.20
B	1.1	14	71,000	13,000	.19
C	1.2	17	53,000	13,000	.24

APPENDIX C

CANADIAN LABOUR CONGRESS — GLOSSARY OF LABOUR TERMS

AGENCY SHOP — A clause in a *collective agreement* similar to the *Rand Formula.*

AGREEMENT, COLLECTIVE — A contract (agreement and contract are used interchangeably) between one or more unions acting as *bargaining agent,* and one or more employers, covering wages, hours, working conditions, fringe benefits, rights of workers and union, and procedures to be followed in settling disputes and *grievances.* (Convention collective.)

AMERICAN FEDERATION OF LABOUR — CONGRESS OF INDUSTRIAL ORGANIZATIONS (AFL-CIO) — A federation of *craft* and *industrial unions,* as well as unions of a mixed structure in the U.S.; the U.S. counterpart of the *Canadian Labour Congress. (Fédération américaine du travail — Congrès des organisations industrielles).*

ARBITRATION — A method of settling disputes through the intervention of a third party whose decision is final and binding. Such a third party can be either a single arbitrator, or a board consisting of a chairman and one or more representatives. Arbitration is often used to settle major *grievances* and for settling contract interpretation disputes. Voluntary arbitration is that agreed to by the parties without statutory compulsion. Compulsory arbitration is that imposed by law. Governments sometimes impose it to avoid a *strike* or to end one. *(Arbitrage obligatoire; Arbitrage facultatif)*

BARGAINING AGENT — Union designated by a *labour relations board* or similar government agency as the exclusive representative of all employees in a *bargaining unit* for the purpose of *collective bargaining. (Agent négociateur)*

BARGAINING UNIT — Group of workers in a craft, department, plant, firm, industry or occupation, determined by a *labour relations board* or a similar body as appropriate for representation by a union for purposes of *collective bargaining. (Groupement négociateur; Unité de négociation).*

BASE RATE — The lowest rate of pay, expressed in hourly terms, for the lowest paid qualified worker classification in the *bargaining unit. (Taux de base).* Not to be confused with basic rate, which is the straight-time rate of pay per hour, job or unit, excluding *premiums,* incentive bonuses, etc.

BLUE-COLLAR WORKERS — Production and maintenance workers as contrasted to office and professional personnel. *(Cols bleus).*

CANADIAN LABOUR CONGRESS (CLC) — Canada's national labour body representing over 70 per cent of organized labour in the country. See *Notes on Unions No. 3 (Congrès du travail du Canada — CTC).*

CERTIFICATION — Official designation by a *labour relations board* or similar government agency of a union as sole and exclusive *bargaining agent,* following proof of majority support among employees in a *bargaining unit. (Accréditation).*

CHECKOFF — A clause in a *collective agreement* authorizing an employer to deduct union dues and, sometimes, other assessments, and transmit these funds to the union. There are four main types; the first three apply to union members only: (1) Voluntary revocable; (2) Voluntary irrevocable; (3) Compulsory; (4) Rand Formula — dues deducted from union and non-union employees. *(Précompte).*

CLOSED SHOP — A provision in a *collective agreement* whereby all employees in a *bargaining unit* must be union members in good standing before being hired, and new employees hired through the union. See *Union security*. *(Afelier fermé).*

CODE OF ETHICAL PRACTICES — A declaration of principle adopted by the *Canadian Labour Congress,* requiring unions to try to ensure maximum attendance at meetings and general participation by membership. Under this code, no one engaging in corrupt practices may hold office in the union or in the CLC. *(Code d'ethique).*

COLLECTIVE AGREEMENT — See *Agreement.*

COLLECTIVE BARGAINING — Method of determining wages, hours and other conditions of employment through direct negotiations between the union and employer. Normally the result of collective bargaining is a written contract which covers all employees in the *bargaining unit,* both union members and non-members. *(Négociations collectives).*

COMPANY UNION — A one-company group of employees, frequently organized or inspired by management and usually dominated by the employer. *(Syndicat de boutique).*

CONCILIATION and MEDIATION — A process which attempts to resolve labour disputes by compromise or voluntary agreement. By contrast with *arbitration* the mediator, concilator or conciliation board does not bring in a binding award and the parties are free to accept or to reject its recommendation. The conciliator is often a government official while the mediator is usually a private individual appointed as a last resort, sometimes even after the start of a strike. *(Conciliation; Médiation).*

CONFEDERATION OF NATIONAL TRADE UNIONS (CNTU) — A Quebec-based central labour body. *(Confédération des syndicats nationaux — CSN).*

CONTRACTING OUT — Practice of employer having work performed by an outside contractor and not by regular employees in the unit *(Impartition).* Not to be confused with subcontracting, which is the practice of a contractor delegating part of his work to a subcontractor.

CONTRACT — See *Collective agreement.*

CONTRACT PROPOSALS — Proposed changes to the *collective agreement* put forward by the union or the employer and subject to *collective bargaining.* *(Revendications).*

COST-OF-LIVING ALLOWANCE — Periodic pay increase based on changes in the Consumer Price Index, sometimes with a stated top limit. *(Indemnité de vie-chère).*

CRAFT UNION – Also called horizontal union. A trade union which organizes on the principle of limiting membership to some specific craft or skill, i.e., electricians, plumbers, etc. In practice many traditional craft unions now also enroll members outside the craft field, thereby resembling *industrial unions*. *(Syndicat de métier)*.

FEDERATION OF LABOUR – A federation, chartered by the *Canadian Labour Congress*, grouping *local unions* and *labour councils* in a given province. *(Fédération des travailleurs)*.

FRINGE BENEFITS – Non-wage benefits, such as paid vacations, pensions, health and welfare provisions, life insurance, etc., the cost of which is borne in whole or in part by the employer. *(Avantages sociaux)*.

GRIEVANCE – Complaint against management by one or more employees, or a union, concerning an alleged breach of the *collective agreement* or an alleged injustice. Procedure for the handling of grievances is usually defined in the agreement. The last step of the procedure is usually *arbitration*. *(Griefs, Réclamation)*.

INDUSTRIAL UNION – also called Vertical Union. A trade union which organizes on the principle of including all workers from one industry, regardless of their craft or whether they are skilled or unskilled. See *Craft union*. *(Syndicat industriel)*.

INJUNCTION – A court order restraining an employer or union from committing or engaging in certain acts. An ex parte injunction is one in which the application for an injunction is made in the absence of the party affected. *(Injonction)*.

INTERNATIONAL CONFEDERATION OF FREE TRADE UNIONS (ICFTU). – An international trade union body, formed in 1949, composed of a large number of national central labour bodies such as the *Canadian Labour Congress*. It represents 50 million members in 96 non-communist countries. *(Confédération internationale des syndicats libres – CISL)*.

INTERNATIONAL LABOUR ORGANIZATION (ILO) – Tripartite world body representative of labour, management and government; an agency of the United Nations. It disseminates labour information and sets minimum international labour standards, called "conventions", offered to member nations for adoption. Its headquarters are in Geneva, Switzerland. *(Organisation Internationale du travail – OIT)*.

INTERNATIONAL UNION – A union which has members in both Canada and the United States. *(Syndicat international)*.

JOB EVALUATION – A system designed to create a hierarchy of jobs based on factors such as skill, responsibility or experience, time and effort. Often used for the purpose of arriving at a rational system of wage differentials between jobs or classes of jobs. *(Evaluation des emplois)*.

JOB SECURITY – A provision in a *collective agreement* protecting a worker's job, as in the introduction of new methods or machines. *(Sécurité d'emploi)*.

JURISDICTIONAL DISPUTE – A dispute between two or more unions as to which one shall represent a group of employees in *collective bargaining* or as to whose members shall perform a certain kind of work. *(Conflit de compétence)*.

LABOUR COLLEGE OF CANADA – Bilingual, bicultural institution of higher education for trade union members, operated jointly by the *Canadian Labour Congress*, McGill University and the Université de Montréal for the purpose of providing a training ground for future trade union leaders. *(Collège canadien des travailleurs)*.

LABOUR COUNCIL – Organization composed of *locals* of *CLC*-affiliated unions in a given community or district. *(Conseil du travail)*.

LABOUR RELATIONS BOARD – A board established under provincial or federal labour relations legislation to administer labour law, including certification of trade unions as *bargaining agents,* investigation of unfair labour practices and other functions prescribed under the legislation. *(Commission des relations du travail.* Au Québec: *Tribunal du travail)*.

LOCAL (UNION) – Also known as lodge, or branch. The basic unit of union organization. Trade unions are usually divided into a number of locals for the purposes of local administration. These locals have their own constitutions and elect their own officers; they are usually responsible for the negotiation and day-to-day administration of the *collective agreements* covering their members. (Section locale).

LOCKOUT – A phase of a labour dispute in which management refuses work to employees or closes its establishment in order to force a settlement on its terms. (Lockout).

MAINTENANCE OF MEMBERSHIP – A provision in a *collective agreement* stating that no worker need to join the union as a condition of employment, but all workers who voluntarily join must maintain their membership for the duration of the agreement as a condition of continued employment. See *Union security. (Maintien d'adhésion)*.

MEDIATION – See *Conciliation and Mediation.*

MODIFIED UNION SHOP – A place of work in which non-union workers already employed need not join the union, but all new employees must join, and those already members must remain in the union. See *Union security, Union shop. (Atelier syndical modifié)*.

MOONLIGHTING – The holding by a single individual of more than one paid job at the same time. *(Travail noir)*.

NATIONAL UNION – A union whose membership is confined to Canada only. *(Syndicat canadien)*.

PER CAPITA TAX – Regular payments by a *local* to its *national* or *international union, labour council* or *federation,* or by a union to its central labour body. It is based on the number of members. *(Capitation)*.

PICKETING — Patrolling near employer's place of business by union members — pickets — to publicize the existence of a labour dispute, persuade workers to join a *strike* or join the union, discouraging customers from buying or using employer's goods or service, etc. *(Piquetage, faire le piquet)*.

PREMIUM PAY — A wage rate higher than straight time, payable for overtime work, work on holidays or scheduled days off, etc., or for work under extraordinary conditions such as dangerous, dirty or unpleasant work. *(Salaire majoré)*.

RAIDING — An attempt by one union to induce members of another union to defect and join its ranks. *(Maraudage)*.

RAND FORMULA — Also called Agency shop. A *union security* clause in a *collective agreement* stating that the employer agrees to deduct an amount equal to the union dues from all members of the *bargaining unit,* whether or not they are members of the union, for the duration of the *collective agreement.* See *Checkoff. (Formule Rand)*.

REOPENER — A provision calling for reopening a *collective agreement* at a specified time prior to its expiration for *bargaining* on stated subjects such as a wage increase, pension, health and welfare, etc. *(Réouverture)*.

SENIORITY — Term used to designate an employee's status relative to other employees, as in determining order of layoff, promotion, recall, transfer, vacations, etc. Depending on the provisions of the *collective agreement,* seniority can be based on length of service alone or on additional factors such as ability or union duties. *(Ancienneté)*.

SHIFT — The stated daily working period for a group of employees, e.g., 7 a.m. to 4 p.m., 4 p.m. to midnight, midnight to 8 a.m. See *Split shift. (Quart; poste; équipe)*.

SHIFT DIFFERENTIAL — Added pay for work performed at other than regular daytime hours. *(Prime de quart)*.

SHOP STEWARD — A union official who represents a specific group of members and the union in union duties, *grievance* matters, and other employment conditions. Stewards are usually part of the work force they represent. *(Délégué syndical; Délégué d'atelier)*.

SLOWDOWN — A deliberate lessening of work effort without an actual strike, in order to force concessions from the employer. *(Grève perlée)*. A variation of this is called a work-to-rule strike — a concerted slowdown in which workers, tongue in cheek, simply obey all laws and rules applying to their work. *(Grève du zèle)*.

SPLIT SHIFT — Division of an employee's daily working time into two or more working periods, to meet peak needs. *(Poste fractionné)*.

STRIKE — A cessation of work or a refusal to work or to continue work by employees in combination or in accordance with a common understanding for the purpose of compelling an employer to agree to terms or conditions of employment. Usually the last stage of *collective bargaining* when all other means have failed. Except in special cases strikes are legal when a *collective agreement* is not in force. *(Grève)*. A Rotating or Hit-and-run strike *(grève tournante)* is a strike organized in such a way that only part of the employees stop work at any given time, each group taking its turn. A Sympathy strike *(grève de solidarité)* is a strike by workers not directly involved in a labour dispute — an attempt to show labour solidarity and bring pressure on an employer in a labour dispute. A Wildcat strike *(grève spontanée)* is a strike violating the *collective agreement* and not authorized by the union.

STRIKEBREAKER; SCAB — A person who continues to work or who accepts employment to replace workers who are on *strike*. By filling their jobs, he may weaken or break the strike. *(Briseur de grève; Jaune)*.

STRIKE VOTE — Vote conducted among members of a union to determine whether or not to go on *strike. (Vote de grève)*.

TECHNOLOGICAL CHANGE — Technical progress in industrial methods such as the introduction of labour-saving machinery or new production techniques. These often result in manpower reductions. *(Progrès technologique)*.

TRADE UNION — Workers organized into a voluntary association, or union, to further their mutual interests with respect to wages, hours, working conditions and other matters of interest to the workers. *(Syndicat)*.

UNION LABEL; BUG — A tag, imprint or design affixed to a product to show it was made by union labour. *(Etiquette syndicale)*.

UNION SECURITY — Provisions in *collective agreements* designed to protect the institutional life of the union. See: *Checkoff, Closed shop, Maintenance of membership, Rand formula, Union shop, Modified union shop. (Sécurité syndicale)*.

UNION SHOP — A place of work where every worker covered by the *collective agreement* must become and remain a member of the union. New workers need not be union members to be hired, but must join after a certain number of days. See *Union security, Modified union shop. (Atelier syndical)*.

WHITE-COLLAR WORKERS — Term applied to workers in offices and other non-production phases of industry. *(Cols blancs)*.

WORK-TO-RULE — See *Slowdown*.

WORKING CONDITIONS — Conditions pertaining to the workers' job environment, such as hours of work, safety, paid holidays and vacations, rest period, free clothing or uniforms, possibilities of advancement, etc. Many of these are included in the *collective agreement* and subject to *collective bargaining. (Conditions de travail)*.

INDEX